MW01484416

The Teachings of
Daoist Master Zhuang

MASTER ZHUANG

THE TEACHINGS OF
DAOIST MASTER ZHUANG

Michael Saso

Los Angeles
Oracle Bones Press
2012

Oracle Bones Press

ISBN 978-0-69280-269-4

PRINTED IN THE UNITED STATES OF AMERICA

To the cherished memory of

PROFESSOR ARTHUR WRIGHT

and

MASTER ZHUANG CHEN DENG YUN

Bai r sheng tian

Contents

LIST OF ILLUSTRATIONS ix
LIST OF FIGURES xi
ACKNOWLEDGMENTS xiii-xiv

INTRODUCTION 1

Part I. Master Zhuang

1. HISTORICAL ORIGINS 13

Introduction
1. Proto Daoists
2. The Beginnings of Religious Daoism
3. The Formation of the First Daoist Canon
4. Great Masters of the Sui and Tang Periods
5. The Age of Sectarian Division (Song and Yuan)
6. Polarization and Political Decline

2. CHILDREN OF ORTHODOXY 47

Introduction
1. Wu Jing Chun and Lin Jan Mei
2. Lin Ru Mei and Chen Jie San
3. Lin Xiu Mei and Zhuang Deng Yun

3. DAOIST MASTER ZHUANG 65

Part II. The Teachings of *Master Zhuang*

4. THE DAO OF THE LEFT   95

Introduction
1. Mao Shan Magic: The Dao of the Left
2. Preparing for the ritual
3. Performing the Dun Jia rituals

5. ORTHODOX RITUAL: THE DAO OF THE RIGHT   149

Introduction
1. Kinds of Orthodox Ritual
2. Ritual Meditation Leading to Union with the Dao
3. Teachings Concerning the Meditations of Union
4. Preparations for Orthodox Ritual Meditation
5. The Jiao Rites of Union
6. The Fa Lu Rite for Exteriorizing the Spirits

6. THUNDER RITUAL: NEO-ORTHODOXY OF THE SONG   181

Introduction
1. Three Styles of Thunder Ritual
2. The Teachings of Master Zhuang on Thunder Ritual
3. Meditations for Gaining Control over Thunder
4. The Practice of Thunder Ritual
5. The Dance of the Ho Tu

NOTES   207
SELECT BIBLIOGRAPHY: DAOIST SOURCES   235
INDEX AND CHINESE CHARACTERS   242

Illustrations

Master Zhuang	Frontpiece
The Su Qi ritual	74
Closing the demon's gate Jin-t'an	75
Fa lu rite	75
Datewood thunder block of Lin Hsiu-Mei	76
Zhuang A-Him performing the Jiao ritual	76
The role of the Daoist in the Chinese community	
A Ming dynasty woodblock print	77

Figures

1. The Battle Chart of the Eight Trigrams   101
2. The eight trigrams arranged in the order
   of the Posterior Heavens.   102
3. The sacred steps of *Yü* arranged as a "magic square"
   in ritual dance.   103
4. The magic square envisioned on the left hand of the Daoist.   103
5. The nine stars in the heavens, seen as a magic square.   104
6. The *Qi Yi Zong* seal.   105
7. The talismans of the Six *Jia* spirits.   107
8. The talismans of the nine stars.   108
9. Arranging the standards of the twenty-eight constellations.   115
10. The twenty-eight constellations.   115
11. The arrangement of the altar for sacrifice.   121
12. The Huang Zhen talisman and left-handed mudra.   123
13. The talisman and mudra of the Jia Xü spirit.   127
14· The talisman and mudra of the Jia Shen spirit.   130
15. The talisman and mudra of the Jia Wu spirit.   133
16. The talisman and mudra of the Jia Chen spirit.   137
17. The talisman and mudra of the Jia Yen spirit.   142
18. The left hand, showing the joints to be pressed in order
    to summon a spirit.   171
19. The *Fa Lu* rite for exteriorizing the spirits.   175
20. The eight trigrams of King Wen; the *Lo Shu*.   189
21. The system for determining the location of the gate of life.   191
22. The *Cao Ren* and the eight trigrams represented in lamps.   193
23. The Battle Chart of the Eight Trigrams unwound
    into the form of a serpent.   201
24. The arrangement of the eight trigrams in the
    order of the *Ho Tu*.   204

Acknowledgments from the First Edition

A great debt of thanks is owed to Professor Noritada Kubo, retired director of the Toyo Bunka, and to Professor Hiroji Naoe of Kyoiku University, Tokyo. Their comments and help corrected many errors. The encouragement of Professor Arthur Wright of Yale University and Professor Arthur Wolf of Stanford, who with Margery Wolf read an early, unrevised version of the text, is deeply appreciated. Fr. Yves Raguin, S.J. kindly loaned the Ricci Institute copy of the Daoist Canon to the project. Murdoch Matthew did an excellent and much-needed job of editing. Finally, the most profound expression of gratitude must be made to Master Zhuang himself, who so graciously revealed his teachings and allowed me to sit equally with his sons, A-Him and A-Ga, during the lengthy evening lessons in ritual orthodoxy. In so doing, Zhuang insisted, he was following a prophecy made to Zhuang's spiritual ascendants by the Sixty-first generation Master of Dragon-Tiger Mountain. According to the words of the Heavenly Master, Zhuang would preserve the texts of Daoist orthodoxy, to be returned to their places of origin, in Mainland China. The following pages represent only a fraction of Master Zhuang's esoteric knowledge, but an essential part nevertheless which had not been described before in a western language. His mijue tradition will be continued, it is hoped, in future work and research, by students and scholars of religious Daoism.

Acknowledgements for the 3rd edition

Thirty-two years and two reprints after the Teachings of Daoist Master Zhuang were first published, a third updated and clarified edition has been prepared. This edition was made possible by to the hard working staff and research assistance of Oracle Bones Press, the Sino-Asian Institute and the requests of scholars in and outside of China. Wordings in the original edition have been edited and clarified and the Romanization updated. In this third edition, emphasis is placed on the oral nature of the Daoist Master's teachings. The traditions found in Zhuang's private mijue—hand written documents explaining the meaning of deliberately obscure passages in the Canon—have been noted. The basic requirements of a scientific approach to the social humanities, i.e., the tried and tested field experience of actual Daoist practices that can be verified by other scholars in the field, have been accentuated. It is hoped that this 3rd edition will affirm the new direction that Daoist studies are taking inside China itself. The Chinese Academy of Social Sciences, The Laozi and Daoism Study projects, Professors Hu Fucheng, and Thomas Yeh, and the scholars of the Daoist Studies Center of Szechuan University, in Chengdu, China, offered inspiring guidance. A great debt of thanks is owed to these unassuming and brilliant scholars, as well as to the Daoist monks and nuns (Dao Gu) of Wudang Shan, Qing Wei Daoists who live near Longhu Shan, and the late Daoist Head Master Min Zhiting, of White Cloud Monastery, Beijing, whose wisdom and sagacity affirmed and verified the widespread use of Master Zhuang's mijue tradition inside China.

Beijing, Fang Zhuang bldg. 2, Zuo-an Men research center, Spring 2010

Introduction

The Oral Tradition of Daoist Master Zhuang

Wisdom is like water. It resides in the lower meditation field, the belly.
The head is for thinking; the heart for willing and desiring. The belly is the place
for wisdom and contemplation. We "return" to Dao's gestating presence,
from this inner womb of intuitive awareness.
—Daoist Master Zhuang

The Teachings of Taoist Master Chuang is a word-for-word account of "Religious Daoism" (Dao Jiao 道教) as it is taught in Taiwan and China today. Religious Daoism began during the Han dynasty (second century B.C. to the second century A.D.) in China, and continues to flourish in the contemporary world. Daoism is an esoteric as well as a popular movement; that is, it has a system of oral teachings meant for the highly trained specialist, as well as a body of common doctrines meant for the men and women of China's cities and villages. The two doctrines are complementary, fulfilling rather than contradicting each other. The esoteric aspects of religious Daoism teach a method for purifying and emptying the inner person, to cultivate interior, mystical contemplation. The purpose of the contemplative ritual of the Daoist is to bring about union with the ultimate, transcendent Wu-wei Dao. After achieving "Union with the Dao" the Daoist master turns to help all men and women to be in harmony with the Dao, either through meditative ritual in the present life, or funeral ritual for those who die before attaining union. The exoteric or every day aspect of religious Daoism teaches the yin-yang five-element cosmology, the proto-scientific basis for change in nature, as well as the model for the festival and religious practices of China's masses.

Due partially to the influence of Buddhism, medieval Daoists built great monasteries, known as Guan, for men or women to lead lives of austere celibacy. However from their beginnings until today they also live as ordinary citizens by the firesides of China's cities and villages, marry, and bear children. Meditating in private, they also come forth to offer "Rites of Passage," as experts in China's popular religion, when called upon by their fellow villagers. Many village Daoists were literati scholars, trained in the classics and expert in literary composition. The texts of the Laozi and the Zhuangzi were their daily companions.

Scholars universally proclaim that Religious Daoism (post 145 CE) and Philosophic Daoism (before 221 BCE) are not identical. Though the two terms referred to different time periods in ancient China, many modern scholars are opposed to identifying Religious Daoism with the explanations they give to the texts of Laozi and Zhuangzi. The Daoist priest will agree in a friendly way that there are many philosophers and scholars who would qualify as Dao Jia—experts in Daoist philosophy—but not as Dao Jiao—experts in religious Daoism. To the religious Daoist, the Laozi and the Zhuangzi are basic texts used to teach novices the first steps of contemplative inner practice. Novices who master these texts are then given a set of five, eight, or ten vows to observe, and only then are they allowed to study the esoteric, private mijue hand written and kojue oral directions, for Daoist liturgical meditation.

Young Daoists are taught that they must be compassionate, unassuming, and selfless, uninterested in the wealth, fame, or social advancement of the literati or the merchant.[1] They are told that they may never use their marvelous powers over nature for anything but good. A heterodox Daoist is one who uses "black" or "left" (sinister) magic for the detriment of others. An orthodox Daoist works solely for good while personally practicing the teachings of the Laozi and the Zhuangzi. It is specifically this latter work, the *Zhuangzi* (*Chuang-tzu*) which is used to teach young Daoists the secrets of mystic prayer. The first seven chapters, known as the *Zhuangzi Nei Pian* are considered essential to the training of a novice in contemplation.[2] As early as the fifth century, Daoists developed a ritual meditation based on the words made famous by the early chapters of the *Zhuangzi*, the "heart fasting, sit in forgetfulness" (Xin zhai zuo wang心斋坐忘), teaching that Dao abides in the heart-mind that is empty.

If the training of a Daoist in contemplative prayer is rigorous and exacting, the liturgical role he or she (men and women can be Daoists) must perform for village temples and households is even more demanding. The religious Daoist is at the beck and call of the needy at any hour. In the role of a spiritual mandarin, the Daoist acts as a mediator between the invisible world of the spirits who govern nature and the world of humans. From a private, or a public temple altar purified by offerings of sweet incense, wine, fruit, and flowers, he/she ascends to the highest heavens, brings literary documents to the spirits who control nature, regulates the seasons, blesses crops and children. The Daoist is also called on to descend into the darkness of the underworld (shared with Buddhism) to free the souls of the deceased from the punishments of hell. Only politicians are not freed from hell from whence they eternally inflict punishments on souls not yet freed from hell or purgatory by Buddhist and Daoist liturgies for the deceased.

In his role as expert in China's popular religion, and celebrant of "the rites and festivals of the masses," the Daoist appears as a proponent of the yin-yang five-element theory of the cosmos, a philosophy worked out after the writing of the Zhuangzi and the Laozi, and now an essential part of Chinese religion. The exoteric or public doctrines of religious Daoism are seen to derive from this common body of Yin Yang Five Element 陰陽五行 knowledge known to all. The Daoist is the expert in this matter, the theologian of Chinese popular religion. He or she acts as teacher and counselor for the masses, while maintaining in private the esoteric and secret meditations and rituals of his or her own inner practice.

Religious Daoism is a newly recognized field of research among China experts. Only in more recent years has it been thought worthy of study by university professors and scholars of Chinese religions. The neglect can be partially ascribed to the secrecy with which the Daoists maintained their esoteric doctrines. The Daoist Canon, a massive collection of works in 1,120+ volumes, was not available for scholarly study until modern times. The present edition of the Daoist Canon was commissioned during the reign of the Ming dynasty Zheng Tong emperor, 1436-1450. Between 1435-1447, 1,057 volumes were printed by woodblock. During the reign of the late Ming Emperor Wan-li (1473-1620) a 63-volume supplement was added to the Canon in about 1607. It was not until 1924-1926 that a modern photo-offset edition of the Canon was printed by the Commercial Press in Shanghai and made available to some of the larger scholarly libraries in the West. Finally in 1962, the Yi Wen Press in Taipei, and in the 1980s the Wen Wu Press in Shanghai produced inexpensive photocopy editions of the Canon, which is now found in almost every major university library where Chinese studies is taught. Thus the possibility of studying religious Daoism from canonical sources is very recent.

A second problem in studying religious Daoism was and is the antipathy felt by many Chinese scholars toward Daoism and even Buddhism. Until the latter half of the 20th century, the overwhelming majority of scholarly endeavor both in China and the West was concerned with the intellectual and moral teachings of Confucius. Since the men who wrote Chinese history were, for the most part, at least publicly Confucian, the Daoist was always relegated with women and minorities to the last place in the biographies of famous people in the dynastic histories. This is not, of course, to deny the Daoists' profound influence at the Chinese court, nor that of their Buddhist confreres. Nevertheless the Confucian literati felt politically compelled to maintain their hegemony as leaders in the courts of the imperial Chinese government. Eternally on the watch lest the separation of church and state be broken by an emperor who overindulged his religious interests at the expense of "good government," the Confucians believed that the balance of powers that maintained China in stability through so many millennia was dependent on keeping the Confucian mandarin on the top, and the Buddhist and Daoist toward the bottom of the political and social pyramid. In modern times, however, especially after the famous May 4 movement in 1918, and the rule of the Chinese Communist Party since 1949, many Chinese intellectuals have consciously rejected the entire past in favor of the scientific modernization felt necessary to maintain China's economic prosperity. Chinese and agnostic western scholars, nevertheless, felt it necessary to analyze, date, and study the basic texts in the printed Daoism Canon. Some of these texts, named below, appear in the commentaries of Daoist Master Zhuang. The titles are not translated, but deliberately left in Pinyin Romanization; the profundity of meaning renders all English versions, the editors feel, somewhat misleading.

Daoists and their role in Chinese popular religion have been brought to the attention of the "West" by social scientists (ethnographers and anthropologists) in the field of Chinese religion and society. Whereas text-based historians and the humanists found abundant materials describing the literate Confucian past, social scientist have found far more field evidence for authentic Daoist practice, visibly active in the villages and cities of the Chinese present. Whether in Taiwan, Hong Kong, Penang, or Singapore, even in Chinese communities in the U.S., and today in modern China, the role of the Daoist remains clearly evident in the practice of modern festival, burial, temple and home ritual.

Many problems in interpreting the newly available Daoist Canon were solved by fieldwork with Daoist priests, who could explain and punctuate passages insoluble to the scholar unfamiliar with the oral tradition of Daoist teachings. The Daoists knew how to explain the Canon, and had manuals in their libraries far more explicit than the materials found in the printed Ming dynasty version. By studying with a Daoist priest, it was possible not only to give meaning to the seemingly haphazard order of the 1,300+ volumes of the Canon, and to find supplementary materials that had not been previously published or were in clearer form than the printed sources.

To illustrate, one need only take a cursory glance at the Ming dynasty Daoist Canon.[3] Traditionally, the canon was divided into seven sections, the first three, *Dong*, or Arcana, which were described by Lu Xiu Jing, who died in 471, and the four *Fu*, or supplements, which were added shortly after.

The Three Arcana were called the (1) *Dong Zhen Bu*, or Arcana of the realized, (2) *Dong Xuan Bu*, or Mystery-occult, and (3) *Dong Shen Bu*, or Arcana of Spirits. The first, *Dong Zhen* section of the Canon is supposed to contain the teachings of an elite Daoist monastic group, the Shang Qing (Highest Purity) sect, practiced ca. 370 in the environs of Mao Shan (Mt. Mao) in Jiangsu province, central China. The second, *Dong Xuan* section of the Canon contains the texts of the Ling Bao order, the popular ritual-oriented Daoists of third and fourth century China, who created grand liturgies of renewal and burial. The third, *Dong Shen* section of the Canon is named after a manual used by the Zhengyi and Ling Bao Daoists, that is, the *San Huang Wen*, the Writ of the Three Emperors, along with the teachings of the earliest Celestial Master Daoists of the Zhengyi Meng Wei school.

Each of the first three sections of the Canon is divided into twelve subsections:

1. *Ben Wen*   Basic Writings
2. *Shen Fu*   Spirit Talismans
3. *Yü Jüe*   Esoterica
4. *Ling Tu*   Spiritual Diagrams
5. *Bu Lu*   Sacred Dance steps and registers
6. *Jie Lü*   Vows and Regulations
7. *Wei Yi*   Liturgies
8. *Fang Fa*   Lesser rituals
9. *Zhung Shu*   Written Formulae and Incantations
10. *Ji Zhuan*   Biographies
11. *Zan Song*   Hymns and Chants
12. *Biao Zou*   Official Documents sent to the Spirit World

The last four sections of the Canon, or the *Szu Fu* supporting passages, are not divided into twelve subsections as are the Three Arcana above. The four supplements not only contain ritual, which adds to the materials of the first three sections of the Canon, but also include books of alchemy, breath control, Daoist philosophy, and dictionaries of Daoist lore.

The fourth section of the Canon is called the *Tai Xuan Bu*, or the section of the Great Mystery. It is said to support the first arcanum, the *Dong Zhen Bu*; that is, it supplements the teachings of the first great monastic school, the Mao Shan Highest Purity order. The fifth part of the Canon, the *Tai Ping Bu*, or Great Peace, is supposed to supplement the second arcanum, the *Dong Xuan Bu*, the teachings of the Ling Bao order. The sixth section of the Canon

called *Tai Qing Bu*, or the Great Purity, is supposed to support the third arcanum, the Dong Shen Bu. Finally, the seventh and last section of the Canon is
the repository of the teachings and holdings of the Heavenly Master school,
the Zheng Yi or Orthodox One order of antiquity.

Here in schematic form is the structure of the Canon:
  1. *Dong Zhen Bu*, Mao Shan, Shang Qing order
  4. *Tai Xüan Bu*
  2. *Dong Xüan Bu*, the Ling Bao order
  5. *Tai Ping Bu*
  3. *Dong Shen Bu*, the San-huang Wen and the registers of the Meng Wei
     order
  6. *Tai Qing Pu*
  7. *Cheng Yi Bu*, holdings and teachings of the Zheng-i order

Having established a theoretical structure for the Canon, the Daoists of
the Ming dynasty seem to have brought their documents to the Zheng Tong
emperor in such haphazard order that the imperial court as well as the Confucian scholars were totally confused about which documents belonged
in each of the seven categories. Thus, one would expect to find the major
documents and teachings of the contemplative Mao Shan order in the first
section of the Canon. But instead, one finds at the very beginning of the Ben
Wen, or basic teachings, of the first section, the basic document and teachings of the Ling Bao order in the *Ling Bao Wuliang Du Ren Shang pin Miao
Jing*, with a commentary in sixty-one chapters. Next, one finds the Dadong
Zhen Jing, one of the basic texts of the Mao Shan Shang Qing school, immediately followed by two documents seemingly adapted from the Buddhist
Canon, the *Hai Kong Zhi Zang* and the *Ben Xing Jing*. Also in the first section
are found the basic doctrines of the various Thunder Vajra schools that are
the Daoist counterparts to the Vajrayana mudra and mantra of Tantric Buddhism, along with the manual of interior alchemy known as *Yin Fu Jing*,
more texts and commentaries of the *Du Ren Jing*, commentaries on the Yi
Jing (I-ching) Book of Changes,—texts and documents which in fact cover
almost every aspect of religious Daoism.

In the second section of the Canon, which should have been exclusively
devoted to the Ling Bao tradition, one finds the basic texts of the first, *Dong
Zhen* section, the Yellow Court Canon, and the magnificent work of the
ninth "meditation" master of Mao Shan, the *Deng Zhen Yin Jüe* of Tao Hong
Jing. The great liturgical sections of the *Tong Xüan Bu* do actually contain
the rituals of the Ling Bao order, including the beautiful jiao festivals of

renewal and the zhai Yellow Registers for burial. In the third section of the Canon, the *Dong Shen Bu*, the *Sanhuang Wen*, or Writ of the Three Emperors, is the remnant of a strange text, a cryptic document mentioned first in the apocryphal texts of early Han China. The *San Huang Wen* was often kept hidden, since the Tang dynasty, perhaps for "protection" of its use by esoteric Daoist masters. Since the text was used by Ling Bao as well as Zheng Yi Daoist masters, the name given to the third section of the Canon may point to a central role played by Ling Bao Daoists from the very beginning, in the formation of the Canon. The third Dong Shen section contains commentaries on the Laozi and the Zhuangzi, the registers and rituals of the Heavenly Master sect, and documents deriving from the military Pole Star sect from Wu Dang Shan in Hupei province.

The eclectic nature of the canon can be further seen in the four supplements. The fourth, *Tai Xuan Bu*, does indeed contain one of the basic documents of the first monastic order, the famous *Chen Kao*. Along with this document, which supports and supplements the teachings of the first Mao Shan monastic order, are texts of internal alchemy, a grand encyclopedia of Daoist lore called the Seven Cloud Tally Box, and texts of inner alchemy. The fifth, *Tai Ping Bu*, further supplements the second or Ling Bao section of the Canon with the basic *Tai Ping Jing*, the Canon of the Great Peace. Also in the fifth section of the Canon is one of the earliest and most valuable of the canonical texts, the *Wu Shang Bi Yao*. This partially complete text can be safely dated to the sixth century, and its teachings figure prominently in the doctrines of Master Zhuang, as explained in the main body of the present work. The sixth and shortest section of the Canon contains the *Tai Shang Gan Ying Pian*, a morality treatise widely used in China's popular religion, and the works of the most famous Daoist philosophers.

The seventh and last section of the Canon is named after the Orthodox One, or Zheng Yi sect. Known from the earliest times as the Celestial Master sect as well as the Meng Wei Auspicious Alliance order, 正一盟威 the twenty four basic registers or Lu 籙 which identify the Daoist of the Zheng Yi order are found in clear and explicit form in this last section of the Canon.[4] The Zheng Yi section, in fact, represents the holdings of the Celestial Masters, the successors of the first Celestial Master Zhang Dao Ling in the southern headquarters of orthodox Daoism at Dragon-Tiger Mountain or Long Hu Shan in the province of Jiangxi. Commissioned by the imperial government from Song times to give licenses of ordination to local Daoist priests, the Celestial Master at Dragon-Tiger Mountain kept in his possession the main books and paraphernalia of the various Daoist orders of south China whose members came to the sacred mountain to be licensed. Thus one finds in the seventh section of the Canon the registers of the Meng Wei order, the Ling

Bao order, the Pole Star, various Thunder Vajra schools, and the ubiquitous Shen Xiao sect of the Sung dynasty charlatan Lin Ling Su.

To the lay reader unfamiliar with the complexities of the Daoist Canon or the various schools of religious Daoists, the above brief description may seem both confusing and brusque. Master Zhuang, in chapter 1 of this work, will bring a Daoist Master's interpretation into the canonical confusion. In fact, the first three early Daoist movements are clearly defined in Master Zhuang's teaching. From the mid Song dynasty ritual, as well as doctrinal unity were preserved by "Three Mountain Alliance" Daoists. The attempts to pull away from orthodoxy or to separate from the mainstream of Daoist tradition were curbed by the Celestial Masters through their right to grant official licenses of ordination. As seen in the documents of Master Zhuang and as will be explained in chapter 5, the various sects of Daoists are carefully graded. The status and rank of a Daoist at ordination is awarded according to conformity to the teachings of the Celestial Masters. In an ordination manual used by the Celestial Masters at Dragon-Tiger Mountain from the mid-Sung dynasty (ca. 1120) until the present, the grades of ordination are:

Grade one: Knowledge of the teachings and meditations of the Mao Shan Shang Qing school, the Yellow Court Canon.

Grades two and three: Knowledge of the teachings and meditations of the Qing Wei Thunder Vajra and the Bei Dou Pole Star schools; Tantric Daoism.

Grades four and five: Knowledge of the rituals of the orthodox Meng Wei Zheng Yi school, the twenty-four registers of the Celestial Masters.

Grades six: Knowledge of the Ling Bao fourteen registers, of popular Daoist ritual.[5]

The manual further names the kinds of Daoists, that is, the schools and orders of Daoists, who came to Dragon-Tiger Mountain for ordination. For each of the orders, the Celestial Master provides teachings and instructions in their own order and in its proper doctrines. Thus if a Daoist from the highly rigorous monastic order known as the Qüan Zhen school approaches the Celestial Master, the integrity of his own order and its practices are maintained. But the rank at ordination will be given according to the monk's knowledge of the above registers or doctrines. There are almost a hundred local schools and orders of Daoist men and women who approach the Celestial Master for documents of ordination, according to official Daoist gazeteers.

The main schools are:

1. The Mao Shan Shang Qing registers, the basic doctrines of which are to be found in the Yellow Court Canon. Meditations of mystical union are the specialty of this order, based on the writings of the Zhuangzi, and the woman Daoist mystic Wei Hua Cun.

2. The Ching Wei, or Thunder Vajra school from west China also attributed to a Daoist woman mystic, Zu Shu. The purification rituals of this order are used to oppose evil black magic.

3. The military Pole Star sect from Wu Dang Shan in Hubei province. The use of gongfu bodily exercises, military prowess involving spirits as well as weapons, and Pole Star envisioning rituals are proper to this early order.

4. The Orthodox Celestial Master Zheng Yi Meng Wei school, with headquarters at Long Hu Shan in Jiangxi province. The Daoists who belong to the order, but live by the firesides of village and city China, call themselves Jade Pavilion (Yü Fu 玉府) Daoists as a sort of identifying secret title.

5. The popular Shen Xiao order promoted by Lin Lingsu during the reign of the Sung Emperor Hui-tsung, ca. 1116, in central and south China. The Daoists of this school were at first considered heterodox; proponents of a kind of black magic for harming people. They were drawn back into orthodoxy by the famous late Song dynasty Daoist Master Bai Yuchan. Their corrected registers are kept by the Celestial Masters at Long Hu Shan. To all of the local Daoists coming to Lung-hu Shan for ordination, the Heavenly Master awarded a license and gave instructions in their preferred form of late Sung dynasty Daoism.

The teachings of Master Zhuang deal with the above themes in an intimate and lively fashion. Trained from youth in the secrets of Meng Wei orthodox Daoism as well as in the elite exorcisms of the powerful Qing Wei Thunder Vajra rites, Master Zhuang imparts in the following pages the secrets of esoteric religious Daoism, as he was taught them by his masters. In chapter 1, the sources of Zhuang's teachings are traced to the beginnings of religious Daoism. A brief but fairly complete history of the origins of religious Daoism and its development into the Song dynasty is given, as he was taught by his masters. In chapter 2, the history of the transmission of Zhuang's teachings from Mainland China to Taiwan is recounted from local archives and from sources found in Zhuang's extensive library. In chapter 3, the role of Zhuang in the community, his effect on his neighbors, and the respect engendered by his battle against evil and prayers for public blessing are described. The first three chapters comprise part I of the book and define Master Zhuang and his role in society.

Part II, chapters 4 through 6, deals with the teachings of Master Zhuang in detail. Chapter 4 describes the terrifying Dao of the Left, the "sinister" magic of the Six Jia spirits, attributed to Mao Shan in Jiangsu. Chapter 5 gives a general description of the Dao of the Right, the beautiful rituals of orthodox Daoism. The second part of the chapter teaches the method of performing one of the earliest meditations of orthodox Meng Wei Daoism, the Fa Lu rite of mandala building. Chapter 6 describes the rites of Tantric Daoism, the famous Five Thunder method, which became popular during the Song dynasty. The ability to perform thunder ritual is highly prized by the orthodox Daoists and a high rank at ordination is awarded for the mastery of its secrets. Thunder ritual is used to counteract the harmful black magic described in chapter 4. As has been observed, the term orthodoxy is applied to Daoists who spend their lives in doing good for their fellow men and women of the Chinese community, and who follow the texts and rubrics of classical canonical Daoism descending from antiquity. Heterodoxy describes Daoists who practice harmful black magic to the detriment or harm of others. But from the viewpoint of an outsider, a marvelous unity is seen to exist among Daoists. In spite of the diversity of sects and rubrics, the mystic experience of unity with the Transcendent Dao and the power over nature resulting from such a union draw all Daoists together in a camaraderie transcending sectarian difference. Yü Tao ho Yi 於道合一 (to be joined as one with the Dao) is the key to Daoist ecumenism, as well as inner cultivation.

PART I

DAOIST MASTER ZHUANG

Note: Chinese words in this third edition are written in pinyin romanization; the 1978 first edition used the Wade-Giles Romanization.

1. Historical Origins
An account of Daoist history as told by Master Zhuang

INTRODUCTION

Master Zhuang is a Daoist of the Celestial Master Tianshi 天师 school, who lived in modern day north Taiwan. Though a thriving industrial nation, its people still cherish the past glories of traditional China. Zhuang was renowned as a teacher of classical religious Daoism, a system of ritual meditations that originated in the first half of the second century A.D., and continued to evolve, grow, and proliferate until the present. To Master Zhuang the origins of his teachings are a sacred oral tradition, unshakable by the theories of modern historians.[1]

In Master Zhuang's opinion, Tianshi religious Daoism was indisputably established by Zhang Daoling 张道陵 the first Celestial Master, who founded the Orthodox One, Celestial Master 正一天师 Daoist school about A.D. 142, toward the end of the Han dynasty. The teachings of Zhang Daoling concern the Zhengyi Auspicious Alliance registers 正一盟威录 i.e., lists of spirits' names and descriptions that the Daoists of his order are empowered to summon and command.[2] Master Zhuang also felt a deep sense of allegiance to the Mao Shan Highest Purity order 茅山上请派, a meditative school founded in the fourth century near Nanking in the central province of Jiangsu. To this order is attributed the difficult text known as the Yellow Court Canon 黄庭经, used by Zhuang as a manual for meditation.[3] Next in the honor and prestige associated with his practice is the Tantric Daoist Qingwei 清微 school, or to hide its identity, the "Celestial Pivot" 天枢. Zhuang puts its origins in the late Tang dynasty and associates it with a famous woman Daoist named Zu Shu, as well as with the sacred peak of the west Hua Shan, near the city of Changan.[4] Along with the Qingwei, Zhuang honors the Pole Star (Beidou 北斗 or Beiji 北极) Daoist tradition, associated with Wudang Shan in the province of Hubei.[5] His own Zhengyi Mengwei school is ranked fourth, after the three monastic centers mentioned above.

In fifth place, Zhuang puts the Shenxiao 神霄 order, a Song dynasty order popular in Fukien, the province of origin for the majority of Taiwan's Chinese population. For two reasons, he felt, the Shenxiao sect is not as respectable as the first four orders. First, said Zhuang, its rituals are a "ministry

of local exorcism," contrived replicas of stately orthodox rituals of the earlier orders. They lack the meditations of inner alchemy that are essential to
traditional orthodox schools.[6] Second, its Daoists sometimes practice black
("left" or sinister) magic to harm men or women of the community and thus
some of its practices are classified as xie 邪 heterodox.[7] The Shenxiao order
was, however, brought under the wings of orthodoxy by the great 13th century Daoist Bai Yüchan. Its beneficent rites are now a part of the repertory
of the Celestial Master, who grants licenses of ordination in its rituals, along
with those of the higher, more traditional four orders.[8]

Zhuang was not unaware of the monastic Quan Zhen 全真 order, or the
other great Daoist movements of Chinese history. His own master, Lin Xiumei, was a devout practitioner of the meditations of Quan Zhen Daoism.[9]
The teachings professed by Zhuang are most intimately related to the first
four doctrines mentioned above, that is, the Mao Shan Yellow Court Canon,
the Qingwei tantric rites, the Pole Star (Big Dipper) meditations and Kung
Fu exercises, and the stately rites of renewal and burial of the Orthodox
One-Celestial Master school. The esoteric doctrines of these schools are
Zhuang's rightful inheritance.[10]

Though there have been a number of excellent treatises published in
Japanese and Chinese within the last three decades on the history and the
doctrines of religious Daoism, there has been very little published in western languages, and no in-depth work on the esoteric mijue 秘诀 practices
of the Qingwei and Pole Star schools. The brief overview of Daoist history
given here is meant only to acquaint the reader with some of the names,
movements, and historical origins of topics discussed by Master Zhuang
concerning the less-known Daoist mijue esoteric tradition. The sources used
are in hand written Chinese; many, but not all, are similar to the sometimes
incomplete Daoist Canon itself, a source that is certainly not critical. Its
biographies are, in fact, hagiographic and filled with pious legend. The following outline is therefore an attempt to describe Master Zhuang's account
of Daoism's liturgical origins, which may or may not coincide with modern
scholars' view of Daoist history.

1. PROTO DAOISTS (The Qin and early Han period, 220 B.C. - 24 A.D.)

Though religious Daoism did not begin as an organized movement until
the declining years of the Han dynasty, that is, the second century C.E.,
historians agree that the court magicians, or fang-shi 方士, of the early Han
dynasty and the violent years which preceded the Han (ca. 221 B.C.) were
precursors of later Daoist rituals.[11] The infamous Qin Shi Huangdi, who
united China under a strict military rule and called himself "First Emperor,"
spent his declining years in search of Daoist formulae for longevity. He died

on a trip to the eastern coast of China from eating poison mushrooms, and his body was spirited back to the capital, bringing about the fall of the Qin and the rise of the Han.[12]

Legend says that Liu Bang, who founded the Han empire in B.C. 206, was assisted to victory by the magic of a Daoist named Zhang Liang 张良.[13] Zhang used a talismanic manual received from Laozi who appeared in the guise of "the Duke of the Yellow Stone 黃石公." The founder of Celestial Master Daoism at the end of the Han period, Zhang Daoling, was said to be the eighth generation descendant of Zhang Liang.[14] The sixth emperor of the Han dynasty, Wu Di 五帝, or the military emperor, surrounded himself with fangshi (proto-Daoists) and established state sponsored cults to Huang-di 黃帝, Hou Tu后土, and Tai Yi 太乙, (Daoist "Yama," ruler of the Underworld), spirits worshipped in later religious Daoism.[15] Both court ritual and popular religious practices during the Han dynasty helped form and influence religious Daoism at the end of the Han period.

Chinese and Japanese historians point to the importance of a strange and little-studied apocryphal literature, the Gu Wei Shu 古纬书, in the formation of early religious Daoism.[16] The Wei apocrypha were popular during the reign of the usurper Wang Mang, who ruled from A.D. 9 to 23, in the middle of the Han period. The emperor Guang Wu Di, who restored the Han dynasty in 25, used the Wei Apocrypha and especially the Ho Tu, 河图"River Chart" to justify his rule.[17] During the later Han period the Ho Tu and its sister chart, the Lo Shu 落书 (writings that came out of the Lo River on the back of a turtle), became an accepted branch of scholarly study. Their use is frequently mentioned in the Hou Han Shu, the history of the later Han dynasty.[18] During the Sui dynasty (589-618), however, the Wei apocrypha were condemned and their study, as well as connection with religious Daoism was forgotten, until the late Ming and 19th century Qing China.[19]

It is useful to examine briefly some of the Wei apocryphal texts to see how much of religious Daoism was in fact drawn from these popular sources. The important early Daoist text, the *San Huang Wen, 三皇文* or *Writ of the Three Emperors*, is mentioned in the Wei apocrypha.[20] The fragmentary texts remaining from this collection are not consistent in describing who the Three Emperors were. They are sometimes said to be Fu Xi, the Celestial emperor; Nü Gua (the wife of Fu Xi) , the earthly emperor; and Shen Nung, the emperor of mankind. In another text the Celestial emperor is called Fu Xi, the earthly emperor is Shen Nung, and the emperor of man is Huang Di.[21] The three emperors are described as having twelve heads, eleven heads, and nine heads, respectively, but the term "head" is interpreted as a single ruler in a dynastic succession of emperors. Thus the Celestial Emperor was a dynastic reign of twelve kings, the earthly emperor a series of eleven kings, and the emperor of humanity a series of nine kings. The Writ of the Three Emperors was assumed into the texts of religious Daoism, and the connections with the Wei apocrypha forgotten.[22]

A second central theme of religious Daoism is the worship of the Five Celestial Rulers, Wu Di (五帝). The five emperors are taken to be personifications of the primordial stuff of the cosmos, the five movers or five elements. The doctrine is taken from the yin-yang five-element cosmology, and is found in adapted form as a part of court ritual in the Yüeh-ling, 月令 or Monthly Commands chapter, of the *Book of Rites* 礼记.[23] Zhang Daoling, the founder of Celestial Master sect Daoism, is said to have used the Monthly Commands chapter in his ritual practices in west China. The later texts found in the Canon show that the names given to the Five Celestial Emperors coincide with titles in the Wei apocrypha; that is, the Daoist texts are similar to rituals found in the classical *Book of Rites*, with names taken from the Wei apocryphal texts.[24]

One of the central documents of religious Daoism, the *Lingbao Five Talismans* 灵宝五符, is also cryptically mentioned in the apocryphal Ho Tu 河图 texts.[25] The apocryphal texts themselves suggest in context that the Five Talismans are a Ho Tu. The following story, relating how the Ho Tu was given to Yü the Great as a talismanic means to control the floods,[26] is changed in later Daoist legends to say that the *Lingbao Five Talismans* were given to Yü to use in controlling the flooding waters, in the same ritual context.

In the story, the Ho Tu is described as a talismanic chart painted in red characters on a green background. It depicts the course of the Yellow River, beginning at Mount Kun Lun and flowing to the sea. At each of the great curves in the river a star in the heavens controls the water for a thousand Li. The river flows in the five directions, east, south, center, west, and north, emptying into the P'o Sea in the east. The person who possesses the chart can control the flow of the river, the stars, and the elements. When the Ho Tu is revealed, it is always brought out of the Yellow River by a spirit horse or dragon. Phoenixes are seen in the royal temple, and vapors of five colored lights come forth from the river. The spirit of the Yellow River who announces the chart is described as having a man's head and a fish's body.[27]

The three ancient kings, Yao, Shun, and Yü, are each given Ho Tu, which enables them to establish a successful rule (N.b., The rulers of Neolithic, Xia, Shang, and Zhou dynasty China were buried with a circular piece of jade called a "Bi" 璧, the symbol of the Imperial Ho Tu gave the right to rule. See the *Lun Yu*, Ch. 10). Yü uses the magic chart to control the floods and, when finished with the powerful talismans, he is told to bury them atop Mao Shan in Jiangsu.[28] Thus there can be seen in the mid-Han period a definite association between the later center for Daoist legerdemain and the apocryphal descriptions of the Ho Tu. The Ho Tu is called a zhen wen, 真文 realized or true writ, the name used exclusively by later Daoists to describe the Lingbao writs and talismans.[29]

Abruptly the apocryphal text shifts to the evil King Ho Lü of the kingdom of Wu. In search of a magic means to conquer the kingdoms of Yüeh and Chu, Ho Lü climbs Mao Shan to find the zhen wen talismans. There he encounters master Lung Wei and commands him to go into the secret recesses of the mountain and bring out the true writs. The text states explicitly that there are 174 characters (zi 字) in the writ.[30] Master Lung Wei complies, but King Ho Lü cannot understand the text. The king takes it to Confucius and tells a lie, saying that a red bird brought it.[31] Confucius is not fooled, and quotes a rhyme sung by the children of the western sea:

> The King of Wu went out one day
> To see a cloud filled lake.
> He met old master Lung Wei
> Who lived upon a peak.
> Climbing up north Mao Shan
> He came upon a cave.
> There was built a secret room
> The writs of Yü to keep.
> The Celestial rulers great writs
> Are forbidden to narrate;
> He who would receive them
> Six hundred years must wait.
> He who takes them out by force
> Brings ruin to his kingdom.

The myth and the poem are found in four different sources, one a fragmentary historical text called the *Yüeh Jue Shu* (*The Demise of the Yüeh Kingdom*),[32] one from the Buddhist Canon, and two from the Daoist Canon.[33] The most interesting of these later references is the diatribe against Daoism quoted by the Tang dynasty Buddhist Xüan Yi in the *Zhen Zheng Lun*.[34] In this Tang dynasty text, the Buddhist master laughs at the notion that the *Lingbao Five Talismans* are a source of blessing. If possession of the famous Daoist charms is so efficacious, the Buddhist says, why did they cause the fall of the kingdom of Wu?[35]

It is apparent, therefore, that the association of the *Lingbao Five Talismans* of the Daoists with the Ho Tu of the apocryphal texts was still made in the

Tang period, even after the Apocrypha and the Ho Tu were condemned during the preceding Sui period. The *Introduction to the Lingbao Five Talismans,*[36] a very early text in the Canon, also recounts the story of Ho Lü. The writer refers to the Ho Tu, specifically, when recalling the story. On the final page of the Daoist canonical text, the Lingbao basic sources are said to be:

1. The hidden secret talismans of the Ho Tu;
2. The Lo Shu found on the carapace of the flying turtle;
3. The Ping Heng, or seven stars of the dipper.[37]

Both the Ho Tu and the Lo Shu, therefore, along with the Pole Star and the rituals surrounding its central place in the northern heavens, were considered to be predecessors of Daoist Lingbao liturgy.[38] (N.b., Neolithic, Xia, Shang, and Zhou burial sites also contained a square piece of jade called a "cong" 琮 with a circle carved from its center, thought to help lead the soul of the deceased from square earth to circular heaven).

The influences of Han dynasty religious practices on religious Daoism go far beyond the few examples cited in the preceding pages. Scholars who have studied the period agree that the popular conjurers, zhou 咒, and their charges, the possessed wu 巫 mediums of feudal China who also figure prominently in the religion of the Han, became associated with a branch of religious Daoism.[39] The use of possessed mediums in popular ritual is not allowed by the orthodox Celestial Master school taught by Master Zhuang. The two professions—that of the stately, literary, orthodox Daoist, and that of the frenzied possessed medium—were distinguished by two separate ministries almost from the beginning of religious Daoism.[40] In modern times, the possessed mediums and the Daoists who control them are often called "Redhead" (hongtou 红头) that is, they belong to a branch of Daoists and a style of ministry called Redhead in popular usage.[41] The Daoists who do not employ medium possession and who follow the strict canonical rules, literary documents, and meditations of ritual alchemy are in some areas called Blackhead or "Back Hat"(wutou 乌头). A distinction between the literary and the military, elite and popular religious Daoism seems to have been made in the very beginning,[42] as can be seen from an examination of the two earliest Daoist movements.

2. THE BEGINNING OF RELIGIOUS DAOISM
The Later Han and Three Kingdoms Period, A.D. 25-264 道教开始

The first saintly man associated with the founding of religious Daoism is the semi-legendary Yü Ji, a mystic and visionary who was born in the area known as Lang Yeh in the province of Shandong, northeast China. Perhaps during the reign of the Shun Di emperor (126-145), Yü Ji was visited by spirits while standing by a river near a place called Jü Yang.[43] The spirits gave him a book, called the *Taiping Qing-ling Shu, The Great Peace Book of Pure Commands*. It had 170 chapters and its doctrines consisted of texts taken from the Yin-yang Five Element theory of the Cosmos, the sayings of the Fang Shi or Dao Shi of the mid Han period, and a new method for commanding spirits to bring blessings and cure illness.[44] According to the message of Yü Ji's prophetic book, heaven had forgotten the principles of yin and yang, thus losing the Dao. Earth had lost the proper functioning of yin and yang, and was experiencing natural disasters. The rulers and ministers of state had neglected the proper balance of yin and yang and were not acting according to the seasons and ways of nature; they were in danger of losing the succession of rule. The loyal minister Xiang Kai, whose biography is found in chapter 60 of the later Han dynasty history, was concerned enough to bring the book to the court of Emperor Huan Di who reigned 147-168.[45] But Huan Di put the prophetic book aside, not realizing that within two decades it would fall into the hands of the Daoist rebel Zhang Jiao, leader of the Great Peace movement, also known as the Yellow Turban rebellion.[46]

There is no doubt of the deep and lasting influence of Yü Ji's book on the formation of religious Daoism. Besides being the basic manual of the Yellow Turban rebels, it also influenced Zhang Daoling, the founder of the orthodox Celestial Master school; Ge Xuan, who is later credited with forming the Lingbao school; and the founders of the third early order known as Mao Shan.[47]

Though the origins of the three early Daoist movements are shrouded in legend, as is the authorship of the *Tai Ping Canon*, the doctrines attributed to Yü Ji that are still found in religious Daoism. The present text of the *Great Peace Canon* has only 119 chapters and many obvious lacunae. It is found at the head of the fifth section of the Daoist Canon, and is used as a title for the entire section, as supporting the doctrines of the Lingbao Canon.[48]

The second great holy man and mystic to whom the founding of religious Daoism is attributed is the first Celestial Master Zhang Ling, known also as Zhang Daoling.[49] Zhang was born in the state of Pei, on the northwest corner of Jiangsu province and the border of Anhwei. Two very sparse accounts of his life are found in the dynastic histories, the first in the biographical section of the Wei history, the second in the *Hou Han Shu (History of the Later Han)*.[50] In these official Confucian sources, Zhang is said to move from his home in Kiangsu to Szechuan province in west China, in search of formulae of longevity, inner alchemy and macrobiotic practice. While in Szechuan, he composed Daoist books[51] that "led the people astray." All those converted to the order were made to pay five bushels of rice. The Confucian historians gave them the derisive name, "Five Bushels of Rice thieves."[52]

Zhang Daoling flourished after the time of Yü Ji, during the years of the Shun-Di reign (126-145). The earliest accounts of his doctrines speak of the composition of twenty-four books of talismanic writings (fu-shu)[53] and the dividing of his theocratic kingdom into twenty-four zhi or administrative districts, with a Ji-Jiu, or grand libationer, at head of each division.[54] The Yueh-ling chapter of the *Book of Rites* and the Lingbao Five Talismans were used to compose his liturgies.[55] Finally, Zhang was credited with creating a ritual which characterizes his sect and its successors until the present day. Documents were composed after the model of memorials and rescripts of the imperial court. The documents were addressed to the rulers of the three realms—heaven, earth, and underworld—to cure illness and win blessings for the people.[56]

A third biography of Zhang Ling is found in the Canon.[57] This account may be modeled on a work missing from the Ming-dynasty Daoist Canon, the *Shen-Xian Juan,* attributed to the third- and fourth-century eccentric, Ge Hong.[58] The Ming dynasty version relates that was a student of the classics when young. He became enamored of the doctrines of longevity in the works of the alchemists, and depleted his family's fortunes in searching for life-prolonging macrobiotic formulae. He is said to have discovered the "Nine tripods of the Yellow Emperor for preparing the elixir of life," but in the process, he became so poor that he had to till the soil and herd cattle for his livelihood.

It was then brought to Zhang Daoling's attention that in the kingdom of Shu (Szechuan) lived a simple and good people who were easy to convert. Zhang immediately gathered some of his followers and went there. He took up residence on the slopes of the mountain where the heron bird sings Mount He Ming. A host of Celestial spirits appeared and revealed to him a doctrine by which the sick could be healed and the land governed in a kind of communal theocracy. It was probably at this time that the book of the Twenty-four Registers was written. Converts flocked to the new religion and their contributions supported Zhang's alchemical experiments. He was soon able to concoct a formula for longevity, which led to immediate dissolution (death) and immortality. Reminiscent of the accounts of the Boddhisattva in Mahayana Buddhism, Zhang drank only half of the potion, thus remaining behind to preach his new doctrines of salvation. After consuming the portion of the drink, Zhang was able to be in two locations at once. Visitors and disciples often saw the master rowing a boat on the lake in front of his retreat while speaking to visitors in the guest pavilion.

The rituals which Zhang Daoling used to govern the villages of Szechuan, were expanded by his grandson and successor Zhang Lu, who many scholars consider to be the systematic organizer of Daoism in West China. Classical sources were used to reconstruct a theocratic kingdom from the ruins of the decaying Han Empire.[59] Taxes were levied, roads repaired, marshes drained, and crops increased. Portions of the grain crops were stored for the poor and the weary traveler. People who committed public offenses were made to confess their sins publicly and to repair a section of a road in penance. If Ge Hong's later account is to be trusted, the early Daoists appear as men of learning and intellectual attainment, trained in chemical experiment and classical learning. Their intent was to found a golden age in the provinces of the floundering Han Empire. As Professor Rolf Stein has observed in a masterful article on Daoist movements at the end of the Han, the political divisions of Zhang Daoling's twenty-four spiritual bishoprics were not unlike the well functioning village leadership of an earlier Han local administrative system.[60] The leaders of early Celestial Master Daoism were indeed the elite of provincial society.

The writings of Yü Ji, mentioned above, were also the basis of a second popular but ill-fated Daoist movement that was to meet a bloody end. In the eastern provinces of China a man named Zhang Jiao (no relationship to Zhang in the west) founded a sect based on the *Tai Ping Jing, the Way of the Great Peace,* of Yü Ji.[61] Zhang Jiao's brand of Daoism, similar in many respects to the Five Bushels of Rice sect in the west, was different in one important aspect. The followers of Zhang Jiao were considered by late Han officials to be rebels intent on overthrowing the court of Han and setting up a new kingdom of *Huang Lao* (Huang Di and Laozi, or, according to some commentators, Laozi as Emperor). According to the teachings of Zhang Jiao, the Blue Heavens—the religion and rule of Han—were dead, and the Yellow Heaven, or, the era of the Great Peace rebellion, was soon to be established. The beginning of a new sixty-year cycle, that is, the Jia Zi year, 甲子 A.D. 184, would see the establishment of the new peace. But instead, in a quick and savage reprisal, mandarin, martial commander, and court arose to obliterate the leader and his converts. The Way of the Great Peace ended in the massacre of its leaders and their myriad followers. Daoism would thereafter be a spiritual rather than a political movement in Chinese history. The Way of the Great Peace was renamed the Yellow Turban Rebellion for the color of the kerchiefs that Zhang Jiao's troops reputedly wore to their death.[62]

In the official dynastic histories, the sparse details and certain common features may make the original Daoist movements seem almost identical.

Closer scrutiny, however, shows that the two were in fact distinct, separated
not only by the plains of east China and the hilly country of the west but by
two distinct styles of religious ritual, some of which still distinguish Daoist schools today.[63] Thus, both the Great Peace movement in the east and
the Celestial Master order in the west worshipped similar Daoist divinities.
But while the eastern group simply honored Huang Lao i.e., The Yellow, or
Imperial Laozi, the west required a specific devotional reading of the *Laozi
Dao De Jing* for membership in the sect. Both movements set up religious
theocracies, but the eastern Great Peace movement divided China's eight
central and eastern provinces into thirty-six Commanderies (fang 方) with a
general at the head of each. The Celestial Master Daoists in the west divided
their kingdom into twenty-four bishoprics or zhi 治, each led by a grand
"Wine Libationer" 祭酒. A group of elders, "surveyors of merit," 督讲 were
put in charge of local village administration. The system, as has been noted,
resembled Han local administration in its age of prosperity.

Both schools considered sickness and disaster to be caused by sinful acts.
The Great Peace movement required its penitents to meditate on their sins
in "Pure Rooms," while the Celestial Master order developed a ritual of repentance. The devout were made to write out their sins on three documents;
the one for the heavens was burned, the one for the earth was buried, and
the one for the underworld was dropped in the water. Thus one sees a definite literary, scholarly spirit in the Celestial Master sect and a military, popular, almost heterodox bent to the way of the Great Peace. The Great Peace
movement clashed openly with the civil government and ended in a bloody
conflagration; the grandson of Zhang Daoling, Zhang Lu, surrendered his
territories to the conquering forces of Cao Cao and the Wei kingdom in the
north. He was rewarded with a noble rank, and his theocratic kingdom continues until the present. Thus the two movements can be distinguished by
the tendency of their ritual and political activities: the one military and the
other literary in religious intent.[64] Daoists still distinguish clearly wen 文
literary, and wu 武 martial or exorcist ritual.

It is interesting to note a further difference in the color symbolism of the
two movements. The three basic colors of the meditative system attributed
to Zhang Daoling are black, yellow, and white.[65] Black-purple, the color of
the sky just before dawn or the winter solstice before the rebirth of yang in
the cosmos, is the color of the deities of the heavens, the symbol of primordial breath within the microcosm of man. Yellow is the color of earth, of
gold, and of the spirit within the center of the microcosm in man. White is
the color of the late afternoon, of the watery underworld, and of the seminal
essence of "wisdom" in the belly of the human body.[66] The Tai Ping Jing of

Yü Ji, on the other hand, takes a different view of the basic colors. Blue-black is made the color of yin, or north, and red the color of yang, or south. The two systems are not contradictory but complementary, as the military and the literary were meant to complement each other in the visible imperial system.[67] The *Zhen Gao* 真诰, a compilation of the basic texts of the Mao Shan order in the sixth century by Tao Hongjing (see below), ecumenically uses both the colors of the *Tai Ping Jing* and the colors of the Celestial Master order for its symbols.[68] It is also interesting that the common people often classify Daoists who are literary, classical, or orthodox as Black and those who are military, popular, or exorcist-or cure oriented as Red. Most important for our present purposes, however, is to note that the two traditions were present from the very beginning of religious Daoism.[69]

Zhang Daoling's kingdom was surrendered by his grandson Zhang Lu, in the year 215, a few years before the final fall of Han and the establishment of the short-lived Kingdom of Wei. By the year 317 and the publication of Ge Hong's *Bao Pu Zi* 葛洪包扑子 or *He Who Embraces Simplicity*, the main themes in religious Daoism had been established, and the books later expanded into the Canon were already known, if only in nuclear form.[70] Thus in the valuable bibliography of books possessed by Ge Hong, there is mentioned the Yellow Court Canon, which will become the basic text of the Mao Shan monastic order, the *Du Ren Jing* and the Lingbao Five Talismans, which are central to the Lingbao order. Surprisingly, the Mengwei or Auspicious Alliance registers of the Celestial Master sect are not mentioned although we know from other sources that they were already extant.[71] The formation of a first Daoist Canon was completed by 471, a hundred and fifty years after Ge Hong's publication of the *Bao Pu Zi*. Note that Zhuang's orally transmitted version of Daoist history differs in some aspects from the studies of western scholars.

3. THE FORMATION OF THE FIRST DAOIST CANON
THE NORTH-SOUTH PERIOD, A.D. 265-581

There is no doubt that the coming of Buddhism to China during the Han dynasty and its widespread acceptance during the north-south period (265-58I) had a profound influence on the formation of religious Daoism. Perhaps two of the deepest impressions were in the emphasis Daoism came to place on burial ritual and the notion of universal salvation. That man should be involved in the care of all souls, not only in the rites for his own ancestors, was a revolutionary thought in the history of Chinese religious expression. Somehow between the sparse accounts of the Han and Wei dynasty histories and the gathering of the first Daoist Canon before the death of Lu Xiujing in 477,[72] a magnificent ritual of cosmic renewal (Jiao) and communal rites for the dead (Zhai) were worked out in something like first draft form.[73] Through a combination of ancient court ritual from the *Book of Rites*,[74] Buddhist canons of merit and repentance as in the *Avalambana* (Chinese: *Yü Lan Pen)*, and the liturgies of the early Daoist popular movements, an esoteric ritual was created and universally accepted as basic to all Daoist orders by the end of the fifth and beginning of the sixth centuries. Three different expressions of these rituals were incorporated into the first Canon, called the *San Dong* or *Three Arcana* by its compiler, Lu Xiujing.[75]

The first of the arcana, the *Dong-Zhen Pu*, 洞真部 or the *Arcanum of the Realized,* evolved around a group of literati-mystics atop Mao Shan in the province of Jiangsu. The order was called the Shangqing 上请 movement, that is, the Highest Pure order. Its organization was contemplative in spirit, based on the experiences of the great Woman Mystic Wei Huacun.The first Daoist monasteries of the order were established atop the three peaks of the Mao Shan range, near the modern city of Nanjing in central China.[76] The second arcana, the *Dong Xuan Bu*, 洞玄部 or *Arcanum of the Mysterious,* derived from a variety of sources, including the classic rituals of the *Book of Rites* and the early Han dynasty Wei apocrypha. The collectanea containing the varied Lingbao texts became the basis for the later magnificent liturgies of the *Dong Xuan* section of the Canon. The third arcana, *Dong Shen Bu* 洞神部 *Arcana of the Spirits* , became the repository for the *Three Emperors Writs* 三皇文 and the spirit-summoning methods or Fa Lu 发炉 of the early Celestial Master order, among many other liturgical materials found in its pages. All Daoists were obliged to learn the Fa Lu and Chu Guan 出管 rites for summoning and sending forth spirits, a meditation used at the beginning of orthodox ritual from the formative period until the present. Zhuang described the formation of the early Daoist Canon in the diagram below.[77]

Formation of the Three Arcanam *San Dong*, the First Daoist Canon
I. Legendary period[78]
    Warring States era, 480-226 BC, and the Western Han, 206 BC to 200 CE
        A. Inner Alchemy 内丹 (*nei-tan*) tradition
        B. Yin-yang 5 Element philosophy
        C. Han dynasty Confucian "New text" rituals, the "Monthly Commands" 月令
        D. The Ancient Wei Apocrypha 古微经.
        E. Yu Ji's *Tai Ping Jing* 太平经 vi. Zhang Daoling's 24 registers, and the Fa Lu mandala meditation (chapter 5).

II. Period of the San Dong (Three Arcana textual Formation:[79]
    Three Kingdoms to CE 200-370, Wei Kingdom, 3 Daoist schools:
        A. Shangqing order
           Founders: Lady Wei Huacun,* Yang Xi, Xu family (father and son)
        B. Lingbao order
           Founders: Ge Xuan (Daoist uncle) and Ge Hong, Ge Chao Fu[80]
           and Wei apocrypha sources
        C. Zhengyi Mengwei order
           Founders: Zhang Daoling* and Zhang Lu

(*indicates a semi-legendary person)

III. Period of collating the first Daoist Canon:[81]
     A.D. 370 to 536; collected by Lu Xiujing (d. 477)
        A. TheYellow Court Canon, and the *Ta Dong Zhen Jing,*
        B. *Lingbao Wu Fu, Lingbao Wu Chen Wen;*
        C. *Wu Yue zhen xing tu,* Lingbao Documents;
        D. 24 Mengwei registers, 24 Zhi dioceses; fa lu mandala meditation;
        E. San Huang Wen, the Three Emperor Writs.
        F. The Mao Shan Shangqing tradition:

Mao Shan master Tao Hongjing, Liang Dynasty court official and Mao Shan Daoist, was the 9th recipient and organizer of the Mao Shan texts. Tao leaned away from the Lingbao canon and favored the Mengwei and Shangqing traditions. Master Zhuang did not associate the Shangqing Mao Shan tradition with popular Mao Shan, or Lü Shan San Nai medium traditions of modern Taiwan and Hong Kong.

Referring to the above chart, the Three Arcana or San Dong traditions are seen to flow almost as a single entity into the final form of the Canon. Zhuang believed that the Shangqing school through its semi-legendary lady founder Wei Huacun, may have been closely allied in its origins to the third Mengwei tradition, as will be suggested in the following pages.[82] Furthermore, the basic rite of the Mengwei tradition, the Fa Lu, is used by all three traditions as an introduction to orthodox ritual.[83] The Daoist schools of the three formative centuries were thus separated more in space than in doctrine or practice.

The first of the traditions, the monastic Shangqing (Mao Shan) order has received by far the most attention from historians, undoubtedly because of the high social standing of the literati-scholars who were converts to its meditative practices. The Mengwei tradition has received the least historical attention, and piecing together its earliest roots is indeed difficult. The tension between the refined scholar who practices inner alchemy for self-perfection, and the demand of the masses for popular salvation liturgy runs like a major theme through the long history of Daoism. Until the Sui dynasty, an elite, scholarly tradition maintained itself above popular folk beliefs and rites of passage.[84] But in spite of Tang dynasty Daoist use of Zhuangzi for inner cultivation, and the Neo-Confucian metaphysics of late Song dynasty intellectuals, other popular historical and social developments eventually resulted in the emphasis on popular Daoist "rites of passage" ritual, exorcism, burial, and Jiao 醮 festivals of cosmic renewal. Whatever the status of Daoism in the minds of China's intellectuals today, from the 3rd to the 10th centuries it was a favorite topic in literate court circles.[85]

The Mengwei tradition, for all the difficulties encountered by scholars attempting to find traces of its existence in the writings of early Confucian historians, was firmly established by the beginning of the Third century in the area of Han Zhung, Szech'uan. The twenty-four spiritual bishoprics of Zhang Daoling, and the twenty-four "chapters" of the book revealed by spirits, appear in the earliest Canon as a series or Lu register of spirits' names and summons.[86] In order to perform ritual properly, Daoists were required to memorize these spirits' appearance, clothing, secret names, and even the sort of perfume used on their apparel. In the performance of public ritual as well as in private meditation, the vision was to be formed in the mind of the adept with immense care that every detail of the garb, countenance, coiffure, and so forth, was complete and accurate. The secrets were passed on by word of mouth, or kept in the rare written mijue 秘訣 registers of spirits names. A special rite was used to send forth the spirits or chu guan, and a mandala-like meditation called Fa Lu, or lighting the incense burner, was performed at the beginning of all orthodox Daoist ritual.[87] The Fa Lu is found in the earliest Daoist texts. Glosses attribute it to the teachings of Zhang Daoling in Han Zhong at the end of the Han dynasty.[88] The Fa Lu meditation, in its orthodox tradition, from the second and third centuries, is taught by Master Zhuang in chapter 5 below. Mengwei Daoism was certainly practiced by Wei Huacun, the lady founder of the Mao Shan Shangqing order. Ge Hong in the *Bao Pu Zi* also mentions the Fa Lu rite, as a "grinding the teeth" like a drum to summon spirits out of the body. Thus the oldest of the traditions of religious Daoism is well recorded, even though the Confucian annals of early religious Daoism did not appear to be aware of its importance.

The second of the great early traditions, the Lingbao texts and scriptures, are also not as well attested in historical writings, as are the works of the prestigious Shangqing founders.[89] One of the basic texts of the tradition, the

Lingbao Five Talismans, was (like the Fa Lu rite mentioned above) found in wide use among all early Daoist masters. One of the more popular rituals in which the five talismans are used, the so-called Su Qi, 宿启, makes use of formulae found in the Monthly Commands chapters of the *Book of Rites* to renew and bless the cosmos. Though Ge Hong in his *Bao Pu Zi* mentions the Lingbao Five Talismans as being efficacious charms to carry on the person as a defense against evil, he does not mention a liturgy such as the Su Qi, which uses them for a sort of cosmic renewal. Historians do record that Ge Hong's nephew Ge Zhaofu multiplied the Lingbao scriptures, forging texts and the like, in order to sell them for a profit.[90] It could be surmised that between the time of Ge Hong's writing and the gross profiteering of the grandnephew, a liturgy of renewal, the canonical Jiao 醮 Gold Registers of the Canon was in wide use. But since Ge Hong does not mention Mengwei or other Jiao rituals, one must conclude that the eccentric scholar was more interested in the formulae of alchemy and macrobiotics than the liturgies performed for the vulgar masses. The very fact that forged copies of Lingbao rituals could be sold supposes a fine market in the fourth century for popular liturgy. Lu Xiujing, when compiling the first Canon in the fifth century, was careful to edit out the forgeries of Ge Zhaofu,[91] which suggests that a detailed Lingbao liturgy of sorts had been worked out by the end of the third century, even though Ge Hong does not mention it in the *Bao Pu Zi*. The Lingpao Jiao rites are among the most detailed sections in the present Daoist Canon. Zhuang assigned their collection to the fifth century, before Lu Xiujing compiled the first Canon.

The first of the great Daoist traditions found in Lu Xiujing's Daoist Canon is the Mao Shan Shangqing scriptures.[92] Where the historical origins of the Mengwei registers and the Lingbao scriptures are difficult to piece together, the Shangqing scriptures are clearly and accurately described from their fourth century revelation to their sixth-century critical edition by the great scholar Tao Hongjing. The founder of the Shangqing or Highest Pure Mao Shan school is a woman, Wei Huacun (251-334).[93] She was the daughter of a literatus-scholar and the wife of an official. In her youth, she was given a classical education and was learned in Daoist texts, receiving the ordination of a Libationer in the Mengwei tradition. Married at twenty-four, she bore two sons, whom she took to the south of China to escape the wars of the times. After both sons had become officials, Wei Huacun turned to spiritual pursuits. She was visited by a host of immortals who revealed to her the basic scriptures of the Shangqing tradition, including the Yellow Court Canon[94] and the *Da Dong Zhen Jing*. After her death, her eldest son passed on her teachings to a young official of the court of the eastern Chin dynasty, Yang Xi.

In the second year of the Xing Ning reign (Jin Ai Di, A.D. 364) Yang Xi began to have nocturnal visitations from the spirit of Wei Huacun, dead some thirty years.[95] Zhuang believes the visions took place atop Mao Shan in Jiangsu province. The noble lady directed that two friends of Yang Xi attend the seances as scribes—Xu Mai, an army official, and his son Xu Hui. First acting as scribes, the two later received visions themselves and became Daoist adepts. A host of Daoist immortals came with Wei Huacun and joined in dictating the revelations that had originally been given to the woman Mengwei Daoist during her earthly life. It is not difficult to understand the need for supernatural authority to support the strange new books and methods that Yang Xi had received from Wei Huacun's eldest son. The nocturnal visions can be taken either as true trance possessions, in which Yang Xi acted as a medium, or as dictations of texts memorized by Yang Xi and chanted during the rituals of meditative alchemy. If the visions of Yang Xi and his scribes were medium possessions, then the roots of Mao Shan would have to be seen as a form of lowly, even heterodox, popular religion.[96] The same must be said for the theory that Yang Xi's dictations took the form of planchette spirit-writing seance. In such a seance, the demon was thought to possess a small chair with a pen attached to one leg; as the scribes hold the possessed chair, the spirit was thought to occupy the seat and cause the leg of the chair to inscribe characters on a piece of paper or in a box of sand held under the moving instrument. Zhuang's Daoist mother had insisted that Shangqing meditation comes from a Daoist woman, not daemon possessed men.

The very literary style of Yang Xi's writings, with the excellent penmanship of the two Xu's, seem to argue against the medium possession theory. Tao Hongjing was able to identify the handwriting of Yang and the Xu's a century and a half later by the fine calligraphy and the excellent literary composition. The revelations of Wei Huacun must be placed with the orthodox classical tradition of Daoist ritual meditation. The appearance of the spirits, the minute descriptions of their clothes, their words, and even the composition of the texts already reported by Ge Hong in the Bao Pu Zi argue for an earlier Shangqing text. The basic Huang Ting Wai Jing (the appendix to the Yellow Court Canon), which now appears as the earlier of Yellow Court texts, is in fact directions for elite meditations of inner alchemy. The Huang Ting Nei Zing, or the new revelations of the Yellow Court Canon attributed to Wei Huacun, is in fact a register or Lu naming and describing a new list of spirits proper to the Shangqing sect and its ritual meditations. The Mao Shan school was, in its beginnings, an order founded by a woman, for and by the highest literati class in the courts of the southern kingdoms.

Yang and Xu made them the center of interest of an elite court society.[97]

News of the revelations atop Mao Shan soon spread widely in the king-doms of south China. The original writings of Yang and the two Xu's were borrowed, copied, forged, and stolen by various interests among the literate elite families. After a lengthy search for the lost documents, Tao Hongjing (456-536) was able to piece together from hearsay as well as fragmentary documentation the odyssey of the Shangqing texts. A critical edition of the fragments was published in the *Zhen Gao*, a work still appearing in the Dao-ist Canon.[98] In chapter nineteen of the work, the following almost humor-ous account is recorded of high society's attitude toward the texts and Tao Hongjing's recovery of the lost documents.

After the death of Xu Hui in 370 and the approaching demise of Xu Mai (376), the written records of Yang Xi's visions were entrusted to Xu Mai's son, Xu Huangmin. Since the transmission of documents was enough to constitute a Daoist adept, it was thought that Xu Huangmin would fol-low his ancestral origins and put into practice the esoteric teachings of the Shangqing school. But Xu Huangmin proved inept as leader and propaga-tor of the new order. The beautiful calligraphy of his grandfather and Yang Xi, contained in trunks full of written scrolls inherited from his father, were soon dispersed throughout the kingdoms of south China. Xu Huangmin, frightened by the wars of the time, moved away from Mao Shan to a district called Shan in Zhejiang province. There his grandfather and father had been highly respected public officials. Xu went to live with two pious laymen, Ma Lang and his cousin Ma Han, who had been friends of his grandfather. Ma Lang was especially delighted that the young Xu had brought along the valuable manuscripts containing the revelations. He took charge of the trunks and tried to keep the precious contents in good condition.

The Ma family was soon to be harassed by visitors from literati and of-ficials of the region, who came inquiring about the famous documents. Un-fortunately, Xu Huangmin gave or loaned the scrolls indiscriminately to all callers, thus causing great concern to the Ma brothers. Some who borrowed the books did not care for them with proper respect and dignity and soon died. When he attempted to read one of the books, a certain Wang Qing saw fire come down from heaven and destroy it.[99] In a gloss of the *Chen Gao* Tao Hongjing relates that the unworthy who received the *Shangqing* scriptures without proper instructions and rites of transmission were punished by the heavens. The revelations of Yang and the two Xu's were not meant for pub-lic dissemination.[100]

There also came a refined scholar named Wang Ling Qi to the home of Ma Lang and begged Xu Huangmin to allow him to have copies of the scriptures.[101] Xu refused but Wang Ling Qi waited outside Ma Lang's home in the snow until Xu relented. We must remember that the Lingbao scriptures, the books of macrobiotic diets and the alchemical formulae for "instant longevity" were very popular from the north-south period through the Sui into the Tang dynasty. The demand for macrobiotic manuals in particular offered a ready fortune for the adept who could produce the latest book on Daoist hygiene or Daoist magic. The motives of Wang Ling Qi were not purely spiritual. Taking the prized manuals home, Wang was disappointed to discover that the Shangqing doctrines were lofty and difficult to follow. The meditations, the high literary style, and the complicated ascesis did not find easy acceptance in the ritual-loving world of Lingbao scripture patrons. Wang therefore took note of the titles that Wei Huacun had promised to divulge at a later date and forged his own versions of these works, announcing that they had been revealed to him in a vision. Xu Huangmin was completely taken in by the forgeries. Ma Lang at first planned to purchase the new books of revelations, but in a dream saw a jade bowl fall from the heavens and shatter. From this he understood that heaven had not after all revealed the new books and called off the transaction.[102]

Xu Huangmin then left the residence of Ma Lang to live with the Du family in the distant city, Qian Tang. He left behind the trunks of precious documents, now somewhat depleted, with strict orders to Ma Lang that no one was to open them or give any more of the documents away. Not even if a letter came from Xu Huangmin himself was Ma Lang to open or remove a box. A few months later, Xu Huangmin fell ill and sent a letter to Ma Lang asking that the trunks be sent to him at the Du residence. Obedient to the earlier orders, Ma refused to let the boxes out of his house. Xu's sickness worsened, and he died in 429.[103]

The pious Ma Lang, meanwhile, refused to let the Shangqing scriptures be taken out of their protective trunks. He appointed two elderly custodians to guard the door of the room where the treasures were kept, burn incense, and sweep the floor. The fortunes of the Ma family increased a hundredfold, because of the care and devotion with which he guarded the scriptures. As Ma Lang approached old age, he decided to have accurate copies of the texts made, lest they be lost to the ravages of time. A fine calligrapher and one-time friend of the family, Ho Daojing, was hired. The temptation of the prized texts proved too much for Ho, who sold many of the best copies to the public, gave transcriptions to his friends and disciples, and even substituted some of his own copies for the originals. Ma Lang discovered the treachery and was furious. More devastating than the thievery was the scandalous conduct of Ho Daojing, who had given copies of the sacred documents to two of his women followers. He was rumored actually to practice the vulgar fang zhong sexual techniques, a means to longevity specifically forbidden in the revelations of Wei Huacun. Outraged, Ma Lang dismissed the scribe and had molten copper poured over the locks of the trunks so that they could no longer be opened.[104]

The actions of Ho Daojing were ruinous to the pious work of Ma Lang. Copies of Ho's manuals reached the court and an official named Lou Hui-Ming went to the Ma household to claim the prized collection. When Ma refused to break the seals, Lou memorialized the court of Song Wen Di and in the year 465 had the trunks brought to the capital. On the way, the Shangqing scriptures were once more rifled. Lou Huiming opened the trunks and removed some of the contents. Thus the depleted collection of spiritual revelations finally came to light officially, where they were first examined by the court Daoists and then, on the recommendation of the emperor, turned over to Lu Xiujing, who incorporated them in the first Canon and transmitted them to his successor Sun Yuyue.[105]

Tao Hongjing, who, as Sun Yuyue's successor laboriously collected the scattered documents from the literati who had avidly gathered them, noted that a great number of those involved in collecting the precious manuscripts were themselves Daoists.[106] Thus Lou Huiming and Shu Jizhen, men employed by the Song court, were accomplished Daoist masters. Lu Xiujing and Tao Hongjing himself received imperial patronage. By the efforts of scholars like Lu and Tao, the Daoist scriptures were collected, critically edited, and preserved as a canonical tradition.

The following Daoists and scholars were directly involved in the transmission of the Shangqing scriptures:[107]

Wei Huacun		(252-334)
Yang Xi		(330-387)
Xu Mai	(305-376)	
Xu Hui	(died 370)	
Xu Huang Shi		(361-429)
Ma Lang		
Ma Han		
Lu Xiujing		(died 471)
Sun Yuyüe		
Tao Hongjing		(456-536)

Tao Hongjing was able to piece together the original fragments of the Mao Shan revelations by identifying the beautiful handwriting of Yang and the two Xu's and rejecting the forgeries of Wang Lingqi. The fragments were put together in the *Zhen Gao,* a scholarly presentation by Tao, for the elite literati society of the early sixth century. In his Zhao Tai pavilion atop Mao Shan, Tao Hongjing lived the life of a renowned master. The three-story Zhao Tai was a gathering place where Tao ruled like a despot from the top floor, over a crowd of copyists and disciples on the middle floor, who in turn cared for the guest rooms and distinguished visitors on the ground floor of the grand residence.

The personality and influence on Daoism of the two great masters, Lu Xiujing and Tao Hongjing, were entirely different. Lu Xiujing was a master of the Lingbao tradition, which he had received through Ge Xuan and Ge Hong. He was also familiar with the Mengwei registers, or the teachings of the three first Celestial Masters, Zhang Daoling, Zhang Heng, and Zhang Lu. Lu Xiujing was an organizer and a synthesizer. It is most probable that by his time the liturgies of the Lingbao tradition had been combined with the rites of spirit-summoning and spiritual memorials of the Mengwei Celestial Master tradition into a prototype of the Jiao. Though Lu Xiujing recognized the immense value of the Mao Shan revelations and accorded them the highest place in the canon of the Three Arcana, he came to them through the patronage of Song Wen Di and not by a prior conversion or dedication to the Mao Shan scriptures as such.[108]

Tao Hongjing, on the other hand, was a perspicacious man. He despised the loud and vulgar Lingbao rites and did not hesitate to discourage their practice on Mao Shan.[109] Right or wrong, he saw the degrading potential of the popularizing tendency in Daoist movements; the popular rites were beneath the interests of the scholars who were the elite of China's ruling classes. The Shangqing scriptures, however, were the supreme Daoist teachings. Tao, who had been a Buddhist, ranked the Shangqing revelations beside the Lotus Sutra and the Zhuangzi. They were the Sarvayana (all in one vehicle); he thought of the three revelations as one doctrine revealing the highest of all causes.[110] To preserve itself in the religious conflicts of the north-south period, Daoism must remain the prerogative of the highest social classes. As history soon proved, the emphasis on the nonintellectual aspects of Daoism, an emphasis that the court preferred to the elite meditations of the scholarly hermit, was to result in its rejection by many literati.

The influence of Tao Hongjing on orthodox classical Daoist ritual is still deeply felt today. It was in the first chapter of his compilation, *Deng Zhen Yin Jue,* that Tao's opinions had an especially deep effect on future masters. More than in the practices of macrobiotic or chemical alchemy, Tao Hongjing taught as part of the Mao Shan tradition that the very act of ritual meditation, in which the spirits are summoned forth from the body and the very center of the microcosm emptied, was a workable method for find-ing immortality and longevity.[111] Thus, by carrying the doctrine of the Yel-low Court Canon to its conclusion, Tao put the final touch on the formation of the orthodox ritual practice. The meditations through which the Dao-ist purified his body and emptied even the spirits of the highest heavens, the meditations that prepared the microcosm for the encounter with the transcendent Dao, gave efficacy to ritual, as well as direction in the prac-tice of spirituality. Thus meditative alchemy was given a visible expression in liturgy, and liturgy in turn derived its power from the meditations that established the contact of the Daoist with the purest powers and forces of the ultimate heavens. The Lingbao rites of the vulgar masses were an empty shell, a chanting of verses and ringing of bells. Orthodox ritual was a thing of power and beauty, expressing the very depths of the Daoist's meditations.[112]

Zhuang delighted in telling these tales of Daoist origins to is disciples, to show how important it was to preserve Daoist esoteric teachings, not using them for profit, self-glory, or "showing off" in front of scholars. A "great curse" of anger and physical disaster will fall on scholars of Daoism who do not observe the strict rules of purity and secrecy, in the transmission of Daoist esoteric texts, he insisted.

4. GREAT DAOIST MASTERS
SUI AND TANG PERIODS A.D. 581-905

The practices recorded by Tao Hongjing, though preserved in canonical and monastic manuals used by the traditional classic orders, were super-seded by his successor the tenth master of Mao Shan, Wang Yuan Zhi.[113] This honored master, who lived through two complete cycles of sixty years to reach an incredible age of more than one hundred and twenty, was only eleven when Tao Hongjing died. Wang learned ritual Daoism from Zang Jing, who chose instead to train him in the Tai Ping Jing and the popular *Jiao* liturgies deriving from the Lingbao tradition. Though he obviously knew the elite meditations of the Mao Shan Shangqing sect, Wang chose to emphasize the liturgical tradition. The fame of Wang's liturgies spread throughout the Sui empire, and in 611 Wang met Sui Yang Di, the second Sui dynasty emperor, who ordered him to perform a Lingbao Jiao ritual atop the famous central peak, Song Shan. Subsequently an official Daoist temple, Yü Qing Xüan Tan, was constructed at the court in Loyang, and Wang was appointed its Master. He lived well into the Tang period and died finally in 635, the ninth year of the Zhen Guan reign period.[114]

During the lifetime of Wang the emphasis on public liturgy superseded the elite ritual meditations of Tao Hongjing. The delight of the court in Wang's fancy Lingbao rituals of renewal echoed the popular Daoist movements, which grew and expanded during the Tang and the Song Dynasties. Lingbao rites were patronized by China's villages and urban temples, as well as by the nonintellectual imperial court. One can almost see the disapproving stares of the Confucian literati, opposing both the fascination of the emperors and the enthusiasm of the people for Daoism's great dramatic liturgies. The development of popular religion, drama in ritual expression, and the patronage of Tang and Song emperors contributed to Daoism's absence in the historical records written by the Confucian intellectuals.[115]

If the preceding accounts of religious Daoism seem overly involved with the Mao Shan tradition, one need look no further than the Daoist Canon to grasp the importance given to other forms of the Daoist liturgical tradition. Much more attention is given to the grand Yellow Register Zhai and Gold Register Jiao rites in the later Ming Dynasty (1435-1447) *Zheng Tong* Daoist Canon. In contrast, liturgical materials are relatively unstudied either in Confucian or western "inner cultivation" studies. The history of Daoism during the Tang and Song dynasties shows a unique doctrinal ecumenism, uniting the urban and mountain centers together in a sense of camaraderie. The Three Arcana were the common possession of all Daoists. The Lu or registers of the various centers were shared with itinerant Daoists who visited the great mountain centers, and incorporated them as a part of the Canon.

Three great masters whose names figure prominently in the Canon typify Daoism during the Tang dynasty. The first, discussed here in this chapter, is the twelfth Mao Shan master, Si Ma Chengzhen (646-735), the descendant of a noble family. His biography appears in the Tang dynasty official histories as well as in the Canon.[116] Six of his works appear in the Ming dynasty Daoist Canon, and chapter 924 of *The Complete Works of the Tang (Chuan Tang Wen)* is dedicated to his writings.[117] In that chapter a fine summary of the Shangqing Mao Shan teachings is found, as well as a discussion of the *Zhuangzi* and its use in ritual meditation. According to Si Ma Chengzhen, the heart is to be emptied by meditation, for "only the heart which has been emptied can be the dwelling place for the Tao."[118] The doctrine is applied to the Lingbao and Zhengyi scriptures, that is, the exteriorizing of the spirits performed in Zhengyi Mengwei and Lingbao rituals are seen as preparations for uniting the Daoist with the Tao of Wu-wei, that is, the Dao of "Non act," or "Transcendent act."

Some of the more startling occurrences in Daoism both before and after the Tang period were the frequent and lengthy journeys of the masters. As if the powers of spiritual meditation conferred the ability to walk great distances with no effort, Si Ma Chengzhen is seen to be master of the central peak, Song Shan; the southern peak, Heng Shan; the great Buddhist-Daoist center, Mount Tientai in Zhejiang; and his own home, Wangshi Shan. He was an expert in Zhengyi orthodox Daoism, as well as in Mao Shan and Lingbao Daoism. The two esoteric traditions of Pole Star and Thunder-Vajra ritual were said by later writers to be part of his repertoire.[119] The Emperor Xuanzong became a patron of Si Ma Chengzhen's Daoist arts and received the Lu registers of the three Daoist orders—that is to say, a Daoist ordination—in A.D. 72I.[120]

The second great Daoist of the Tang period, whose works were ecumenical and to whom texts in the Canon are credited, was Zhang Wanfu (active ca. 712).[121] The extant writings of Zhang Wanfu show a clear continuity between the three original movements of the early north-south period and the Daoist unity of the Tang. Volume 990 of the Canon contains a complete list of the registers and the times for transmitting them to the Daoist novice.[122] Zhang, like his predecessors, unites all three of the orders—Mengwei, Lingbao, and Shangqing—into a single body of revealed doctrine. The young Daoist, beginning with the basic twenty-four Mengwei registers, receives the San Huang Wen, the Precious Ho Tu Register, the Jie precepts and *Zhang* documents of the *San Dong (Three Arcana),* the *Laozi Dao De Jing,* the *Lingbao Five Talismans,* and the teachings of the Mao Shan Shangqing sect.[123] Zhang Wanfu thus presents Daoism of the Tang dynasty as an ecumenical union of monastic centers and great masters.[124]

The third great master of the Tang period was the renowned Du Guangting A.D. 842-926). A favorite of both emperors and mandarins, Du Guangting is credited with having composed or contributed to twenty-eight works in the Canon.[125] A collection of his writings for the court are included in *the Complete Works of the Tang.*[126] As the last great master before the sectarian movements of the Song dynasty, Du Guangting towers above his contemporaries and later generations as a scholar who commanded a view of the totality of religious Daoism. Du left behind a grand summary of the unified system he envisioned in a number of important works in the Canon. In the *Tai Shang Zhengyi Yue Lu Yi (Tai Shang Ritual for Transmitting the Daoist Rules and Registers),* orthodox, traditional forms of religious meditation and ritual are clearly listed:[127]

1. The introductory ritual is given in the first section of the chapter. Du Guangting describes the classical, orthodox manner of performing the initiation ritual (outlined by Master Zhuang in chapter 5 below) - the solemn entrance of the Daoist into the sacred temple area, the offering

of incense, the beginning of the meditation, the sounding of the drum, (while grinding the left, front, and right teeth), the and the emptying of the microcosm in preparation for union with the Dao (See chapter 5, part 6, below).

2. The main body of the rite contains the registers of the classical orders. Du Guangting lists the twenty four registers of the Zhengyi Mengwei sect, the Ho Tu registers, the Pole Star registers of military or exorcistic Daoism, the Liu Jia spirits (chapter 4) but mentions only briefly the Thunder Vajra sects, which developed later in the Song dynasty.[128]

3. The rite closes with the Daoist restoring the spirits to their places inside the microcosm, (Fu Lu) from whence they had been sent forth before the meditation of union with the Tao.

In a second section, which follows shortly after the rite for transmitting the registers of an orthodox Daoist, Du Guangting describes the ritual of the Ho Tu, the magic chart used by Yü the Great to control the floods.[129] The Ho Tu ritual differs in one important aspect from the earlier Yue Lu liturgy. The rite for transmitting the Lu registers was meant for the Daoist priest alone and therefore was filled with esoteric meditations and allusions to union with the transcendent Tao. The ritual of the Ho Tu, on the other hand, was meant to alleviate the sufferings of the common folk of village and countryside. Du Guangting begins by enumerating the uses of the Ho Tu ritual. It is to control natural disasters, bring thunder and lightning under the Daoist's control, stop warring armies, and the like. The preparation of the Daoist altar is splendidly described: lanterns are set up representing the four directions, the eight trigrams, and the twenty-eight constellations. After the model of the Lingbao Five Talismans, but in a much more complicated mandala, the entire cosmos is symbolically represented in scrolls, hangings, food offerings, and lanterns. With the altar arrayed, the ritual is performed according to the classical model outlined in the preceding paragraph and described more fully in chapter 5 below.[130]

With Du Guangting, the classical period of Daoist ecumenism and unity came to an end. During the following five dynasties and the Song period, sectarianism and reformation threatened the structural unity of religious Daoism. But before the Song dynasty revolution in Daoist orders, the seeds of change could be seen in the writings of some of the Tang masters. This brief overview of the Tang must include three of these precursors of change to indicate the direction from which growth was to come. Of the three masters, Li Chunfeng, an historical personage and early Tang court Daoist, is easily identified in the Canon. Wang Zihua and Lady Zu Shu, on the other hand, are almost legendary figures and their existence was barely mentioned in historical writings before later Song times. The sources of change, however, are clearly identifiable in the thunder-vajra ritual which was to become popular in the Song period. Both the austere Chan (Zen) teachings, and the tantric Buddhist schools, this latter with their colorful rituals, mudras, and mantric charms, were taken as the basis for many of the liturgical reforms in the Song dynasty Daoist canon.[131]

Li Chunfeng was a Mao Shan Daoist who was active at the beginning of the Tang period, about A.D. 632. Two works in the Daoist Canon are attributed to him, both of which describe the use of left-handed mudras, Siddham-Sanskrit mantras, and thunder rites to control and exorcise evil spirits.[132] The Bei Dou Pole Star rituals are highly developed in Li's two works, and the paraphernalia used in later Song dynasty Thunder ritual are described in rudimentary form.[133] The style of ritual described by Li is later developed into a distinct set of rituals associated with Lady Zu Shu, and the Qingwei Thunder-Vajra sect.[134] Qingwei thunder vajra ritual is an essential part of the teachings of Master Zhuang, and is described in chapter 6 below.[135]

The semi-legendary Wang Zihua was born in 714 and died in 789. He resided on Heng Shan, a southern peak in Hunan province where he practiced meditative ritual and allegedly developed a style of thunder rite called Qing Jing style.[136] The rituals of Wang were developed under the influence of the great Si Ma Chengzhen, and were supposedly influential throughout southeast China. His school of Thunder Ritual was mentioned by famous Song dynasty masters, such as Wang Wenqing, and Bo Yüchan.[137]

Lady Zu Shu is a legendary figure active towards the end of the Tang dynasty, ca. A.D. 880.[138] One of Daoism's three great woman teachers, (Wei Huacun and Sun Bu-er are the other two) she is said to have been born in Yung Zhou, Guangxi, to have had long black hair and a dark complexion, becoming an immortal at age 132 years. All of the Daoist schools credit her with founding the Qingwei Thunder or Vajra school of Daoism. She traveled extensively throughout China, to the city of Chang An, and the sacred peak of the west Hua Shan.[139] The late Daoist master Min Zhiting was a Quan Zhen as well as an ordained Zhengyi Daoist who learned from Weibao Shan and Jizu Shan in Yunnan. She taught that her Thunder ritual differed significantly from that of the Shenxiao school, attributed to Wang Zihua, and Lin Lingsu. Just as Daoists of the "Three Mountain Alliance"— Lunghu Shan, Mao Shan, and Gozao Shan—use Thunder rites during Jiao and Zhai liturgies, Quan Zhen Daoists have an especially ornate rite used at the beginning of the Pu Du ceremony for "freeing all souls," which Min Zhiting used, different from the Zhengyi tradition (cf. Chapter 6).

5. THE AGE OF SECTARIAN DIVISION
THE SONG AND YUAN [MONGOL] PERIODS, A.D. 960-1341

Historians agree that the Song dynasty was a period of great intellectual and organizational change for China. Some historians even name the Song dynasty as the beginning of China's modern period.[140] The great Japanese scholar Noritada Kubo, whose book *Chugoku no Shukyo Kaikaku (China's Religious Reformation)* is a classic work on Quan Zhen Daoism, contrasts Daoist sectarianism of the Song with the Protestant Reformation in sixteenth and seventeenth-century Europe.[141] The differences are striking. Multiple schools developed in religious Daoism, without the fury of doctrinal debate, that typified the protestant revolt in the west. Daoist schools developed throughout the length and breadth of China. Each province and county had its own variety of Daoist expertise, without the intense rivalry or acrimony found in Europe.

Daoist rivalry, as will be seen in the teachings of Master Zhuang, was limited to functional rather than doctrinal differences. That is, the disputes of the Daoist masters of the Song and later times were not concerned with the basic doctrines of the Yin-yang Five Element cosmology, the Three Pure Ones, the Five Emperors, or the other common teachings of Daoist belief. Instead, the masters of the traditional orders opposed the use of ritual for harmful magic, the performance of liturgy purely for pecuniary gain to the detriment of meditation, and the trend towards heterodoxy or popular sectarianism that brought down the wrath of the mandarin and the court on the heads of the beleaguered local Daoists. Though Song and Yuan Daoists may have argued about the proper color to be envisioned during a ritual meditation,[142] they presented a unified front when faced with outside opposition, whether Buddhist, mandarin, or imperial. Differences occurred in different forms of monastic living, the introduction of many new kinds of popular rituals, and a trend towards multiplying local and provincial fraternities of Daoist brethren.[143]

Modern scholars tend to identify two great orders of religious Daoists: the Quan Zhen sect in north China and the Zhengyi or Celestial Master sect in the south. But field based research has shown a far more complex picture. The Quan Zhen sect represents, in some ways, the Daoist response to the influence of Chan (Zen) and other forms of monastic Buddhism in China. Like the Buddhist monasteries of China, Quan Zhen Daoists aimed for a rigorous life of simple monastic discipline.[144] Like Buddhism in both China and Japan, they eventually turned to the performance of popular ritual as a means of financial support.[145] The Zhengyi sect, the successors of the first Celestial Master at the end of the Han dynasty, experienced a renewal during the Song period and became the court-sanctioned leaders of religious Daoism throughout south China. The hegemony of Zhengyi Daoism in liturgical matters continues to the present day.[146]

The founding of the Quan Zhen sect is attributed to Wang Zhongyang, who was born in 1113 in Ta Wei village, Xien Yang county, Shenxi province. The first monastery of the order was probably established in the Shandong province, the district of Ning Hai.[147] The monastic headquarters of the order was later established in Bai Yun Guan, Beijing, where it is still maintained to the present day. Wang stressed Confucian and Buddhist doctrines as well as the texts of inner alchemy and self-perfection of religious Daoism. *The Confucian Canon of Filial Piety*, the *Laozi Dao De Jing*, the Buddhist *Pan-juo Hsin-ching (Prajna Paramita Hrdaya Sutra)*, and the *Chang Qing Jing* of religious Daoism were used by the order.[148] The influence of Buddhism on the Quan Zhen masters can be seen from the secondary title of the sect, Golden Lotus Orthodox Religion, (Jin Lien Zheng Zong). The Quan Zhen sect was the parent organization for many later Daoist groups, including the Long Men school, and the Qing Jing contemplative order founded by Lady Daoist Sun Bu-er.[149]

Other noted schools of the Song period were the Zhen Da group of Liu Deren, the Tai Yi order of Xiao Baochen, and the Qing Ming sect of Ho Zhengong. All three were flourishing at the beginning of the southern Song period, between 1138 and 1140.[150] The last of the three, the Qing Ming school, claimed to originate from a third century Daoist master named Xu Xun, who was made one of the legendary founders of Thunder Ritual. Devotion to him was approved at the court of Emperor Hui Zong, in 1112.[151] By far the most popular form of Daoism during the Song period were the prestigious Thunder Rites, propagated by a number of local Daoists and Daoist schools, Though historians have not yet established which of the thunder schools appeared earliest, it is certain that its patronage by the Hui Zong Emperor encouraged the spread of this new form of Daoist Vajra-Thunder ritual.

In 1116 the Thunder rites of Deng Yugong were introduced to the court of Hui Zong, through the presentation of a systematic manual called *The Secret Method for Assisting the Nation and Saving the People*.[152] Teng called his order the Tian Xin Zheng Fa and derived many of his teachings from the Zhengyi Celestial Masters.[153] The new doctrines of Deng were centered on the use of Five Thunder magic, 五雷法 that is, the power of thunder seen as a moving agent for the five elements. The sect used mudras and mantras modeled after the mudra and mantra of Tantric and esoteric Buddhist orders, similar to those found in the Buddhist texts of Tian Tai (Japanese: Tendai) and Zhen Yan (Japanese: Shingon) Buddhism. The use of Siddham-Sanskrit words, as foreshadowed in the writings of the Tang master Li Xiangfeng, and the various thunder mudras are clearly seen in the extant works of the *Tian Xin Zheng Fa* found in the Canon.[154] Thunder rituals attributed to Deng are cited by Master Zhuang, in Chapter 6 below.

In 1117 the famous Daoist master Lin Lingsu was introduced to the court of Hui Zong. Born in Yung Jia, Wen Zhou district in southern Zhejiang, a step away from Fujian province where his doctrines were to become so popular, Lin Lingsu is credited with being a great propagator of Shenxiao style Thunder Magic in the Song dynasty. So powerful a personality was Lin that he was given free access to the emperor, and his Shenxiao magic was awarded imperial patronage. The order was given brief mention in the Song dynasty official history, under the biography of Lin Lingsu.[155] A lengthy biography of Lin is found in The Mirror of Perfected Immortals, a Ming dynasty hagiography of famous Daoists. But Lin is given credit for none of the writings in the present Canon, although his biography mentions books he allegedly had written.[156]

The Song dynasty Longhu Shan orthodox masters, as well as Master Zhuang in the present, are somewhat ambivalent toward the Shenxiao order. One reason is that the Shenxiao masters are not consistent in their manner of performing meditation. Sometimes the orthodox colors are switched or new versions created without reference to the canonical tradition of the past.[157] At other times the Shenxiao Daoists perform ritual without regard for inner alchemy or any form of meditation.[158] Doubly reprehensible is the fact that the lower ranking local masters perform the stately Jiao and Zhai liturgies with no real knowledge of the proper rubrics or of the true content of the ritual.[159] Such is often the case in modern Taiwan, where pecuniary motives have destroyed the spirit of generosity as well as downgrading the inner spiritual cultivation that was typical of the Daoist sage in the past. Finally and perhaps worst of all from the orthodox Daoist's viewpoint, Shenxiao Daoists were and are sometimes accused of performing black, "Dao of the Left, "Sinister" or harmful magic. This last is true not only of Shenxiao Daoists but of local, self-termed "Mao Shan" and other village magicians as well.[160] In making such accusations, however, the critic immediately must add that there were many great Daoists of the Shenxiao tradition who have won the respect of all of their Daoist brethren.

Perhaps the most influential Daoist master of the southern Song dynasty (1127-1278) was the gifted scholar, Bai Yuchan.[161] Born on Hainan island of a literati family originally from Fukien province, Bai is credited with fifteen works in the Daoist Canon and is respected as one of the greatest masters of religious Daoism. A man of ecumenical breadth, Bai brought together the various sects and movements of his time and was considered the leader of Daoism in south China.[162] Among the many titles given to him are "Propagator of Shenxiao Daoism," and "Master of Inner Alchemy." It is clear from his writings that he sought to give legitimacy to the Shenxiao rituals that were popular throughout his native Fukien province.[163] In a massive compendium of Thunder Magic literature, compiled from the writings of noted Daoist experts including Bai himself, is a list of the various Thunder Rite schools of the Song, propogated by the "Three Mountain Drop of Blood Alliance" (Mao Shan, Gezao Shan, Longhu Shan):[164]

1. Sanskrit Primordial Breath Thunder Rites, Qingwei school[165]
   a. Dong Zhen—Hun Dun Thunder rites from Mao Shan
   b. Qingwei Thunder rites from Hua Shan, Hunan, Zhejiang, and Fujien
   c. Lingbao (Gezao Shan propogated) Thunder Rites
2. Qingxu Thunder Magic, used by the Tai Yi school.[166]
3. Shenxiao Thunder Magic, attributed to Wang Wen-Qing (born 1093),[167] corrected by Bai Yuchan.
4. Yu Fu Thunder Magic, of the Zhengyi Celestial Master school[168]
5. Beiji Pole Star Thunder Magic, of the Bei Dou school from Wudang Shan, in Hubei[169]

Perhaps the most significant fact about the various kinds of Thunder Magic is the distinctive Lu that typifies each school. Thus, the "Three Mountain" related Qingwei sect uses a specific Lu, or register of spirits' names, and a style of Siddham-Sanskrit peculiar to its own order. The other schools were distinguished from the Qingwei order by their own style of ritual as well as by their list of spirits summoned to perform Thunder rites. The above list is also found in the *Dao Jiao Yuan Liu*, a private manual circulated by modern Daoists who teach in Taiwan and southeast China. Both sources decry using black magic, betraying the very purpose of Daoism, which was meant to help and not harm the people who came for aid.[170]

The role of Bai Yuchan was that of unifier and religious leader in the southern Song period. The famous Daoist Jin Yunzhong wrote in the Daoist Canon against the Shenxiao order and some forms of Thunder Magic in his Shangqing Lingbao Da-Fa.[171] Because of the efforts of Bai and his disciples, the criticisms of Shenxiao Daoism were mitigated. Since the various styles of Thunder Magic will be more fully described by Master Zhuang in chapter 6, it is sufficient here to point out the complexity of Daoist movements in the late Song and early Yuan periods, and the need of historical scholarship to be nonpartisan as it traces development of Song sectarianism. Pai Yu-

Chan sought to eradicate from Shenxiao Daoism the elements that brought criticism from his fellow Daoists. As a result he was given the honorific title, "Propagator of Shenxiao Daoism" (see note 163). It is interesting to note, however, that in signing his official Daoist statements, Pai Yu-Chan did not use a Shenxiao rank but an orthodox Mao Shan Celestial Master and Pole Star title.[172] The trend to learn as many registers as possible and to use the more prestigious in signing ritual documents can be clearly seen in the southern Song and the Yuan period. Daoists began to be ranked according to the number of registers that they could master.[173]

6. POLARIZATION AND POLITICAL DECLINE
Ming dynasty, A.D. 1638 to the present

The Ming dynasty was noted in the beginning for its patronage of religious Daoism. The trends begun in the Song period were confirmed and consolidated during the Ming. The present Daoist Canon was commissioned and completed by 1447, under the reign of the emperor Cheng Tong.[174] The trend toward sectarianism was brought under control by decree of the court. Three monastic centers in south China—Mao Shan in Jiangsu province, Lung-hu Shan, and Ko-tsao Shan in Jiangsi province—were given authority to grant licenses of ordination, without which the local Daoist masters were supposedly not permitted to practice. The manual called *Dao Jiao Yuan Liu*, which is found in the libraries of Master Zhuang and almost all Taiwan Daoists, explains how the licenses of ordination are given.[175] The Celestial masters of the three mountains were empowered by imperial authority to grant licenses of ordination in the following styles of ritual:

1. The Yü Jing or Mao Shan Shangqing style of meditative ritual.
2. The Qingwei or Tianshu style of Thunder Magic.
3. The Beiji or Pole Star (Bei Dou) style of military exorcism.
4. The Yü Fu or Zhengyi style of orthodox Jiao and Zhairitual.[176]
5. The Shenxiao style of popular ritual and exorcist healing.

In the Dao Jiao Yuan Liu, each of these five styles of ritual are divided into nine grades of perfection, from the lowest grade nine, or Jiu Pin 九品, to the highest grade one, or Yi Pin. 一品[177] The grades are carefully listed, and the Daoist masters are required to sign their official documents, ritual memorials, and rescripts with the title given them at ordination. Thus the custom described at the end of section 5 above was standardized for southern Daoism by decree of the Ming emperors.[178] Furthermore, the Celestial Master at Longhu Shan preserved a special manual in which the rite of ordination and the titles given to the Daoist masters were recorded. The manual is still in use by the Daoists of Taiwan, Longhu Shan, Mao Shan, and Bai Yun Guan in Beijing. It was purchased at Longhu Shan by a Hsinchu Daoist named Lin Rumei (see chapter 2) in 1868 and brought to Taiwan. The manual is now possessed by Master Zhuang and a copy is in my microfilm collection. The book, called *Ji (Gei) Lu Yuan Ke*, describes the qualifications required for receiving each grade of ordination:

Grade one:	The Da Dong Zhen Jing, or the Yellow Court Canon, and its registers
Grades two and three:	Qingwei Thunder, and Pole Star registers
Grades four and five:	the Mengwei registers of Zhengyi Daoism
Grades six:	the Lingbao registers, i.e., "Three-Five Surveyor of Merit" 三五度功
Grade Seven:	Du Jiang and Fu Jiang Cantors
Grade Eight:	Procession Leader
Grade Nine:	Incense bearer

The above list differs somewhat from the lists of Du Guangting, Zhang Wanfu, and the sixth-century Wu Shang Bi Yao only by including in second place the Thunder Rites of Qingwei school.[179] Thus all Daoists, no matter what their sect or creed, were made to learn the registers of classical antiquity as well as the Song dynasty version of Qingwei Thunder Rites in order to receive a license of ordination. The tendency to sectarianism of the Song dynasty was thus effectively blocked with imperial sanction by the practices of the various Celestial Masters during the Ming. Daoists were ranked according to their ability to perform orthodox ritual. A high grade as a Daoist master and the imperial sanction to teach and perform liturgy were given for following the ritual of the classical, canonical Daoist orders of the Tang and the North-South period. The publication of an official canon during the Ming dynasty was a further step toward controlling the proliferating local Daoists.

If the traditional Daoist centers sought to block the trend to diversity and local sectarianism, the popular Daoist movements continued to multiply and spread during the Ming and the later Qing and modern period. There occurred a polarization between the classical, traditional orders and the Daoists of local origin. The former orders were given the name zheng, or orthodox, and the latter were sometimes called xie, or heterodox, though the last term was more often applied to any Daoist or group of Daoists who practiced harmful magic. Though the efforts of Daoists like Bai Yüchan helped to bring the Shenxiao style of popular ritual into the fold of orthodoxy, local groups calling themselves Shenxiao continued to flourish. The

Ming dynasty Celestial Master Zhang Yüchu, in the canonical text *Dao Men Shi Guei (Ten Norms of Religious Daoism)*, decries the falsification of texts and the multiplication of local styles called Shenxiao devoid of both the spirit and proper practice of orthodox Daoism.[180] Local Daoist orders continue to flourish into the present and occupy much of the discussion in chapters 2 and 3 below.

The people of Taiwan call popular orders "Redhead," and the orthodox orders "Blackhead."[181] One of the most popular of the local Fujien Redhead orders is the Sannai, or Three Sisters order, also known as the Sannai Lü Shan orders. The order is named for three legendary ladies who practiced a form of medium possession and healing ritual, mythically associated since Tang times with Lü Shan in Liaoning province in Manchuria.[182] This popular Fujian and Taiwan sect of today, however, has no known connection with Lü Shan in Liaoning other than the name of the mountain. The order is identified in the popular mind with the "Gate of Hell"; the term Lü Shan refers to the place in the cosmos through which the demonic forces attack the world of the living. The ritual role of the Lü Shan Daoists is to capture the demons and send them back to the world of darkness from which they attack the men and women of the community.[183] The magic of the Lü Shan Daoists, although based upon oral rather than written traditions, is respected by their Blackhead Daoist brethren. Interestingly, however, when members of these and other local sects approach the Celestial Master at Longhu Shan for a license of ordination, the Redhead orders are invariably given an ordination in the Shenxiao style of ritual, which shows both the low opinion of the orthodox orders for the sectarian movements of the local provinces and the last place of the Shenxiao registers in the canonical tradition.[184]

In concluding this Daoist oral history introduction, it must be pointed out that the esteem in which the Ming emperors held the Daoist masters did not last into the Qing dynasty. Granted high official titles by emperors of the Ming, the Daoists were stripped of almost all authority and rank by the Manchu Qing emperors.[185] Even harsher treatment was given the Daoists during the Japanese occupation in Taiwan, and the Communist revolution on the mainland. That Daoism has survived in modern Taiwan, China, and overseas communities, even into the modern period, indicates the important place it holds in the hearts of the Chinese people. It is significant that in present day Chinatown communities in the US, Chinese communities still support Daoist priests and folk temples. Far from being obliterated by the coming of technology and industrialization, Daoism has survived as the younger generation turns again to Asian roots for a sense of mystical union and festive celebration. The Chinese communities of the diaspora are witnessing a revival of traditional customs in a secular world.[186] In such circumstances the teachings of Master Zhuang take on a new and timely significance.

In a brief introduction such as this, much material has been omitted. The great disputes between the Buddhists and the Daoists have been slighted, and many important historical figures have not been mentioned.[187] The selection of materials from a rich historical tradition has been made solely to give the necessary background for presenting the rituals and meditations taught by Master Zhuang in contemporary Taiwan.

2. Children of Orthodoxy

INTRODUCTION:
DAOISM IN 19TH CENTURY NORTH TAIWAN

The island of Taiwan is a long, mountainous stretch of land just off the coast of southeast China. Behind its well-watered and fertile western plains are a series of high-rising mountains, which have been compared to a gigantic dragon asleep in a semi-tropic climate. Winds from the China mainland whistle down the straits of Taiwan, blowing sand and dust into the eyes of the inhabitants. The great mountainous backdrop acts both as a watershed and a barrier to typhoons coming in from the Pacific Ocean. Chinese from southern Fujian and from the Fujian-Guangdong province border till the terraced fields of the lowlands, while Austronesian tribes dwell in the rugged mountains. Taiwan belonged first to China, and was a thriving province of the Qing empire during the late nineteenth century. After the Japanese war of 1895, it was forcibly appropriated by Japan and became a part of the Japanese colonial empire until 1945. With the end of the Second World War, Taiwan continues to preserve its cultural heritage from traditional China. It is the home today of twenty million plus Chinese who live in a thriving, modern economy.

Daoist Master Zhuang lived on the northern part of the island in the city of Hsinchu, which is seventy-two kilometers south of the capital city of Taipei on the northwest tip of Taiwan. His ancestors emigrated to Taiwan eight generations ago at the end of the eighteenth century and their descendants have lived in Hsinchu City as practicing Daoists until the present. Zhuang proudly traces his teachings to monastic centers on the China mainland. From his maternal grandfather Chen Jiesan he received the Mengwei registers of an orthodox Celestial Master order Daoist. From the library of the eminent Lin Rumei, he inherited a collection of books brought back from the sixty-first generation Celestial Master at Long Hu Shan, Jiangxi province, on the mainland. From the family of Wu Jingchun he received manuals from Mao Shan and Hua Shan, great centers of Daoist learning in central and western China. The names of the three men—Chen Jiesan, Lin Rumei, and Wu Jingchun—are well known in Hsinchu. Zhuang's accounts of his

Daoist antecedents can be verified from the local gazettes and the Jiapu 家 谱 family histories of the three great Daoists.

In the following pages the history of the texts in Zhuang's possession and the sources of his teachings are traced from their origins on the mainland of China to the bookshelves in the second floor of the Zhuang residence in Hsinchu. The story begins with the coming of Wu Jingchun to Taiwan.

1. WU JING CHUN AND LIN CHAN MEI

Wu Jingchun came to live in Hsinchu on Taiwan in spring 1823, the third year of the emperor Daoguang's reign.[1] The son of an illustrious Mandarin family, Wu Jingchun boasted ten ancestors in the preceding twenty-three generations who had attained the rank of Jinshi, doctor of letters. Three other forebears had been military officials and nine had been ordained Daoist priests. When Wu Jingchun's father was forty-three, the Lin clan of Hsinchu were looking for teachers for the newly founded academy of letters, the Mingzhi Xuyuan,[2] a school for training the children of wealthy Hsinchu families in Confucian learning. The school's first Jinshi had been awarded in the year that Wu was hired.

Weighing the pros and cons of the life of a poor scholar in a wealthy Fujian Mandarin family, under Manchu rulers, against a life of relative affluence in the frontier town of Hsinchu, Wu's father decided to leave the ancestral home. Packing the family belongings and taking his wife and three sons, Wu made the long journey, first by overland route to Amoy Harbor and then by boat across the straits to the port of Nanliao near Hsinchu. Wu was a man of devout piety; before sailing, he burned incense to Xuantian Shangdi, the Daoist god of the Pole Star, and to Mazu, the virgin patron of sailors who crossed the Taiwan straits. Their passage was uneventful.

Hsinchu City in the year 1823 was a thriving prefectural capital, housing a Yamen magistrate with the government offices of the Tamsui district in north Taiwan. Two great families, the Lin and the Zheng clans, controlled respectively the military and the civil affairs of the city. It was not only for his learning in the Confucian classics that the Lin clan had summoned Wu Jingchun and his family. The elder Wu was an accomplished Daoist, trained in the monastic traditions of his ancestors. The fourteenth, fifteenth, and sixteenth lineal ascendants of Wu Jingchun had practiced Daoist ascetics atop Hua Shan in west China. A member of the clan, twenty-three generations previously, was ordained at Mao Shan in Jiangsu. Wu the elder had trained his son in the classical Daoist learning of his ancestors. The rites the younger Wu had learned from his father were a far cry from the vulgar popular rituals practiced by the Redhead Daoists of Hsinchu City. Rather than follow the practices of the professional Daoists, the younger Wu preferred to spend his days in the opulent surroundings of the Lin family villa. Daily parties, poetry reading contests, and performances of classical music were among the pastimes there. Wu Jingchun was content to leave the support of the family to his father.

Unfortunately, the elder Wu did not thrive in his new occupation. Though the elite patronized the Mingzhi academy and he was much sought after as a scholar in Confucian learning, Wu soon fell ill and had to curtail his teaching. The winds from the Taiwan straits came whipping into the city and curbed the summer heat but filled the air with choking dust. The wet rice paddies around the city were breeding places for malarial mosquitoes, cholera, and dysentery. Wu died three short years after his arrival. Wu Jingchun, then twenty-four years of age, was left as heir and head of the family.

Unable to support his mother and two brothers, as had his scholarly father, Wu Jingchun turned to Daoism as a means of making a living. Going to the book trunks of his father, Wu broke the locks and opened the heavy lead binding. There before him were the tattered manuscripts of orthodox Celestial Master order Daoism. To use the meditation manuals and the prognostication techniques was a simple matter, but the complicated rituals of renewal and the lengthy ceremonies of burial could only be performed with an entourage of trained musicians and assistants. When his father was buried and the time of mourning passed, when indeed the family fortunes had dwindled so that it was no longer possible to pretend affluence, Wu Jingchun went to the door of the Lin family and presented his credentials.

When Wu entered the gates of the Lin family villa in autumn 1826 and displayed his legacy of Daoist legerdemain, the Lins were taken by surprise. The Lin clan was noted for its patronage of both Daoist and Buddhist ritual. But Wu Jingchun's collection contained manuals never before seen in Hsinchu. There was a complete set of the grand Jiao 醮 festivals of renewal, with the documentation and the rubrical directions of mainland monastic sects. There were the dreaded Mao Shan manuals of military black magic, the so-called Dao of the Left, used in repelling an attack or winning a battle in war. Finally, there were Qingwei Thunder-vajra manuals from Hua Shan in Shensi, which were powerful enough to counter the Mao Shan Dunjia magic. The presence of Wu Jingchun in the city therefore offered the Lin clan a way to insure its elevation over the other political leaders in the city, as well as superiority in fighting the clan and ethnic battles that broke out every autumn and winter when the young men were not needed in the fields. The seasonal wushu martial arts wars drained the city coffers and depleted the male population.

The Lin family of Hsinchu, one of the most influential and wealthy clans of north Taiwan, is commemorated in all the gazetteers and local histories of Taiwan for its famous martial son, Lin Chanmei.[3] He was six years old in 1826 when Wu Jingchun offered his services; the twenty-four-year-old Wudang Shan Daoist was put in charge of training the boy in the arts of wushu military Daoism. Lin Chanmei, who was destined to be the great pacifier of north Taiwan, was thus brought up in the traditions of Confucian literary learning and Daoist martial arts. With the help of the military magic of Wu Jingchun and the wealth of the Lin family, he was able to discipline and train a fine private army and become a force of peace in north Taiwan. The tenure of Wu Jingchun in Hsinchu was most welcome to the Lins, who patronized his styles of Daoist ritual, and saw that they were adopted by Daoists who lived within the inner confines of Hsinchu City.

Winning acceptance for Wu Jingchun's strange new ways among the resident Daoist brotherhood was a problem requiring adroit political maneuvers to solve. In the diary kept by Wu are written the simple words that he was made an apprentice in the entourage of Guo Daojing, one of Hsinchu's better known Daoists. The arrangement was facilitated by a gift of money in a red envelope so both sides had reason to be satisfied with the pact. Guo Daojing was evidently too old to function without an assistant and Wu Jingchun had an entourage of musicians to train in the ways of orthodox ritual worship. Wu practiced under Guo Daojing for ten years, sharing his unique ritual manuals with the Daoist brethren of Hsinchu City and subordinating himself in all things to the aging master. At the end of the waiting period he was given the daughter of another Daoist, Master Wang, for his bride. With the blessing of the older Daoists, Wu then set up his own Tan or Daoist altar within the inner city. The first center for orthodox Daoist ritual in north Taiwan was established with the Lin family Westgate villa as its headquarters.

The difference of the ritual of Wu, compared with the other Daoists of the old walled city, was immediately apparent to the populace. With a little persuasion from the Lin clan, an agreement was reached that all the "little" Daoists, that is the Redhead or the Shenxiao heterodox orders, were not allowed to perform in the city Cheng Huang temple.[4] Only orthodox Blackhead Daoists who performed liturgy after the manner of Wu Jingchun were allowed to work there. Residents who wished to hire a medium or watch the dramatic tumbling or climbing of sword ladders typical of the popular local orders had to go outside the city walls to hire a heterodox practitioner. Temples and clans within the city walls patronized only the Lin-supported Daoists. The prohibition of heterodox Redhead rites was eased in the modern period. The Cheng Huang temple of Hsinchu still frowns upon mediumistic practices, but allows the popular Redhead Daoists to perform daily rituals within the temple precincts.

The scion of the house of Lin, Lin Chanmei, was sixteen years old in 1836 when Wu Jingchun began his professional career as a Daoist master. The early manhood of Lin Chanmei was spent in schooling, in swordsmanship, and in travel. The Lin family, the gazettes say, hired a swordsman from Japan to train the youth in fighting. During the wars of pacification, he carried a sword bought in Japan, and wielded it with great efficacy. Soon the first wushu forces were formed under Chanmei's direction, the Fei-hu Jun or Flying Tiger troops, named after a chapter in the book of Mao Shan *Dun-jia* magic. They quickly moved throughout north Taiwan, venturing as far south as Dajia and into the city of Zhanghua, seeking to end the bloody ethnic and clan wars. With Chanmei away, the Hsinchu gazette relates, the city feared for its life; with Chanmei near, the city knew no enemies.[5]

Besides the wars, which depleted much of the Lin family wealth and lasted almost to the end of Chanmei's life in 1868, much of the young warrior's free time was spent in the more refined pursuits of poetry, painting, classical music, and partying. The Westgate villa echoed with the sounds of musical ensemble, dance, and song. The gazettes tell little about Chanmei's Daoist activities. The subject is hardly mentioned by his living descendants. Yet when the great warrior posed for his family portrait, he sat with the insignia of a Daoist high priest around his shoulders. In the oral legends of his exploits his victories were attributed to powerful Mao Shan Dunjia magic as well as to the strict discipline of his well-trained troops.

2. LIN RUMEI AND CHEN JIESAN

In its attempts to control the spiritual and temporal destiny of Hsinchu, the Lin family did not spend its money exclusively on wars. Members of the family were also devout patrons of the religious movements of the late Qing era. Much of the Lin fortune was spent in building Buddhist temples outside the city as well as in supporting the orthodox Daoist fraternity within the city. The person mainly responsible for the spiritual control of the city was the fifth son of the family, Lin Rumei. The favorite younger brother of Chanmei, Rumei was born in 1834. The Hsinchu gazettes record that the precocious child was often carried around the inner city on the shoulders of his brother, who spoiled him with endless gifts and favors.[6] Lin Rumei was given the nickname Wu Lauyeh, 五老爷 or "Little Elder Brother Five," since he followed his respected older brother to many of the city's councils and watched the deliberations on politics and war. Lin Rumei soon came to be as respected as much as his powerful elder brother.

Where Lin Chanmei gave lavish parties and led a flamboyant, colorful life, Rumei was given to study and learning. He began to train as a literatus in the Mingzhi academy and was outstanding in his study of the classics. At the same time he was encouraged by Chanmei to study orthodox Daoism with Wu Jingchun; he became a devout practitioner of inner alchemy and ritual meditation. Many of the elders of Hsinchu city who still remember the famous man of religion say that Lin Rumei did not have the stamina for the long and rigorous rituals of a Zhengyi Daoist. The difficult ascesis proved too much for him. Nevertheless it is sure that in 1851 the secrets of the Mao Shan manual of Dunjia magic (see chapter 4 below) were given to him, when Rumei was only sixteen years old.[7]

From Daoism, Lin Rumei turned to join his brother Chanmei in the wars. In that more violent adventure, he was singularly unsuccessful. Returning from a bitter conflict covered with wounds, Lin Rumei was long in recovering. Since the gazettes are often least clear in relating embarrassing moments in the lives of great men, the conversion of Lin Rumei to Buddhism is glossed over in most written accounts. His sudden penchant for Buddhist monasteries is attributed to a strange sort of "mental weakness." (Both Chanmei and Rumei committed suicide). The emphasis of Chanmei's wars changed with Rumei, who built Buddhist and Daoist shrines instead. The Westgate villa became filled with Daoists, Buddhists, and other religious practitioners, who were beneficiaries of Lin's lavish charities. The former parties of Lin Chanmei had filled the inner rooms of the villa with artistic scrolls and literary compositions; now the eaves and walls were covered with the religious poetry of Lin Rumei, done in inlaid mosaic tiles. It was his dream to make the Westgate villa a center for the spread of religious ideas, a sort of school in inner alchemy and ritual meditation.

Two events delayed the accomplishment of Lin Rumei's lofty ideals for another two decades. The first was the death of Wu Jingchun in 1858, which left the Daoists of Hsinchu without a master. The second was the death of Lin Chanmei in 1868, which left Lin Rumei in charge of the family fortunes. The demise of Wu Jingchun was a serious loss for the cause of orthodox Daoist ritual within the city walls. The less orthodox ways of the Redheads began to come back as the people demanded popular rites of exorcism and entertaining drama, rather than the stately orthodox monastic rites patronized by the Lins and Wu Jingchun. The elite families who came to the Westgate villa were distressed but none of them were low enough in the social scale to demean themselves by performing Daoist ritual in public. Hsinchu desperately needed a successor to Wu Jingchun, leading Lin Rumei to plan a trip to Longhu Shan, the nearby Daoist headquarters just over the Fujian border with Zhejiang.

The energies of Lin Rumei first had to be devoted to replenishing the fortunes of the Lin family, totally depleted by the wars of Chanmei. Though successful in pacifying the north, Chanmei had not been a perfect businessman. Lin Rumei was forced to sell much of the family land west toward the sea and north to the dry lake districts in order to keep the family solvent. This was a full-time responsibility that diverted him from his interests in Daoism. Meanwhile, the successor to head of the orthodox Daoist movement was born to a neighbor behind the Westgate villa.

The Chen clan of Hsinchu, which vied with the Lins and the other elite families for status and power in the politics and economics of the city, owned land directly behind the Westgate villa. On it lived a rather unfortunate branch of the family, not so elevated in its economic or social standing as the other branches. When a son was born to the family in 1861, the boy, Chen Jiesan, was entrusted to Lin Rumei for his education.[8] Lin's plans for the boy were quite different from the expectations of the upward aspiring Chen family. Chen Jiesan was first brought up in the classics and trained in the Mingzhi academy. But at the proper and tender age of ten years, he was apprenticed to a Daoist. There are still elders alive in Hsinchu today who recall the frail, intelligent Chen Jiesan and regret the decision to make the boy a Daoist. The first problem was Jiesan's health; he was plagued with and eventually died of a serious heart condition. The second was his intellectual potential. The boy would certainly have passed his Jinshi exams had he been allowed to pursue his course of Confucian learning. There is no question, however, that he became an expert and accomplished Daoist. By the age of twenty Chen Jiesan was the leader of the orthodox Daoist association inside Hsinchu City and the trusted associate of Lin Rumei in the Westgate villa. Lin Rumei's long-planned center for Daoist studies was now a clear possibility.

Lin Rumei was not to be denied his desire to lead a Daoist fraternity. In 1866 he adopted into his family as a younger brother a Guo fang zi (the son of a paternal, i.e., same surname uncle) named Lin Xiumei.[9] Lin Xiumei was given the task of learning the meditations of inner alchemy, while Chen Jiesan was accorded the more lowly duty of performing public ritual. Thus the intellectual leadership of the Daoists, and the influence of the elite clans of Hsinchu's wealthy families, was kept within the Lin household. Chen Jiesan became the leader of Hsinchu's Blackhead Daoists, and Lin Xiumei was made the instructor in inner meditation for the elite families who came to study at the Lin family villa. It is interesting to note that neither the offspring of Chen Jiesan or Lin Xiumei continued Daoist practice. Chen Jiesan's heirs, who received the great library of Wu Jingchun and the

books of Lin Rumei, went into real estate and made a fortune, while Lin
Xiumei's descendants offer only a once-a-year memorial service in front of
his Daoist altar. But these outcomes were not foreseen by Lin Rumei, who
went ahead with his grand plans for founding a lasting school of orthodox
Daoism. With the family fortunes replenished, Lin undertook the greatest
adventure of his life, a trip to Longhu Shan, Daoist headquarters in mainland China. There, at the source of orthodox Daoism, Lin hoped to gain the
power to found his school.

The Hsinchu local gazettes are agreed in reporting Lin Rumei's motives.
They say that he was worried about the low state of Daoism in Hsinchu
City. The vulgar rites of the Lü Shan and Shenxiao Redheads were popular
inside the city proper; Daoism was no longer a socially respectable religion
for the upper classes. It was to restore Daoism to pristine orthodoxy that
Lin Rumei planned his 1868-69 trip to Long Hu Shan to visit and study
with the Sixty-first Generation Celestial Master. The records of the Cheng
Huang temple in Hsinchu reveal a further motivation for Lin's journey.
Worried about the Japanese threat to Amoy and Taiwan, Lin Rumei in 1874
petitioned the court to make Hsinchu's city god, Du Cheng Huang 都城隍,
protector or guardian of north Taiwan. From the Sixty-first Generation Celestial Master, Lin also sought and obtained a protective talisman to defend
Taiwan from foreign invasion. The journey is recorded in the gazettes, in
the temple archives, and in a journal kept by Lin, which is still a part of his
personal library collection.[10]

The pilgrimage left Hsinchu in the third lunar month of 1869. Lin Rumei took along his adopted ninth brother, Lin Xiumei, but left behind the
brilliant young Chen Jiesan, (he was only 8 years old), whose health and
age would not permit him the long and strenuous journey. The pilgrims
set out from Nanliao harbor, at the mouth of the Hsinchu river where a
narrow delta emptied into the sea, almost sixty-four years to the day after
Wu Jingchun set sail from Amoy harbor to Hsinchu. Unlike the uneventful
voyage of the Wu family, Lin's crossing encountered storms and danger. So
seasick was Lin Rumei that he vomited blood. The party was delayed for a
month in Amoy harbor, and an oracle was consulted who determined that
the cause of the illness was an evil spirit. A Jiao was offered, in which the
powerful Thunder Spirits were invoked to effect a cure. The small party set
out again in the fifth month and finally arrived at the village of Qingzhou
at the base of Long Hu Shan in Jiangxi. There a second Jiao of thanksgiving
was offered in the presence of the Sixty-first Celestial Master. The gratitude
of Lin Rumei for his cure and safe arrival in the very center of orthodox
Daoism was celebrated in a grand document that is still extant in the Lin

collection. The details of the journey, the cure, and the arrival are recorded in a Shuwen 疏文 document, dated on the seventh day of the seventh lunar month, 1869. Lin had at last come to the very source of orthodoxy, and his joy was unbounded.

In all some two thousand silver taels were spent by Lin Rumei at Long Hu Shan. He purchased a library of ritual and meditative manuals from the Sixty-first Celestial Master, including an ordination manual and a complete set of Thunder Vajra rituals more advanced than those brought to Hsinchu by Wu Jingchun in 1823. Finally a great Fu talisman of blessing was drawn by the sixty-first Celestial Master to be hung in Hsinchu's Cheng Huang temple. Lin was rewarded with a high level Grade Two (Er Pin) Daoist ordination. The party returned to Hsinchu in June, 1869. Bringing the talisman for the Cheng Huang temple was the crowning point of Lin's triumphal return.[11] Now indeed the Lin family villa could be established as the center for orthodox Daoist learning in northern Taiwan. Establishing the Zhengyi Citan, a fraternity of orthodox Daoist priests, was Lin's first act back in Hsinchu.

Long Hu Shan was visited again by Rumei's adopted brother Lin Xiumei, between 1889 and 1892. This quiet and contemplative man chose to return and learn more of Daoist practice. He outlived the sixty-first generation Celestial Master and was ordained in two distinct orders, the Qingwei Thunder-Vajra sect, deriving from Hua Shan in Shensi, and Quanzhen meditation, brought from Baiyun Guan in Beijing to Long Hu Shan during Lin Xiumei's stay. The picture of Xiumei in the modern family residence shows him with the cap of a Quanzhen monk.[12] When Xiumei finally did return to Hsinchu in 1892, a few years before the Japanese invasion, he chose to remain quietly outside the ritual arena and did not make his influence felt in the thriving Zhengyi Citan. He moved out of the Lin clan villa and established a household across from the Cheng Huang temple on Zhong Shan street, where it remains to this day.

The Zhengyi Citan meanwhile continued working under the leadership and guidance of the scholarly but frail Chen Jiesan. When Lin returned to the Westgate villa, he turned over all the Long Hu Shan manuals to Chen Jiesan and appointed the young Daoist as chief instructor in the Zhengyi school of Daoist ritual. Chen was a devout student and soon mastered the new styles and ceremonies. Daoists came from all over Taiwan to study under Chen Jiesan. He was careful to keep a list of all those who came, taking a prescribed stipend for the privilege of learning orthodox Daoist secrets.[13] Lin Rumei was either unaware of the growing number of disciples, or was not concerned. The new orthodox ways of the Zhengyi Citan had become famous even as far away as the Zhangzhou and Quanzhou prefectures on the mainland. In the daily diary of Chen Jiesan are the names of four Daoists who came across from Fujian to Taiwan to study.[14] Nevertheless, the joy of Lin Rumei in his school was premature. The seeds of destruction were sown by the profit-making motives of Daoists from outside the Zhengyi Citan school. With the Japanese occupation (1894), the fraternity he had established survived by keeping its manuscripts out of site, and well hidden.

The death of Lin Rumei was as tragic as his life had been fortunate. The local gazetteers carried no accounts of the demise of the great spiritual leader. Worn out from the harrowing experience of crossing the straits and his later devotions, Rumei never quite recovered from his journey to the sacred mountain. The depressing specter of Japan invasion hovered just over the horizon. After attaining the protective talisman from the Celestial Master and the edict from the Guangxu Emperor making Hsinchu's Cheng Huang deity a king over the island temples and their spirits, he began to sense the impending failure of all his spiritual labors. The spirits of Buddhism and Daoism in ever-increasing numbers came to haunt his dreams. In a fit of depression on the eve of the Japanese invasion, Lin Rumei killed himself in the Westgate villa. The shock to the Zhengyi Citan and its widely spread members was so great that the organization did not recover. Except for a few loyal members, the Orthodox Daoist center kept a low profile in Hsinchu. The immediate family of Lin Rumei was the hardest hit by his death. The son became an alcoholic, haunted by dreams of the returning soul of his father. The eldest daughter made off with the paraphernalia, the talisman, and the Daoist implements of her father, giving them in time to her eldest son, Tong, the artist.

After the death of Lin Rumei, the manuals in the possession of Chen Jiesan were not returned to the Lin family. They were kept in Chen's own library and seldom used. Chen soon made his move into real estate investment. So wealthy had he become as master of the Zhengyi Citan that he was able to invest in land and associate with the highest of Hsinchu's elite families. Futhermore, the invading Japanese frowned on the practice of indigenous religions. The temples, that had had their social roots in local popular government, were changed into more politically stable and controllable forms of local organization. Buddhism and Shintoism became the state-patronized religions, where Daoism was only tolerated at best. The Zhengyi Citan was dispersed and the grand collection of books and manuals distributed among its members. Only a few of the original clan member—the Zhuang, Guo, Wu, Chen, and Meng families—continued to practice ritual in the public forum.

3. LIN XIU MEI AND ZHUANG CHEN DENG YUN

The beginning of the 20th Century

When Chen Jiesan gave up the vocation of a Daoist priest for the affluence of a real estate agent, he had no intention of giving up entirely the practice of inner alchemy or the ritual meditations of orthodox Daoism. If the tasks of burying the dead, curing a child's ills, or blessing a temple were now behind him, the prestige accruing to him from his years as master of the Zhengyi Citan could not be easily forgotten. Futhermore, the only other leader of the fraternity, Lin Xiumei, refused to emerge from his retirement in the Zhongshan residence. Chen therefore decided to keep the Daoist legacy within his own family by training one of his two children as a Daoist. His older child, a girl named Chen A-Guei, was brilliant, strong, and diligent — the perfect choice had she been a male. The second child, a boy named Chen A-Gong, had no inclination and was in any event too young to be instructed seriously as a Daoist. Chen Jiesan therefore began training his daughter in the ways of an orthodox Daoist priest in the classic tradition of Wei Huacun, Zu Shu, and Sun Bu-er.[15] A-Guei responded well and soon surpassed her peers, the orthodox Blackheads of Hsinchu, in ritual perfection. A-Guei's training, however, was kept within the immediate family circle, her status as a daughter of one of the elite clans of Hsinchu keeping her from performing in public.

In order to propagate the Daoist line under his own name, Chen Jiesan called in a Zhaoxu 诏婿 husband for A-Guei. A marriage was arranged with the Daoist Zhuang clan, and a contractual agreement was made with the new husband that the eldest son of A-Guei would be brought up as a Daoist heir to the documents of Chen Jiesan. The Zhuang clan in return would be privileged to share in the secrets of Chen's orthodox registers and manuals. Thus, at the turn of the century, Chen A-Guei was given in marriage and went to live in the narrow alley behind the Cheng Huang temple, a ten-minute walk from her father's mansion. Unfortunately Chen Jiesan's always delicate heart failed and he died in 1901, a few months after his daughter's marriage and before a son was born to the hopeful union.

Ch'en A-kuei gave birth to her first son in 1911, the year of the Xin Hai revolution. The boy, who was given the name of Zhuang-Chen Dengyun (Zhuang-chen who ascends to the clouds), inherited the brilliance of his mother and the bad temper of his father. Because of the contractual arrangements, it was expected that the young Zhuang would go to the home of his maternal uncle, Chen A-Gong, for his education. This strange man, A-Guei's younger brother and heir to their father's fortunes, was an astute businessman but a noted habitué of the city's courtesan houses. Owing to prolonged association with women of ill repute, he had contracted a social disease and could not father children. Chen A-Gong thus welcomed the Zhuang child into his residence and treated him as his own son. A double surname was given the boy; thus Zhuang-Chen Dengyun became the official title used by Zhuang to sign documents. He was to receive, besides the splendid library of Daoist books that Chen had inherited from the Wu and Lin libraries, the wealth of the Chen clan inheritance.

Zhuang-Chen Dengyun was a brilliant student and took first place in school competitions. He was also an apt pupil of Daoism, and was trained by his real father and mother, the elder Zhuang, and Chen A-Guei, in the performance of Daoist ritual. But the brand of Daoism that Zhuang's father practiced was a far cry from the orthodoxy of the Lin and Chen clans. After the death of Lin Rumei, the heterodox practices of the Redhead Daoists had again entered the city. The elder Zhuang was, in addition, a practitioner of Mao Shan Dunjia magic. Zhuang's mother was greatly alarmed at the bad training being given to her eldest son. She appealed to Lin Xiumei as well as to Chen A-Gong to intervene. Nevertheless, for a brief time the elder Zhuang had the greater influence over Zhuang-Chen Dengyun, during the years of his youth. It was not until 1926, in Zhuang's fifteenth year, that a series of fateful events brought him back into the fold of orthodox Daoism as practiced by his mother and maternal grandfather Chen Jiesan.

The first of the changes in Master Zhuang's life came when a book of his poems in classical Chinese was published by a local press. As a reward for the excellent style and calligraphy, the city government rewarded Zhuang with a trip to Kyoto. After several month's absence, Zhuang returned from Kyoto to find that his uncle Chen A-Gong had married a concubine. Not only the courtesan, but now two adopted brothers and a sister were established in the household of his maternal uncle. Chen A-Gong, out of devotion to his newly found love, had allowed the woman to adopt children of her own and make them heirs to the Chen family fortune. The situation was too much for the youth; Zhuang Teng-yün gathered his few personal belongings and returned home to his parents.

The portrait of Chen A-Guei still hangs over the family altar in the Zhuang residence. From a wide and honest forehead her two eyes stare down at the visitors, expressing the resolve and strength of character that undergirded her hopes and aspirations for her Daoist son. Furious with her useless and profligate brother, Chen A-Guei strode through the dark and narrow streets to her father's house and confronted the concubine. What right, the concubine demanded, did the married sister have to determine the inheritance of the Chen household? A-Guei did not deign to speak to the woman of the streets. Her eyes flashed as in the picture over the family altar; she turned and spoke to her brother. "There was a contract made between my father and me," she said in a soft and firm voice. "According to that contract my son, Zhuang-Chen Dengyun, was to retain the Daoist books of my father. "

Terrified by the apparition of his sister and the wrath of the courtesan, Chen now had an easy solution to the problem. Coolies, always waiting at the street corners to make an extra piece of silver, were immediately summoned. Five cases of books and manuscripts were loaded on the sweating, bent shoulders. The whole of the Westgate populace watched as the Daoist library of Lin Rumei and Wu Jingchun was moved from the Chen mansion to the poor house of Zhuang behind the Cheng Huang temple. Good riddance, said the courtesan, as the unwanted books disappeared into the darkness. A-Guei now had her son and her father's library and was content.

Zhuang was by Chinese reckoning sixteen years old in 1926 when he returned to the home of his father.[16] Delighted, the elder Zhuang contracted to do a day-long ritual at the Cheng Huang temple, using his own son as chief cantor and assistant. To the ritual were invited many of Hsinchu's illustrious families, among them, the celebrated hermit, Lin Xiumei. Reluctant as always to appear in the limelight, Lin agreed to come to the temple simply because the occasion demanded an appearance. During the ritual performed by Zhuang, the elder Lin was heard to cry out in a loud voice that the ritual was not being performed in the orthodox manner. To make things worse, a sudden wind blew out the lamps. The Daoists, temple custodians, and the pious faithful were all terrified.[17] Lin strode out of the temple, followed shortly by the two Zhuangs, father and son. After two days of entreaties and promises, Lin Xiumei agreed to take the young Zhuang Dengyun as a disciple. The agreement was made on two conditions—that Zhuang act as leader of the Zhengyi Citan and propagate only orthodox forms of Daoist ritual, and that each year, for nine days preceding the festival of the Pole Star on the ninth day of the ninth lunar month, Zhuang and the living members of the Zhengyi Citan offer a Jiao festival in honor of the late Lin Rumei.

The discipleship of Zhuang lasted for two years, from his eighteenth to his twentieth year. During that time he was instructed in the meditations of the Yellow Court Canon and given three annotated manuals brought by Lin Xiumei from Long Hu Shan in 1892.[18] He was also instructed in Qingwei Thunder Ritual, to be used as a remedy against harmful Mao Shan Dunjia magic. Finally, he was taught the orthodox manner of performing the Jiao ritual of renewal, after the manner learned by Lin Xiumei at Long Hu Shan and promoted by the original Zhengyi Citan of Lin Rumei in 1869. In 1928 Zhuang Dengyun was ordained by Lin Xiumei, as a grade four Mengwei

Daoist, with a knowledge of Qingwei Thunder Vajra rituals. When Zhuang
asked the aging master why he was not given a higher grade, the prestigious grade two that Lin Xiumei and Lin Rumei had received at Long Hu
Shan, he was told that he needed to observe three strict jie rules: First, high
level Daoists must renounce vulgar Fang zhong "sexual hygiene" - these
practices were in fact forbidden by Wei Hua-ts'un in the Zhen Gao. Second,
the three rules of Laozi, compassion, simplicity, and "never putting self over
others" were required for higher stages of ordination; (only those tested in
merit and virtue could be given a grade two or three ordination). Third,
"one must promise never to give away the Higher Registers to scholars or
postulants outside of one's own lineage."[19]

Lin Xiumei died peacefully in 1928, shortly after ordaining Zhuang
Dengyun in the orthodox Long Hu Shan tradition. Except for the brief
period in which he instructed Zhuang, Lin never made known his Daoist
secrets and practiced his ritual as well as his meditation at a private altar
erected in the rear of his house. After being admitted to the orthodox ranks
of Celestial Master sect Daoism, Zhuang never again performed the heterodox rites learned from his father. Instead, he practiced breath control exercises, meditations of inner alchemy, and the elite rituals that Lin Xiumei had
preserved in the privacy of his own apartments. Like Lin, Zhuang became
something of a recluse and did not often appear in public. Instead of publi-
cizing his new ritual powers, he chose to remain hidden and practiced ritual
in the public forum only when called upon to do so. From 1928 until 1945,
Zhuang supported himself and his family by working as a calligrapher and
secretary in the city offices. In 1944, because of the heavy American bombing, Zhuang took his family to Hualien on the rugged east coast of Taiwan
and remained there until the war ended. In the quiet and unhurried beauty
of the mountains about Hualien, Zhuang spent long hours alone, studying
the manuals of Lin Xiumei and preparing macrobiotic formulae and other
herbal recipes from the great collection of books he had received from his
spiritual ancestors.

Late in 1945 Zhuang returned with his family to Hsinchu. The old household behind the Cheng Huang temple had suffered in fires caused by the
bombing and a part of the valuable Daoist library had been burned. But
Zhuang had taken the most important books with him to Hualien and
shortly after his return was able to establish a Daoist center. The postwar
years were difficult and jobs were scarce. There was no recourse but to
turn to the ministry of public ritual in order to support his growing family.
With his wife and seven children, Zhuang was forced to rely on meditations taught to him by his aging mother to establish the new Zhengyi Citan.

Ch'en A-Guei, who had dreamed for years that her son would fill the role of Lin Rumei in Hsinchu, now saw her hopes about to be realized. Zhuang once more practiced the songs and melodies, the drumming and document writing, and began to train a fitting entourage of disciples to perform in the old orthodox ways of his fathers. The fame of the Zhengyi Citan began to spread and disciples came to learn orthodox Daoism from him.

But the joy of Ch'en A-Guei was short-lived. The new disciples were not the same sort as those from the elite families who had come to her father's house in the late Qing dynasty. The new trends in education begun by the Japanese and furthered by the Nationalist government emphasized technology, progress, and industrialization—all of which worked to secularize social values. The families that had patronized Lin Rumei's association for Daoist meditation now were the entrepreneurs who brought factories, roads, and technology of all sorts to Taiwan. The Zhengyi Citan was filled with the idle, the riffraff, lower-class laborers who were anxious to make an extra "New Taiwan" dollar moonlighting as Daoists. To perform once in a rite of burial, for instance, earned enough money for a week's living. Zhuang's new disciples studied only long enough to learn the external rubrics for performing ritual and then left to set up their own Daoist altars. A religious revival was in full swing and the temples and private households throughout Taiwan were demanding the services of professional Daoists. Once again the Redheads flocked into Hsinchu City, and Zhuang, in disgust, withdrew from active leadership in the fraternity of Daoist brethren.

It is interesting to note from both written and oral sources that none of the orthodox Daoists from the time of Wu Jingchun to the succession of Zhuang Dengyun took up the practice of external public ritual unless forced to do so by poverty. The profession of a popular ritual master in the public forum was considered low enough by the socially elite to be undesirable for their own sons. Wu Jingchun did not become an active Daoist until 1826, after the death of his father. Chen Jiesan left the profession as soon as his wealth permitted. The profession of a Daoist master was passed on to his daughter's eldest son, who did not practice Daoism until financial need forced him to do so. All of these Daoists were orthodox; that is, they practiced classical, canonical liturgy and considered the meditations of inner alchemy to be an essential part of the preparation for ritual performed in the public forum. The books of Wu Jingchun were copied out and put into the collection of Lin Rumei. These were in turn, along with the grand collection brought home from Long Hu Shan, given to the keeping of Chen Jiesan. Chen passed on his teachings to his daughter A-Guei, and she in turn taught her own son, Zhuang-Chen Dengyun. Since inheritance constitutes one of the main elements in ancestor worship, Zhuang brought into his family residence the ancestor tablets of Wu, Lin, and Ch'en, honoring the tablets of his spiritual ancestors next to those of the Zhuang clan. Canonical orthodoxy was therefore considered the distinguishing feature of the ritual practiced by the leaders of the Zhengyi Citan tradition. The conditions for orthodoxy in the tradition were: 1) Texts from the original pre-Song dynasty Daoist Canon, 2) Performance of ritual according to the classical rubrics of antiquity, and 3) Orthodox ritual must be accompanied by the meditations of inner alchemy.

The main books used by Master Zhuang Dengyun in teaching orthodox Daoism are of two kinds: those relating directly to the correct performance of ritual in the public forum, and those concerned with private meditation, breath control, and macrobiotics. In this book I present texts of the first classification, saving the second sort of meditative manual for another study. My reason is simply that the Qingwei and Zhengyi tradition have not been written about in western languages or in Chinese, aside from the incomplete form found in the Daoist Canon. There are many works available in English concerning the techniques of breathing, yoga, and so forth, as practiced in Asian monastic traditions. There are few works explaining in exact detail the application of these exercises to the performance of public ritual. In my presentation, I shall try to remain faithful to the teachings of Master Zhuang, who presented the materials to me in the format found in the pages that follow.

The teachings of Master Zhuang were always given with reference to one or more manuals from the collection of Lin Rumei or Chen Jiesan.[20] Whenever possible I attended the teaching sessions with the corresponding volumes of the Daoist Canon in my own possession, to compare them with Zhuang's version of orthodoxy. At first Zhuang resented my audacity in comparing canonical texts to his hand written manuals, but he soon came to welcome the opportunity to correct the canonical version, which was often less clear or even corrupt when compared with his own texts and the oral explanations he had learned from the aged recluse, Lin Xiumei. Since Zhuang was endlessly busy with the calls of his clientele, it was sometimes necessary to wait for several hours before time could be set aside for a lesson. Zhuang usually expounded his doctrines on days that the almanac (Tungshu) considered fortunate, or on days when burial ritual was forbidden. Since burials were preceded by night-time rites, it was often necessary to come at an odd hour, hoping that Zhuang would be free from the rigorous demands of burial ritual or the obligations of entertaining his many callers. The lessons always began with a period of light conversation, followed by a scolding for his sons and disciples who failed show respect for the sacred doctrines.

It was often necessary to wait a long time before Zhuang got to the point. Only the patient are rewarded with the revelation of orthodox Daoist secrets, Zhuang explained, when he chose to speak of them.

3. Daoist Master Zhuang

A study of the teachings of the Daoist master Zhuang would be incomplete without a sense of the surroundings in which Zhuang lived, the effect of his ritual and inner practice on his community, and the place accorded him in society. Perhaps more important than the spiritual content of Daoist ritual are the uses to which it is put in a modern Asian setting. It is most interesting from the social anthropologist's viewpoint to ask what sort of friends Zhuang has, what classes of people patronize his liturgies, and what the residents of Hsinchu City think of the Daoists in their midst. It would be a mistake to suppose that a Daoist is universally a popular person, a person whom one is proud to call a friend or relative. Since the ministry in which the Daoist engages is often concerned with sickness, ill fortune, or death, the very mention of a Daoist's name can bring memories of unpleasant events which occasioned summoning him, events which most people would rather forget.[1] Thus when funeral ritual is needed, one might try to recall a noted Daoist who would perform a burial service for a reasonable fee; but the family Daoist would not ordinarily be the subject of conversation at a public gathering or a festive occasion.

It is, furthermore, most difficult to meet a Daoist master. Though the villagers are well aware that there is a local Daoist in residence, the questions of the young anthropologist or student of Asian Studies are often put off with a shrug or a noncommittal answer. This is because the Daoist assiduously avoids all contacts either with Chinese or foreign scholars, owing to the esoteric nature of the doctrines professed and the rituals practiced. The Daoist does not appreciate being asked about inner meditations, and is not even eager to admit practicing them unless called upon by a person in extreme need. Introductions must be arranged in advance, through an acquaintance or go-between. An unwanted caller is often rejected or the introducer cursed by the reclusive master. It is of the essence of religious Daoism for the master to hide his powers behind a frugal and simple façade. "The person who claims expertise in Daoism is an imposter; the person who denies knowledge is an expert," is the lesson taught to the disciples by the master. The villager's image of a Daoist is usually that of a spiritually gifted man or woman who talks to spirits, who preserves esoteric secrets, and who comes and goes at will. There is something sinister about expelling evil and exorcising demons, that sets the Daoist apart from the rest of the community. Friends are few, and his or her liturgical presence is feared. Thus the Daoist is not often introduced to outsiders.

Master Zhuang lived in the center of Hsinchu City in an alley behind the Cheng Huang Temple. On one side of the Zhuang residence was a candy shop and pool hall, and on the other side was a Sento public bath built during the Japanese period. Directly opposite the Zhuangs' front door is the house of the wealthy Cai clan, which holds itself aloof from the other, poorer families in the narrow alley. The Cai family had recently constructed a three-story building with polished terrazo floors and inner courtyards for its children where they can play away from the noise and bustle of the alleyway. Next to the Cai residence lived another Daoist family, the clan of Chen Pang "the Fat," who make a living from their proximity to the Zhuang clan. Next to the Chen family lived a woman medium of the Lü Shan school, the famous Mrs. Wu, (not her real name) who is possessed every morning at ten o'clock by the spirit of the benevolent goddess-saint Chen Nai Ma.[2]

Housewives on their way to and from the central market stop to chat and watch the spectacle of the possessed woman talking in the voice of the goddess. When in possession, Mrs. Wu can be made to pick up a pen and write in a strange illegible script the answers of the goddess to the questions put to her by the housewives. Redhead Daoists, called Hoat-ah by the people, are consulted to interpret her talismanic writings. Though Zhuang is opposed in principle to the brand of Daoism practiced by Mrs. Wu, he and his family are on very good terms with her and exchange gifts on festive occasions.

The house of Chen the Fat is very poor, filled with children and grandchildren in a hot corridor that passes for their residence. So many demands are put on the services of the prestigious Zhuang clan that the Chens manage to survive on the overflow of business that finds its way to their doorstep. The eldest son of Chen, himself rotund and jolly, joins in the rituals of Zhuang by default whenever another Daoist cannot be found. In or near the alley also lived a blind masseur, a family that makes cakes and cookies for wedding ceremonies and other festive occasions, a manufacturer of household Christmas tree lights, a welding and metal shop, and a home that caters to funeral banquets. With the exception of the Cai clan and the manufacturer of Christmas tree lights, almost all the inhabitants of the alley depended on Zhuang for their customers. Musicians, disciples, and stragglers were found in the pool hall next door, when not engaged in ritual performances. The street was always filled with children, people coming and going, passing motorcycles, and clients seeking Master Zhuang's ritual attention. When home, Zhuang pontificated from a wicker chair in his front room, facing the street with the door open—a peaceful scene in a lively neighborhood. The Zhuang residence closed, and was abandoned after his death. His sons opened Daoist altars in other parts of Hsinchu city.

My introduction to Zhuang was originally suggested by a woodcarver named Su, who lived on a street west of the Zhuang residence, and served as porter for the guardian gods in the Cheng Huang Temple's statuary. He got no further than a brusque refusal from Zhuang, who had no interest in meeting a foreign student and threatened to curse Su for even mentioning his name to a foreigner. As head of the Zhengyi Citan, however, Zhuang was the Daoist in residence of the Cheng Huang Temple, a hundred yards or so from the front door of his residence. It was more proper that Mr. Zheng, head of the temple committee and the man who paid Zhuang's retainer, should arrange the introduction. Zheng was a descendant of a famous clan, which produced a Jinshi (doctor of letters) in 1823; he himself was a graduate of Tokyo Imperial University. He had been three times elected mayor of Hsinchu City and was spending his years in retirement as beneficiary and controller of the temple's funds. Zheng and Zhuang had been friends during the Japanese period, but their relationship became more formal after Zhuang inherited the role of Daoist Master from his mother and father. I had the suspicion that Zheng's willingness to introduce me to the Daoist had less to do with any intended honor to me than with the opportunity to issue a reminder to Zhuang, who despised the daily routines at the temple and neglected his duties there. Yet the temple staff assured me that there was no more knowledgeable Daoist in north Taiwan—nor one more difficult to meet.

The first meeting with Zhuang began with a traumatic scolding. What purpose could a foreign scholar possibly have, Zhuang demanded, other than to destroy the traditions of his ancestors? Daoism was an esoteric discipline and the secrets could be revealed to none but his immediate descendants. Luckily I had brought with me a photocopy of a Daoist ritual manual I had found on the shelves of the British Museum.[3] When I showed the manual to Zhuang, his attitude visibly changed. It was a copy of the canonical Su Qi rite that had somehow found its way to the British Museum in 1872; the original had been signed by a Zhangzhou Daoist named Chen who was a fifth level ascendant of Zhuang's maternal grandfather Chen in 1736. Zhuang was both startled and pleased that I should have the manual and immediately accepted me into the entourage of his followers. From the very beginning I made it clear that my purpose was not to disturb his professional ministry or his role in local Daoist liturgy. Where most of the disciples in Zhuang's entourage came to learn ritual and eventually set up their own business, my purposes were purely spiritual, as well as intellectual. I hoped to study and understand the texts that Zhuang used in his liturgy.

Zhuang, much to the dismay of those who wanted only to learn the bare minimum of ritual performance in order to set up a money-making Daoist practice, intended primarily to give instructions in Daoist Yin-yang philosophy, the proper understanding of the *Laozi Dao De Jing,* the *Zhuangzi,* and the practice of inner alchemy. To the motley crew whiling away the hours between liturgical performances in the neighboring pool room, the lectures on breath control, exercise, macrobiotic diet, and the like were wasted. The halcyon days of the Zhengyi Citan (Heirs to Daoist Orthodoxy) when meditations were taught in the halls of Hsinchu's elite clans were gone forever. The only hope for an intellectual revival of religious Daoism lay in two of Zhuang's sons, A-Him and A-Ga. As the latest disciple, I seemed to function as a catalyst, moving Zhuang to teach his two sons more frequently and thoroughly than if I had not been there. The elder son, Zhuang A-Him has since opened up a school for Daoist spiritual practice, Qigong exercise, and meditation. Medical doctors and university graduates now attend A-Him's classes, continuing the original Zhengyi Citan tradition.

To each of Zhuang's lessons I brought printed versions of the Daoist Canon, in order to compare them with Zhuang's own manuscript collection.[4] Where the Canon was corrupt, unpunctuated, or incomplete, Zhuang's texts were clear, punctuated, and completed by his own knowledge of the koujue 口訣, orally transmitted esoteric rubrics. The Ming dynasty Zheng Tong Daoist Canon contained many more variations and schools of ritual than Zhuang had thought possible. For this reason, he asked to see the Japanese studies on the subject and read the works of such noted scholars as Yoshioka, Obuchi, and Noritada Kubo.[5]

In one of Professor Kubo's field trips to Taiwan I was able to introduce the professor to Zhuang; Zhuang reciprocated by performing a Dao Chang ritual and the steps of the Ho Tu sacred dance as described in chapter 6.[6] At my urging, Zhuang read the work of Maspero translated into Japanese, commenting on the differences and similarities to his own grasp of Daoist history and theory. To Zhuang, the maintenance of a high standard of scholarly knowledge on the state of Daoist studies was part of the orthodox tradition that he had inherited. He had withdrawn from the circle of mercenary functionalists because there was no kindred spirit with whom to communicate the results of his own study and thinking, along with his methods of meditative alchemy and ritual perfection. His opposition to the local Redhead orders and to many of his own disciples arose from their disinterest in intellectual or spiritual matters, including the higher stages of inner cultivation in inner alchemy meditation.

Zhuang did not treat all scholars who came to his door with the same trust and openness, though to all he extended a warm welcome. To each visitor he offered the hospitality of his table and the camaraderie of tea or beer to drink. But to most he feigned ignorance, telling outlandish tales and downing large cups of rice wine. In subsequent conversations about the proper conduct for a master of ritual, Zhuang scolded me soundly for being competitive with other scholars, for showing off my knowledge of Daoist secrets, for feeling superior in any way. The first requisites for perfection in Daoist cultivation were peace of heart, frugality of life, and compassionate respect for all others. Both the master, and even more the disciple, are always required to plead ignorance and never make a display of knowledge, lording it over others. This was vividly illustrated by an event that occurred at Zhuang's front door during a popular religious festival.

On the fifteenth day of the tenth lunar month, the mediums of north Taiwan are accustomed to perform the rite called "Passing Through the Gates of Peril." In the dramatic liturgy a local medium is possessed by the boy god, Tai zi ye—Ne Ja, and twelve times leads all the children through a "Gate of Peril" constructed of paper and wood. Passing through the gate is thought to protect the children from sickness and peril for the next twelve months. A Daoist is hired to lead the procession and blow on an exorcist cow horn trumpet. At the end of the procession dances the medium, imitating the steps of the naughty child god. I had alerted a number of young anthropologists and visiting foreign scholars to the event, which, by chance, was to take place in front of Zhuang's house.[7] The medium, Mrs. Wu, was to be in trance and Chen the Fat in his faded vestments was to lead the procession.

At the height of the ceremony, with the foreign cameras clicking and the lady medium in the midst of her possession, a drunk man walked through the front door of Zhuang's residence. He was delighted to see foreigners, but worried about their lack of reverence and misunderstanding that might offend the spirits. He began to scold Zhuang for allowing foreigners to be present.

Zhuang's youngest son, A-Ga, bristled with hostility, and wanted to expel the drunkard violently.

"Leave him alone," said Zhuang. "He is my friend." Even though he had never met the man.

"Is he," I asked, "or are you trying to keep A-Ga from fighting?"

"He is my friend," repeated Zhuang and protected the man from A-Ga, who by now had clenched fists and bulging eyes in defense of his father. With gentleness and restraint, Zhuang spoke quietly to the drunkard and led him out the door and around the corner. I followed and assisted in seeing the man off. We exchanged name cards and parted friends. To Zhuang the man in trouble was the most important person in the assemblage. Although he had never seen the man before, he treated him as a comrade. More urgent than the important visiting scholars or even the fury of his own son was the distress of the man who had temporarily lost his senses. To Zhuang, his role as a Daoist was fulfilled in first assisting those in need. All other duties were secondary.

During the sacred rituals of renewal and the burial ceremonies for the dead, Zhuang, and all those hired to perform Daoist ritual, are required by strict Daoist jie rules to refrain from the use of alcohol, not to eat meat or fish, and to remain celibate. All Daoists are required to observe these rules from a month before the Jiao, while Zhuang and his sons observed the ruled for full 81 days before the celebration of Jiao cosmic renewal. The laity were required to observe the same rules for a week before the Jiao; the wearing of leather, wool (both "dead" objects) and white underwear (the color of the west, used at burial) are also forbidden throughout Taiwan, when entering the Daoist sacred Tan 坛 ritual area.

There were times, however, when Zhuang insisted that guests share an alcoholic drink with him. One such time was the evening of my acceptance as a disciple.[8] Zhuang ordered three bottles of Gaoliang wine, which he, A-Ga, and I were supposed to drink. When "under the influence," Zhuang suddenly pressed me again to say truthfully why I wanted to study Daoism. "To practice Zhuangzi's Heart Fasting and Sitting in Forgetfulness" (心斋坐忘) were the first and only words that came to my befuddled mind. "OK, you can be my disciple" Zhuang answered. When my dizziness had subsided enough to demand that we stop drinking, Zhuang suggested that we walk to the Cheng Huang Temple to thank the spirits and the temple committee for our introductions. By the time we reached the temple, Zhuang was sober, though A-Ga and I were still unsteady.

Whenever I could not show up in Zhuang's front room for an evening lesson or when Zhuang felt like escaping the noise of the grandchildren, the visitors, and the street in front of his residence, he would appear at our door and sit on the tatami regaling my Japanese wife Nariko, daughter Theresa and me with stories of his exploits in fluent Japanese. On one such night, we told him of the coming birth of our second child, to be named "Mari." To

celebrate I opened a small bottle of aged Scotch, of which Zhuang immediately drank half. The quantity was not too great, but the short span during
which the whiskey was quaffed proved too much even for Zhuang. I summoned a cab, but before we were halfway home, the effects began to wear
off. Zhuang demanded that the cab stop. There before our eyes was the
great courtesan house of Hsinchu, the Moon Palace where great maternal
uncle Chen A-Gong had got his mistress, and afterwards gave up his Daoist legacy, giving all of Grandfather Chen's Daoist Mijue manuals to Master
Zhuang's mother, A-Guei.

I begged Zhuang not to go in, first because scholars, especially foreign
scholars, did best to keep out of such places, and second because Zhuang
should not really have another drop. Umbrage was taken at my last statement, and we entered. The magical effect of Zhuang's appearance was a
revelation to me. Still somewhat mollified by the earlier dosage of Scotch,
he was in a mellow and jovial mood, but the clientele who knew him disappeared with some fear.

"Bring the manager!" Zhuang demanded.

A chubby man, who was obviously quite nervous, appeared from behind
a counter. "The manager was just taken ill and has gone home," he mumbled.

"Get us a room and two bottles of wine." Zhuang headed for a booth before he could be denied entrance.

We entered and sat down, followed by a very determined and straightfor-
ward younger woman, who was certainly not a courtesan and was perhaps
the owner's daughter.

"What did you want?" she asked rather abruptly.

"Bring us four bottles of rice wine," Zhuang answered. "Two for each."

"No," I said very firmly. "That would ruin the effect of high quality Scotch,
which all experts know must not be ruined by mixing with any extraneous
beverage."

"Oh," said Zhuang, deeply impressed. "What should we have?"

"It is the custom to have Coca-Cola," I lied, grasping for some way to get
the Daoist out of the place and home while he and I could walk easily.

"Fine," said the young lady, "I'll bring four bottles." In no time we had four
open bottles of Coca-Cola and a full glass before Zhuang, who took one sip,
then gasped in dismay.

"This is terrible!" he spat it out, after the first swallow.

"Let's go," I insisted. "We must get home and get up early tomorrow to
study." Zhuang again called for the manager, and the determined young
lady reappeared. Tonight's drinks would be on the house, she assured us.
There was no bill. I steered Zhuang down the stairs and out the door. The

hallway and entrance were bare of people except for the young lady and the
weak rotund man.

"I always drink for free when I go there," Zhuang said. We walked down
the back streets leading to his home, skirting a puppet show in front of the
temple of Eastern Peace, and finally coming to the cookie shop at the corner
of Zhuang's street.

"Here," Zhuang offered, now quite awake and sober; "let me buy you some
cookies for Theresa and Nariko." He peered through the locked windows of
the residence at a light burning in the interior. The family was still up, packing boxes of cookies and cakes for a wedding ceremony on the morrow.
"Wedding cookies?" I asked. "2 year old Theresa is not getting married."

"They always taste better the night before," Zhuang knocked on the door,
"while they're still fresh."

A high school girl opened the door. Seeing Zhuang with a worried foreigner, she laughed and ran to get her mother and father. The whole family
came. Zhuang ordered *NT$500* worth of cookies for Theresa.[9]

"That is far too many," I objected. "We will never finish them."

"That's all right," said the lady. "They are free; we don't want any money
for them."

"It's still too many. Just a bag will do."

Relieved, they gave me a bag full of freshly baked cookies and we arrived at last at Zhuang's front door, where Mrs. Zhuang, a battle-scarred
and long-suffering woman, let us in. She put her husband on the couch in
the front room where he went straight to sleep.

"Don't worry," she consoled me, for I must have looked terribly crest-
fallen at Zhuang's condition on returning from our house, "He'll be all right
shortly."

The people who knew Zhuang as neighbors did not fear him as much as
those did in more distant establishments, who knew him only by reputation, but no one wanted to risk his possible anger. Neighbors as well as associates did anything not to offend him. That is why neither the courtesan
house nor the cookie factory would accept money for his patronage.

His wrath once aroused, some said, could mean the punishment of the
"Tao of the Left," (zuodao 左道) though in my estimation the fear was un-
founded; Zhuang had vowed never to use his powers to harm anyone,
which is one of the strictest rules for receiving a Lu register higher than
Grade Six.

Zhuang's ocasional anger was not typical of all those who followed the
profession of a Daoist. Both in China and Japan training in Zen, as well as
Daosim, is accompanied by the master's anger, a sign of inner approval.

Zhuang's bad temper was feared, however, for the wrong reasons—lest it lead to a supernatural punishment. Among the older Zhengyi Citan, there were few who were willing to learn the discipline of inner meditation from him, and none whom Zhuang himself trusted enough to teach. Yet there were many members to whom Zhuang had a fierce loyalty and whom he would call to help at public rituals from as far away as Jeelong, Taipei, Zhunan, and Taizhong. It seemed, in fact, that Daoists from far-away cities were more friendly to Zhuang than his disciples within Hsinchu City. This state of affairs can be explained partially by professional rivalry; most of the Daoists whom Zhuang had trained became his competitors if they stayed in Hsinchu but were collaborators and associates if their ritual performance territory did not impinge on Zhuang's. There were, of course, exceptions to this rule. The son of Chen the Fat, for instance, and the lesser Daoists whose mere competence was no match for Zhuang's rubrical perfection were often included in Zhuang's entourage of musicians, acolytes, incense bearers, and cantors. But most of these men were not spiritually loyal to Zhuang and managed after a few years of training to set up their own T'an or private Daoist altar. Thus the disciples watched his ritual performances avidly, hoping to gain for their own more of the great power and ritual perfection for which he was famous.

Zhuang's dealings with his confreres within Hsinchu City were thus not spiritually satisfying for him. There was no reason on Zhuang's part why cordiality should be extended to any who came simply to learn the secrets of Thunder ritual, to counter the Dao of the Left, or learn the external performance of the lower Meng-wei registers below a minimal Grade Six or Liu Pin 六品 ordination. To those who did come to him, Zhuang imparted a bare minimum of knowledge until he could ascertain whether the novice desired to practice meditation, the ascetic fasts of a hermit, and other forms of religious perfection, or only to learn the external rote of funeral liturgy, or memorize the tunes and rubrics of Jiao rites of renewal. For the latter, six months to a year were sufficient.

It was advantageous to be included as a member or acquaintance in Zhuang's entourage simply to share in the great fortune accruing from his ritual practice. There were so many requests for funerals, exorcisms, and Jiao rites of renewal that Zhuang's full retinue of followers, disciples, and other associates usually contained around thirty members, that is, two complete ritual teams. To Zhuang himself were reserved the elite duties: in a three day funeral service, his total performance lasted only forty-five minutes, yet that was enough to win him the highest stipend and to make the funeral the most expensive and prestigious possible. When Zhuang

The Su Qi ritual. A-Ga on the left, and A-Him with back to the camera. The Daoist Kuo at the far right.

Closing the demon's gate Jin-t'an.
Page 209

Fa Lu rite
Page 227

Datewood thunder block
of Lin Hsiu-Mei.

Zhuang A-Him performing
the Jiao ritual.
Honolulu, Hawaii.
1980

The role of the Taoist in the Chinese community: Ming-dynasty woodlock print, Yushu Jing.

performed the rites of renewal, the well-known Dao Chang, Su Qi, Morning, Noon and Night Audiences, Daoists and laity assembled from miles around to watch the perfection and beauty of his liturgical performance.

There were, of course, another dozen Daoists available within Hsinchu City for the ritual needs of the people. There was Chen the Fat, who could be obtained for half the price of Zhuang and who was often seen in the smaller temples performing the Pu Du banquet-sacrifice for freeing the orphan souls from hell or the simple day-and-a-half rite of burial used by families of lesser economic means. There was also the family of Guo the Large-toothed, and the kindly Redhead clans of Zhang and Qien, both specializing in rites such as "Calming a child who suffered fright at night," or reading simple exorcisms, prayers for blessing, and prognostications in the local temples. The Zhang and Qien clans were also highly respected. People turned to them in doubt, since a sick child in the arms of the worried parents calls for any and all sorts of care and attention. The worried mothers of Hsinchu could be seen carrying their children to the famous pediatrician, Dr. Zhou, in the early morning to receive an injection of antibiotic then to the Daoist by ten or eleven o'clock to be soothed and assured by the ringing of small ritual bells, the lighting of incense, and the casting of fortune blocks which assured the loving parents that the spirit world as well as the material world was working for their child's recovery. Others brought their children to the great Cheng Huang Temple, where for a fee of NT $20, the child could be given in adoption to the Cheng Huang deity, an efficacious way to preserve children from future harm.[10]

Perhaps Zhuang's greatest rival in Hsinchu was the fellow orthodox Blackhead Daoist, Chen Dingfeng, or Chen the Thin in distinction to Chen the Fat. Chen the Thin was not related to either the Zhuang-Chen clan or to the Chens of southern Taiwan, also noted ritual experts. This man's father had come to Taiwan in the 1890s to study in the Zhengyi Citan. Instead of returning to Zhangzhou on the mainland, he stayed behind to set up his own business from a busy Daoist office in the central market just south of the Cheng Huang temple, in the middle of the meat and poultry section of the market. Chen Dingfeng inherited the business from his father and turned a fine profit by reading fortunes, burying the dead, and performing at the festivals of the deities in Hsinchu's local temples. Chen Dingfeng was a man of slight build and cautious heart, who kept strictly to himself. In all ways the opposite of the colorful Zhuang, he was a man who never lost his temper, who spoke in a quiet, mild voice, who was respectful and cautious in his dealings with others. The ritual of Chen was well patronized, and his reputation was built on the fine quality of his liturgical performance.

Chen was an accomplished musician, sang in a good voice, and trained his disciples in a quiet and disciplined manner. When not engaged in funeral or renewal ritual, Chen busily studied medicine and was a licensed Chinese herbalist as well as learned in western pharmacy. Mothers who brought their children to Chen found an expert not only in ritual exorcism but in curing by means of Chinese herbs and western drugs. Chen built a two-story residence in a suburb and traveled back and forth on a Honda motorbike; he lived as a gentleman of learning as well as a man of devout religious piety.

Zhuang and Chen were not on good terms, the colorful ways of Zhuang, his sometimes violent temper, and his largesse in teaching the riffraff who came to make a living from the leavings of his table being far removed from the close and frugal demeanor of Chen. But the children of Zhuang, A-Ga and especially A-Him, respected the elder Chen and visited him frequently. Chen was himself without an eligible male offspring, and so arranged to pass on his Daoist secrets to the husband of his eldest daughter, a young man named Meng who worked in the city offices. As perfect and polished in attire as his father-in-law, Meng was soon made a member of Zhuang's entourage, too, a welcome change from the idlers in the poolhall who often marred the splendor of Zhuang's ritual. The sons of the two warring masters became close friends. All agreed that Zhuang's successor as head of the Zhengyi Citan was to be A-Him; the decision was confirmed by Chen Dingfeng, who as the next in age to Zhuang was highest in prestige and therefore by right the leader of the group after Zhuang. Despite the rivalry between the two masters, Chen Dingfeng was wise and gentlemanly enough to see that the teachings of Zhuang had been well learned by the elder son. A-Him was in fact the most accomplished Daoist after his father, as all the other Daoists realized. Out of deference to the age and prestige of Chen Dingfeng, A-Him frequently visited the elderly Chinese herbalist and Daoist and went with him as a son to the various meetings of the Daoist society, which his own father refused to attend. It thus was evident that, although the Zhengyi Citan was divided by its leaders' rivalries, it was brought together again by the gentility of the leader's son A-Him and his father's elder rival.

My own dealings with Chen Dingfeng were warm and polite. Chen was too much a gentleman to speak against Zhuang, though at first he seemed to resent my discipleship in the school of his rival. The resentment was gradually ameliorated by two sets of events, which perhaps reveal more of the personal characteristics of the two men, Zhuang and Chen, than do my descriptions. The great English musicologist, John Levy, had come to Taiwan searching for Daoist music to study and publish and asked both Zhuang and Chen to record from their repertoire of ritual music. Zhuang insisted on being paid for his performance, while Chen allowed Levy to record at no cost during a public performance. The arrangements with Chen were made quietly during several hours before and after the performance in his busy office in the marketplace. Chen cooperated to the extent of holding the microphones during the performance and was in all ways cooperative in demonstrating his various musical instruments; he seemed reluctant to get on with his daily round of sick calls and ritual business, in deference to the elderly visitor from England.

Zhuang, on the other hand, insisted not only on being paid for his services at the rate he would charge a local customer, but demanded that his entourage have several days practice in advance and asked Levy to drive him all the way to Zhanghua in central Taiwan to get the proper bell and drum to be recorded in stereo. Through the forbearance and patience of the London gentleman, Zhuang got his instruments, his entourage, and a recording studio for the performance. But getting him to identify the texts, write out the koujue, or oral secrets, which he had used, and explain his actions was like pulling wisdom teeth. All the while that the Englishman and the Daoist were together, however, Zhuang was at his best, demonstrating breath-holding techniques, songs and rhythms, telling tales of magical powers, and laying on several fine banquets with the fanciest cooking of Mrs. Zhuang.

The second friendly encounter with Chen Dingfeng, which led to a sort of understanding and incipient friendship, began with an attempt to find a missing text. Zhuang, in the carelessness of his daily life and the confusion of his cabinets of ritual documents, noticed that a book was missing. The volume was not just an ordinary ritual manual used in the daily burial services but an extremely valuable rite reserved for Zhuang himself to perform on the occasion of a liturgy of renewal. The manual was in fact a copy of the *Su Qi*, (the same text of which I had brought a copy from the British Museum), an esoteric ritual in which the Ling-pao Five Talismans, the bringers of good fortune, blessing, and cosmic renewal, were planted in the community.[11] The *Su Qi*, Zhuang insisted, is modeled after the Ming Tang —the imperial ritual used in the Temple of Heaven in Beijing, and in Changan city during the Tang dynasty. Zhuang was worried lest the manual had been lost or stolen, since only he and Chen Dingfeng, of all the Daoists within Hsinchu City, knew how to perform the rite in full. The moment was most inopportune. I was in the process of photocopying all Zhuang's documents and making a supplement to the Canon of the well-punctuated texts and commentaries in the inherited collection. Zhuang wondered if the document hadn't been taken by another Daoist named Guo.

The recovery of the manual was first undertaken by the more sanguine son A-Ga, who faced Guo publicly in the central market. Guo denied that he had the book, asserting that the guess was misplaced. He did not know how to perform the rite even if he did have it. The last statement being true enough, A-Ga returned home in defeat. A-Him and I carefully discussed the next step with the Master Zhuang. It would be possible, I reasoned, to ask Chen Dingfeng to intercede. If I asked Chen where a copy of the rite might be, he could perhaps convince Guo or whoever had it at least to loan it to me to be photocopied. Zhuang agreed that it was worth trying and so, with my wife, Nariko, and our daughters, Theresa and Mari (now born), as company, we rode with A-Him in a taxi to the residence of Chen Dingfeng.

It was eight o'clock in the evening when we arrived. Chen had not yet returned from a funeral ritual but Mrs. Chen and the elder daughter welcomed us with great warmth. The conversation shifted from Japanese to Taiwanese to Mandarin, according to the generation and the person addressed. A-Him was treated as a son just returned to the family. As Mrs. Chen served plates of candied fruit and glasses of soda water, with cooled milk for the children, Chen Dingfeng came in, exhausted from his daily liturgical routine. It was obvious that the elder Chen held A-Him in high esteem. He heard the explanation of my project, finding and analyzing the Daoist manuals held by the members of the Zhengyi Citan, and he cooperated splendidly, opening his own trunks and showing us manuscripts that A-Him had never seen. Among Chen's collection were two of the manuals brought back from Long Hu Shan by Lin Rumei, which had been given directly to his own father and had never been a part of Zhuang's collection. But he did not have a copy of the *Su Qi*. I explained as gracefully as possible that I knew where perhaps one could be obtained, if Chen could help us in our arduous search for it. Chen smiled and replied that if I could come to his office at eleven the following morning, he might have been able to locate a copy of it.

Since our family shopped each morning in the central market, it was easy enough to combine a trip to the market with another visit to Mr. Chen's tidy office. The interior had not changed since my first visit there with John Levy in 1969. The musical instruments were on the wall, the books in neat rows behind the locked windows of bookshelves. Chen was at work delicately writing with a Chinese brush on a sheet of yellow rice paper.

"I have the book you want," he said, looking up. "A disciple of mine, named Guo, had it."

He took a tattered manuscript from a drawer of his desk. On the front was pasted a new strip of red paper on which was written, "From the collection of Chen Dingfeng." The book was, indeed the *Su Qi*, but I could not tell whether it was from Zhuang's collection. The personal seal of Chen, obviously newly printed, was to be found on every third page or so, and the signature at the end was signed with Chen's name.

"May I make a copy of this with my camera ?" I asked. "I will be able to return it to you by this afternoon." Chen readily agreed and again queried me about my project with the books of Daoist liturgy. I explained that the books held by the Daoists of Taiwan were invaluable additions to the printed Canon, since most of the Taiwanese manuals were punctuated and had commentaries and detailed rubrical explanations, while the published canonical works were bare and dry, with no sign of punctuation.

"You should have come to me earlier," said Chen. "Had I known what your purpose was, I would have been glad to explain to you what I know of Daoism. "

I was startled and grateful for his offer, since it was difficult for any Daoist master to agree to reveal his teachings. "What can I do for you in return?" I asked. "There is so little which I have that can be of use to a master. "

"I would be grateful to see some of the copies of the published Zheng Tong Canon, which you have in your library."

With the copy of the *Su Qi* tucked safely under my arm, I returned home and photocopied the entire manual as quickly as possible. I was anxious to see what use Chen would make of the canonical texts that I could bring him. The Dong Xuan section of the Canon, with the great liturgies of renewal, was the obvious choice, since it had the texts closest to those in Chen's own collection. I hurried back with four of the hardbound brown volumes and appeared at Chen's office door at one o'clock, before the first of the afternoon callers had appeared.

"Thank you for the use of your *Su Qi*," I said. "Here are some of the copies of the Canon." I waited to see what he would do with them. With restrained but obvious delight at seeing the Canon, a set of such price that he could never afford to buy it, Chen opened the volumes carefully and located the *Su Qi*, the Morning, Noon, and Night Audiences, to compare with his own copies.

"You were quick about copying the *Su Qi*," he said, seeing my interest in what he was doing. "Have you finished with it?"

"Yes, thank you," I replied, wondering how to ask respectfully what use the printed versions of the Canon were to him. As I hesitated, he paused and looked up, as if to answer me before I could ask in the proper manner.

"You see," he said, "the text here is the same as the *Su Qi* which you borrowed. But I am looking for the name of the spirit which the ancient author summoned to act as liaison to carry the documents to the heavens. We must study continually to know if we are indeed summoning the proper liaison spirit-officials."

He continued to glance through the pages of the Canon. I promised to bring more copies from my library and he in turn promised to loan me other copies from his collection to photocopy. With the *Su Qi* on microfilm, I was able to give Zhuang a printed version of the lost text, while Chen kept his copy of the manuscript. It was interesting, I thought, that only Zhuang was sure enough of himself not to refer to the Canon for the names of the various liaison officials. Indeed, Zhuang's manuscripts contained several volumes of Lu or registers containing the names, descriptions, and proper occasions for using the communicating spirits in orthodox ritual. Further, Zhuang had memorized the entire text of the *Su Qi* and did not need the book during the public performance of ritual. Chen later admitted that only Zhuang knew how to perform the rite properly. The Daoists of the Zhengyi Citan were waiting for A-Him to become head of the fraternity, hoping to learn from him the orthodox rubrics known only to the Zhuang family.

As mentioned above, splitting up collections of written texts and not returning a borrowed book to a master was a common practice among the Shenxiao Daoists of north Taiwan. The noted Master Huang, a Hakka Daoist who lives in Zhong Li City to the north of Hsinchu, had an extensive collection, dispersed generously among the Redheads of Hsinchu, Taoyuan, and Taibei counties. It is common to see as many as fifteen Daoists traveling from village to village in the Hakka farming communities, each performing his own liturgical specialty in various village temples on a rotating schedule. Thus the fraternity of friendly Redhead Shenxiao brethren protect each other in a community of economic interests, insuring that no one master will monopolize the trade in Jiao liturgies of renewal.

It must not be thought that the practice of stealing, forging, or copying texts is peculiar to Taiwan or to the local Redhead Shenxiao orders. The early history of Mao Shan, described in chapter I, shows the literati families of the north-south period competitively struggling over possession of the prized Shangqing revelations of Wei Huacun at Mao Shan. Tao Hongjing spent many years retrieving the lost books and completing the Mao Shan collection. In view of such past and present threats to the integrity of collections, Master Zhuang in modern Taiwan was rightly concerned about preserving his library. When called upon to perform a Jiao liturgy of renewal, Zhuang and his sons alone were accountable for the entire ritual performance. The result was a liturgy so perfectly executed as to make Zhuang the most sought-after and expensive master in north Taiwan, and a minimal opportunity for attrition to the texts.

Even though social encounters with Zhuang were avoided by those who did not know him and were feared even by his own disciples, there were occasions when the Zen like violent temper and scolding were subdued and the warmest expressions of camaraderie and friendship emerged. Friends from Zhuang's high school days or fellow office workers from prewar times saw a different Zhuang when they came to his residence. To such guests Zhuang always served healthy fruit juices or drinks made from almonds and peach juice, a formula supposedly good for longevity. Zhuang also made a fine millet wine flavored with the essences of black sesame and dried mushrooms, another Daoist formula for longevity. Long hours were spent talking with friends, drinking, and meditating. If it were not necessary to perform ritual for a living, Zhuang said, he would spend his days talking with his friends, and his nights in internal alchemy or nei dan 內丹 meditation.

When I first met Zhuang, the house was poor and untidy, the children many, and the standard of living frugal. But through the marriages of his sons and daughters, the fortunes of the family visibly improved. For the eldest son, who had chosen the career of an army officer in order to further his education, Zhuang found a wife from an upper-class wealthy family. The Zhuang household received a new coat of paint and fine furniture as part of the dowry. The second son married into a shoe salesman's company and moved away from his father's residence. The third son, A-Him, had put aside thought of marriage until his ordination as the successor of his father, and spent his free time pursuing Daoist perfection with meditations, breath control, and physical exercise. The fourth son, A-Ga, who stayed at home reluctantly to help his father in ritual, found his own bride in the farming village of Nanliao near the birthplace of his mother. A-Ga's bride was a wealthy farmer's daughter and the Zhuang home received a television set, refrigerator, and automatic washing machine as part of her dowry. The daughters of Zhuang likewise married well. The eldest daughter, who was trained as a medical technician, married a public official. The second daughter married the son of a paper manufacturer, and the third daughter a wealthy merchant's son. All three daughters visited home frequently, bringing their children to play in the family rooms and be spoiled by the doting grandparents. The second daughter often lived at home in order to help with writing the lengthy documents used in ritual sacrifice. Her children were dry-nursed on the breasts of their grandmother or were carried by their grandfather as he entertained guests in the front room of the busy residence. Zhuang was indulgent, kind, and totally unable to discipline his grandchildren.

A-Him married, and now has four children. Three of his sons are trained in orthodox Daoist liturgy, and perform the Jiao ritual with him when asked. Since he had been chosen to succeed in the ministry of military Daoism, that is, the ministry of exorcism, much of his energy was given to wushu martial arts exercises for self-strengthening. The techniques of Fang Zhong sexual hygiene, however, are strictly forbidden to orthodox Daoists. This last practice, A-Him told me, was part of the Tao of the Left and not practiced by the more orthodox Daoists of the "Three Mountain Drop of Blood Alliance," who receive a Grade Five or higher ordination. A-Him's rigorous wushu training included running and jumping with heavy weights on each shoulder so as to be able to jump great heights when the weights were removed, strengthening the fists and the arms by hitting hard objects, and sitting in the lotus position while holding the breath for long periods of time. During the breath-holding exercises, A-Him said that he could in effect breathe through the pores of his skin; he always meditated bare from the waist upward. The secrets of Zhuang were gradually being revealed to him, but in such a way that no doctrine or method was ever completely revealed at one time. Zhuang's greatest fear was that A-Him in his youth and enthusiasm would let slip the secrets to friends and sycophants who cultivated A-Him's company in order to exploit his talents. And, indeed, A-Him had already a large coterie of followers to whom he taught his wushu exercises and breath-control techniques. In order to receive a grade five "Lu" ordination from his father, he renounced "sexual hygiene" and all thoughts or actions of "impure" origin (see p. 31b, *Long Hu Shan Ordination Manual* 给录元科). Whatever doubts Master Zhuang had concerning his son, there was no denying that he was an excellent Daoist and had far surpassed his father in many of the feats of physical endeavor and ritual perfection. This both pleased and slightly upset the elder Zhuang. Furthermore, A-Him showed a kind of generosity not typical of the other members of the Zhengyi Citan fraternity; he refused to receive any fee from the poor and often turned down payment when he felt the donor could not afford it. There was no doubt that Zhuang A-Him would be a worthy successor to his father and an able leader of the Zhengyi Citan brethren.

My position among the disciples and children of the Zhuang family was passive and unobtrusive. I took photos of the grand liturgies, a practice that proved helpful in winning friends among the Daoists, the musicians, the temple committees, and the laymen who patronized the liturgies. To all who appeared in the photos, I gave copies, which were treasured by the recipients and still hang in many of the temples and the homes of those who received them. During the great liturgies of the Jiao festivals of renewal in the local temples, I also recorded the music and helped in some of the lesser roles not requiring the years of training that Zhuang's sons had been through. In many of the intricate ceremonies requiring incense to be put into small holders or tiny cups of wine to be laid on the altar tables for the heavenly worthies to witness, Zhuang's hands shook too violently to accomplish the tasks. In all such instances I was given the task of writing talismans, handling the incense wine, offerings, fetching the memorials, burning documents, and doing the other small duties to assist the temple custodians who were unfamiliar with the intricacies of Daoist rubrics.

Finally, there were many times when the writing of documents was lagging far behind with a ritual deadline imminent, or when the need for talismans was pressing; on such occasions all hands were brought into the meditation room or the front room of the Zhuang residence to assist. It was during the preparation for one grand festival that I first noticed A-Him's inability to draw talismans. I asked if I might help and A-Him replied with great gratitude that he would teach me how to write the talismanic charms if I would agree to sit through the process with him and follow his precise instructions. The practice of the Wushi Daoism, A-Him explained, had made his hands too stiff to write with the necessary flourish. He could no longer control the pen, nor did he have the talent or feeling for composing the lengthy literary documents. That was why his unwilling brother, A-Ga, had been pressed into ritual service. A-Ga was truly a most unwilling disciple and obeyed his father only out of filiality. But he was quick of mind and fast of hand and could use the brush to compose memorials, rescripts, documents, and other ritual compositions faster than any other member of the family. To A-Him fell the duty of executing the sacred dance steps, turning exorcistic somersaults in midair, fighting the demons with sword, spear, halberd, and axe, and summoning the proper spirits into the talismanic charms drawn by others.

I followed A-Him's instructions and, using the models in Zhuang's manuals for rubrical composition, drew the five Ling-pao talismans, the twenty-eight stellar talismans, and the Pole Star charms. When done, A-Him lit incense and, chanting in a voice loud enough to fill the whole house, called down the proper spirits into the charms, sealing each in a large folded paper container. We then both left the front room, while Zhuang slept on the couch, to have an evening *dianxin* (dimsum) snack in the temple concession. A-Him's favorite stall was noted for a sausage made of glutinous rice, seasoning, and smoked ham, a delicacy proper for the cold winter evening. With a bottle of beer to add cheer to the occasion, A-Him spoke of his frustrations, his hopes, and his future plans for the Zhengyi Citan.

"A-Ga does not want to be a Daoist," he said. "He is terribly jealous of the literary secrets my father has revealed to him, yet does not truly believe in the spirits he has been taught to summon."

"Yes, but A-Ga is filial," I replied. "He knows that the Zhengyi Citan needs both of you in order to make your father's work a success."

"It may seem that way to you because whenever you are here he listens closely and seems to study. But did you know that A-Ga once ran away?"

I did know that A-Ga had gone to the port of Keelung and taken a job as a radioman on a merchant vessel. Zhuang had gone after him, creating a grand scene on the dock, demanding that the master of the shipping company allow his son to return. Chastised, A-Ga returned reluctantly to his father's household and continued the role of a Daoist, but with no heart for the rituals.

"It is because my father's hands shake that A-Ga is necessary to him. Only A-Ga can write the memorials and rescripts in a hand fast enough to keep up with the demands on my father's and my own ritual performance."

I told A-Him how important I thought it was that his father reveal all of his secrets: "He has kept so many to himself that if he chooses to reveal some to you and some to A-Ga, at least we are sure that more of what he knows will be passed on to future generations." I said that I hoped A-Him's resentment of his recalcitrant brother would not prevent him from seeing the necessity of having Zhuang pass down for posterity what had been taught to him by his three Daoist masters.

"You are right in fearing that much of what my father knows may be buried with him," A-Him agreed. "The secrets of the meditations are simple. I have learned them as well as the dance steps, the mantras, talismans, and mudras. But what my father keeps from us is the most essential part of our instructions."

"And what is that?" I was thinking that I might be able to find in the Canon the secrets that Zhuang kept from his sons.

"What do you think it was that the Daoist Chen wanted when he asked to see your copies of the Canon ?" Warmed by the beer and sausage, A-Him grew bolder.

"He wanted to know the name of the proper liaison official to be sent off during certain rituals."

"More important, he wanted to know the description of the spirit; without knowing what the spirit looks like, how can he summon him or her?"

"Has your father told you the descriptions of the various spirits ?"

"Only for some," A-Him answered. "He has told you some, and others to A-Ga. But the main spirits, those for the Su Qi ritual, the Morning, Noon, and Night Audiences, he keeps to himself."

"What else has he not yet revealed ?"

"The dance of the Ho Tu," he answered. "You will see him do it soon."[12]

"But surely the rubrics must be written somewhere in one of his manuals. You should be able to figure out which spirits are summoned according to the rubrics of the Pole Star "yuejian" method and the other techniques that he teaches (see chapter 6)."

"True, but without the koujue (oral transmission) it is difficult to fathom."

The hour was already late, and we returned to the front room of Zhuang's house to complete the preparations for the Jiao festival. Zhuang had already left the room to attend to some details in the temple. A-Him described the spirits that he could summon and I in turn promised to find what I could in the volumes of the Canon in my own room. The dance of the Ho Tu for which A-Him had such admiration was soon to be used by Zhuang in a manner that well justified the son's respect for the rite and his desire to learn it.

Having spoken something of Zhuang's relationships with the ordinary people of Hsinchu, with his friends, and with his own family, I must say something about how Zhuang behaved towards the spirits and other Daoists when summoning his magical powers from the heavens. If his magic was more powerful than others', it was likely that the practitioners of the Tao of the Left would be reluctant to pit themselves against his method. That this was indeed the case can be seen in the following instances observed and recorded during my stay with Zhuang in Hsinchu. Since it was often necessary to corroborate Zhuang's stories by interviewing villagers who witnessed the events, I have included an account of the impressions of the witnesses who saw Zhuang's performance.

The first case involved the use of Mao Shan black magic, in which the Six Jia (Liu Jia 六甲) spirits were invoked to harm a fellow Daoist.[13] One day while I was sitting in the front room of the Zhuang residence, a man from the Hakka district near Zhubei, ten kilometers north of Hsinchu, entered in a state of great agitation and begged to see Zhuang. Turning his head as if bothered by an intruder, Zhuang asked what had occurred.

"My brother, a Daoist whom you know, is being attacked by Mao Shan magic," the man said, holding his farmer's hat in both hands and bowing his head in supplication. Zhuang sat up suddenly as if an electric shock had run through him.

"Mao Shan?" he glowered. When Zhuang is angry, his eyes open very wide, an expression he assumed when exorcising evil demons as well as when scolding his subordinates. "Where are you from?"

Upon hearing the location, Zhuang immediately put on his grey overcoat

and walked out the door, telling his wife he would soon be back. He mo-
tioned A-Him and me to stay where we were and took a taxi to the distant
farming area. In about two hours he was back, somewhat intoxicated and
pleased with his prowess.

Upon arriving at the farmhouse, Zhuang had found the afflicted man,
a minor Daoist, gasping in bed with a high fever. The family insisted that
another Daoist was using black magic against him. Zhuang computed the
Jia spirit of the day (see chapter 4) and then summoned the spirit of the
Pole Star, Po Jun i.e., the *Gang* spirit of Thunder Ritual, to subdue it. He
then paced the steps of the Ho Tu a total of twelve times, as described in
chapter 6, sealing off the room from the attack of the Mao Shan Daoist.[14] He
finally commanded the Jia spirit to return and attack the Mao Shan Daoist
who had caused the trouble. Satisfied that the attacker would be punished
and the sick man relieved, Zhuang declared the ritual ended. The man soon
arose, feeling much better, and served Zhuang a bottle of warm rice wine
and other refreshments. Zhuang finished off the bottle of wine on the spot
and took the waiting taxi back to Hsinchu.

Within a few moments of Zhuang's return, while he was still boasting of
his success, a stranger entered the front door. Obviously shaken, the man
announced himself as the practitioner of the Left Dao whom Zhuang had
just overcome by his Thunder Magic. With abject apologies, he promised
never to use the evil magic again and backed out the door, disappearing
hastily down the alley too rapidly for me to question him about his state
of mind. Before long the farming family appeared, bringing a catered feast
of various soups, noodles, and sashimi (raw fish with green mustard). The
word of Zhuang's victory soon spread around the neighborhood. A-Him
told me privately that the previous year another such battle had taken place
in which another Daoist had died after attempting to oppose the Mao Shan
Daoist's black magic. Whatever the explanation for Zhuang's success and
the previous exorcist's failure, it was certain that the man who had just apol-
ogized and fled was visibly shaken. The reputation of Zhuang as a powerful
master was confirmed in the neighborhood by the event, and Chen the Fat
came from across the alley to ask about being instructed in Thunder Magic.

The second event concerned the exorcism of a man whose possession
occurred during the performance of one of Zhuang's solemn liturgies of
renewal.[15] The incident took place during the festival of renewal for the
temple of the goddess Matsu in Zhong Gang ward of Zhunan City, south
of Hsinchu. Zhuang was in the process of performing a Su Qi ritual, and I
was able to record the entire event on tape and on film, with the mudras and
mantras used by Zhuang in the expulsion. The Su Qi ritual, according to

the earliest rubrics in the Canon, is supposed to begin between 11 P.M. and 1 A.M., the time to correspond to the symbolic renewal effected by planting the Five Talismans. But Zhuang, despite the rubrics, and his own prognostications indicating that the later hour was more propitious, decided to perform the rite between 8 and 10 P.M. One reason was to accommodate the village elders, all of whom wished to witness the beautiful event and were reluctant to wait up until midnight. The second reason alleged was the need to begin the rite called Morning Audience at 3 A.M.[16] By putting the Su Qi earlier in the evening, we could all be assured of a few hours rest before the strenuous rite of the Morning Audience. But Zhuang's real motive was his own physical condition. After the first full day of ritual, he was exhausted and his hands were shaking from the effects of the fast and abstention from alcohol. The only people in the temple who knew that the rite was beginning at the wrong moment were A-Him and I, and although I attempted briefly to suggest we sleep earlier and perform the rite at the proper time, Zhuang was adamant.

A violent wind was blowing from the Taiwan straits as the rite began, echoing through the temple and distorting the sounds on the recording. By the time of the fa lu mandala building, the wind had subsided and the interior of the temple was peaceful, presaging good fortune. Suddenly, during a particularly lyric moment in the ritual, the whole gathering was disturbed by the obvious possession of the local medium, right in the center of the temple. The man had stripped to the waist and taken on the strange features of the possessing god, whose name everyone breathed forth in unanimous recognition.

"Tai Zi yeh—Ne Ja!" the temple custodian whispered into my ear. The village elders and the other Daoists seemed pleased that such a propitious deity had come into the temple, but Zhuang was angered. He continued to perform the rite as if nothing was happening. But then the demon seemed to become enraged and followed Zhuang, imitating his every motion. As if to add insult to injury, the medium began to speak in the boy god's weirdly high and piercing voice. To the horror of the entire entourage he was saying: "The rite was begun at the wrong hour! The rite was begun at the wrong hour!" Zhuang turned and faced the possessed man, his eyes wide with rage. Taking the posture of the Pole Star mudra, he breathed deeply and used the Thunder Magic rubric to expel the deity.[17] In a moment, the possessed man left the center of the temple, collapsed, and came out of his trance. Zhuang then declared his own right to determine the hour when ritual was to be initiated.

When the rite had ended, the temple committee came to ask Zhuang if indeed the ritual had begun at the wrong hour. Voices were raised, but

Zhuang insisted on his own privilege to decide when the various liturgies should begin. Neither A-Him nor I said anything, and the medium, of course, could remember nothing of his possession or what he had said during the trance. The matter was dropped, but the head of the temple committee, a large man who was a devout Buddhist, begrudgingly admitted to me later that the power of Zhuang was indeed great to have expelled the spirit so easily. The remainder of the Jiao festival was a great success and no bad effects were seen to come from the wrong timing, proving Zhuang's power over the heavenly spirits to be indeed effective.

Many other anecdotes could be told to convey the impression Zhuang made on the community around him, his relationships with his friends and neighbors, and his attitude towards the spirits. For instance, whenever I came for a lesson in ritual Daoism, Zhuang always began by worshiping his ancestors, burning incense to the two tablets on his main family altar. One of the tablets honored his own forebears, the Zhuang clan, and the other contained the tablets of all the Daoists from whom he had inherited his manuals. There were memorial scripts for the Wu, the Chen, and the Huang clans, as well as the memory in Zhuang's own mind of the powerful Lin brothers, Rumei and Xiumei, who had contributed so much to his own tradition. He also had a deep and abiding devotion to the Daoist spirits on his altar, especially to the eight-armed four-headed statue of Dou Mu (Marishi), the Mother Goddess of the Pole Star, patron of Pole Star and Qingwei Daoism.[18]

Zhuang's approach to his spirits was one of complete devotion and strict observance of propriety and rubrical perfection. Where other Daoists allowed their disciples to do things such as eat from the sacrificial offerings or drink the sacrificial wine, Zhuang would not allow any talking or whispering during his ritual and looked neither to the left or right when engaged in public prayer. He was ferociously loyal to the men who worked for him, forgiving their weaknesses, even their cheating him on innumerable occasions. Chen the Fat, for instance, had taken many ritual objects from Zhuang's home, even from his altar, and never returned them. Many of his closest disciples had broken away to form businesses of their own. It was essential to Zhuang's character to make nothing of any of his possessions, his reputation or his knowledge, hiding his talents from all but the closest disciples and his own sons, living in a carefree manner. Zhuang was, in all ways, a Daoist and took joy in his ritual profession.

The relationship of Zhuang to the belief of the common man, that is, to what many social scientists call "folk religion" or "Chinese religion" was basic. This institution, which is very hard to delineate, is not an organized

religion but a belief shared by the Han Chinese people with myriads of local variations; it can be defined basically as the religion of the Han people,
based on the cosmological theory of yin-yang and the five elements. That
is to say, the yin-yang five element theory, when euhemerized or personified as a system of spirits and demons who rule the invisible world, is the
basic tenet of the system called Chinese religion. A Daoist as such is a firm
believer in Chinese religion and participates in all the local rites, ancestor
worship, and whatever else is considered to be of faith by the people whom
he serves. Thus Zhuang believed in the spirits that the citizens of Hsinchu
City believed in. He offered religious sacrifice on the birthday or feast day
of a popular local deity, he freed the hungry souls from hell in the Pu Du
ritual of general amnesty for the deceased, and he performed funeral ritual
in which the spirit of the deceased was led through the labyrinth tortures of
hell's bureaucracy to the heavenly realms of the immortals. These practices
were basic to Chinese religion in Taiwan's cities and villages; and to all the
underlying beliefs, Zhuang ascribed with a deep and convinced devotion.

At the same time Zhuang was externally a man of the world, one educat-
ed by the Japanese and in the mandarin literati traditions of his forebears.
To the agnostic, Zhuang said nothing of his Daoism, and to the common
man, everything of the theology of folk religion. But for himself and his sons
he kept secret the esoteric doctrines of monastic Daoism, the techniques of
breath control, inner alchemy, refinement of the spirits, and meditation. In
the following pages I shall describe a minute part of Zhuang's beliefs and
practices, but a part nevertheless basic and not well known either in the
west, or in China. The secrets of religious Daoism, even those contained in
the printed Canon, must depend upon men like Zhuang for preservation
and proper explanation.

PART II

THE TEACHINGS OF DAOIST MASTER ZHUANG

4. THE DAO OF THE LEFT

INTRODUCTION

When Master Zhuang gave lessons in Daoism to his sons, A-Him and A-Ga, he did not begin with the esoteric "Dao of the Left" or the elite meditations of inner alchemy, but with the practical first steps of drum playing, ritual dance, and song.[1] To A-Him, the elder of his sons destined for the profession of ritual Daoism, Master Zhuang taught the military exorcisms, the handling of sword and spear, tumbling, and the art of self-defense.[2] To the younger son A-Ga, Zhuang taught the arts of literary Daoism, the composition of official ritual documents, brush stroke, and song.[3] The older son was a much better student than the younger and learned his own role and that of his brother to perfection. A-Ga, on the other hand, was at first embarrassed to perform ritual in public and wanted a more acceptable, modern profession. My acceptance by Master Zhuang as a disciple had a beneficial effect on A-Ga, who suddenly realized the value of his studies in the eyes of a foreign scholar. Much to the delight of the elderly Zhuang, his two sons, and more especially A-Ga, attended the instructions given for my benefit. Because of my presence and my questions concerning the sources of Zhuang's teachings, A-Ga tried to outdo his brother A-Him in the esoteric knowledge of meditative Daoism and became proud of his role as ritual expert in the public forum. My presence lent prestige to A-Ga's performance and led him to study Daoism in a scholarly manner.

Zhuang's selection of the Dao of the Left as the first manual to use in my instruction was at first puzzling. The manual was both extremely elite and difficult to master. Zhuang insisted that he had learned the manual first from his own father, but further questioning made clear that he did not teach the method to his own sons. Nowhere else in his documents was there such a clear explanation of how the spirits were to be commanded and summoned at the Daoist's discretion. The book was the most detailed in Zhuang's library in explaining the method of forming mudras, reciting mantras, and performing the accompanying meditations.[4]

I. Mao Shan Magic: The Tao of the Left

"Today I shall speak of the Dao of the Left," Zhuang said. He told A-Ga to bring the manual called Qi-Men Dun Jia[5] from the shelves in his bedroom. The manual was wrapped in white cloth, and consisted of four juan 卷 or paperbound texts, each with forty or so handwritten folio pages. We passed the four books around, examining the rice-paper pages. The text had been copied out in 1851, the first year of the Emperor Hsien-feng's reign. At the end of each section was written the date and the name of the copyist, a teacher of Lin Rumei who had been hired to copy out the text in Lin Rumei's name. The original text was later stolen; only my photocopy of the original remains.

"The book comes from Mao Shan," said Zhuang. "It was brought to Taiwan by Wu Jingchun in 1823, and came originally from Wu's grandfather, twenty three times removed." He brought forth an ancient and tattered manual with the title *The Family History of the Wu Clan* (*Wu shi Jia pu*) written on it.[6] On the first pages of the family history could be seen the account of how the first Daoist in the Wu clan had gone to Mao Shan and been ordained a high-ranking monastic priest. "The manual was acquired by the Wu clan at Mao Shan, but in fact it must be classified as a sort of military magic that originated at the famous Wu Dang Shan, a Daoist center in Hubei province noted for its military ritual." Zhuang told again the story that we had heard many times, of the origins of the Wu Dang Shan military school, of the supposed founding of the order by Zhu Ge Liang during the wars of the Three Kingdoms, and the emphasis of the order on military arts, and battling with the sword. Since most of Zhuang's stories were hagiographic, that is, pious folk stories rather than historically accurate accounts, I challenged his description, using the preface of the Qi Men Dun Jia manual as proof.[7]

"Surely the manual here has no relationship either to Mao Shan and the famous Shangqing sect or to the Yellow Court Canon, the basic text of the order. It is difficult to see how it relates either to Mao Shan, where Wu's ancestor is said to have acquired it, or to the Wu Dang Shan military tradition, since the manual mentions nothing of either mountain."

"You are not wrong in supposing that the manual does not belong to the Mao Shan Shangqing sect, which is wholly orthodox and historically from a tradition quite different in content from the text we have here." As he spoke, Zhuang opened the first volume of the manual and quoted from the preface.

"The manual was copied out at the beginning of the Ming dynasty, and was entitled *Qi Men Dun Jia*, a marvelous method for hiding the Six Jia spirits in the microcosm, and calling them forth to do battle. The early Mao Shan sect was concerned with inner alchemy and attaining longevity by ritual meditation. Like all other Daoists, Mao Shan monks later began to bury the dead and perform rituals of renewal. The present manual, therefore, is called Mao Shan Magic only because it was propagated there many centuries later, during the Sung period (960-1278). I say that it must originally have come from Wu Dang Shan because of the preface. Here we see that the method explained in the manual is attributed to Zhu Ge Liang, the famous general of the Three Kingdoms period (221-263). Methods of military magic are traditionally said to have come from Wu Dang Shan in Hupei, the place where Zhu Ge Liang practiced his battle tactics and developed the Ba Zhen Tu, the Battle Chart of the Eight Trigrams." Zhuang opened the first manual to the pages where the battle chart was explained.[8]

"Then the manual cannot be a *Qi Men Dun Jia* like the popular pamphlets that can be bought next door at the Cheng Huang temple."[9] I showed Zhuang the pamphlet I had just purchased, with the same title as the manual in his collection. He took the book, peered at the first few pages, and returned it with a chuckle.

"This sort of manual is very late, and cannot be traced back earlier than the Sung. The only similarity in the two volumes is the title. In fact, these four volumes, which I have just taken out of my collection, are a Lu or register of the spirits' names and appearances, and the secret charms and talismans for bringing them under the Daoist's power. They are only called *Qi Men Dun Jia* to offset the idle and curious who might chance upon the book in my library. In fact the book of military magic is very dangerous and must not be lightly shown to the outsider, who may put it to evil use. Because it is Zuo Dao, the Dao of the Left, officialdom has condemned the book and punished those who practiced it throughout Chinese history. Orthodox Daoists have the manual only in order to combat those evil Daoists who practice black magic to harm the men and women under their spiritual care. I explain it to you only so you may use it to help, and never to harm by its powers."

Zhuang settled back into a more comfortable position before beginning his lesson. A-Him, the elder brother, sat straight and alert. A-Ga, the younger, looked for some avenue of escape. Zhuang began to repeat his injunctions about preserving the secrets he was going to reveal and never using the feared Dao of the Left except to help one's fellow man. Orthodox Daoists like himself and his sons were never permitted to use such techniques except in the most extreme conditions.

A-Him complained about his father's long introductory discourses, which were designed to make us restless and unwilling to wait for the truly important revelations. Today's lesson was not like the others. In a brief few sentences, Zhuang got to the point. There were three preliminary warnings, he said. The heart must first be made to control the impulses and the phantasms which entered the mind. Before such a dangerous doctrine was imparted to the disciples, the master must assure himself that their hearts were pure and their motives simple. Anyone learning these secrets who intended to use them for gross profit or for harming others needlessly would be punished drastically by the spirits. The second warning had to do with self-discipline. The spirits will only obey those who are upright and who have practiced the rubrics so thoroughly that not the slightest detail is missing. The third point concerned the method of bringing the power of the spirits into one's own body. The mind had to be emptied of all cares and worries and the body purified in all respects before the power could be brought into the microcosm of the body.

Paraphrasing the text, Zhuang chanted:

> The heart and the mind must be as one,
> Purified from any sullied desires.
> Only the pure of mind can touch the heavens
> Only the upright of heart can assemble spirits.
> Nature obeys the upright and orthodox.[10]

A hundred days before beginning the rite for internalization of the spirits, the disciple must begin by regulating the mind and senses. The exercise of breath control and meditation on the purest of the heavenly spirits must be practiced daily upon arising and before going to bed. The Daoist must envision the three principles of life in the center of the microcosm, the Yellow Court within his own body, and see himself contemplating before the eternal, Transcendant Dao. When the Three Principles of Life—Primordial Heavenly Worthy, Ling-pao Heavenly Worthy, and Dao De Heavenly Worthy—are present, then mystic contemplation on the Eternal Dao is possible. As the time for beginning the ritual approaches, the Daoist must abstain from meat and practice celibacy. He must be particularly careful to give good example to his neighbors, by acts of benevolence and mercy towards the poor, loyalty to his friends, and filial respect to his parents. Only then will it be possible to perform the Dun Jia rites; if at any time during the period of preparation or of ritual enfeoffment the Daoist fails to act virtuously, the spirits will immediately refuse to obey him.

Though ritual perfection is demanded in every detail, the vestments worn by the Daoist during the ceremonies may be of his own choice. He may wear the white robe with square hat of the southern monastic orders, the black robe with the fish hat of the Quan Zhen sect, or the bright red embroidered robes with the gold crown of the Zhengyi Daoist. The clothes are not important, as long as the rubrics are performed with ritual perfection. Quite unlike the literary Dao of the Right, there are no musical instruments, percussion pieces, or other paraphernalia used (see chapter 5). The ritual objects, the sacrificial offerings, and the meditations are described in section 2 below. They are listed as they occur in the Dun Jia manual, with Master Zhuang's oral explanations.

II. Preparing for the Ritual

1. Selecting a site for the Daoist altar.[11]

Choose a site where a river flows between two mountains. It must be an area where gentle breezes blow and the air is fresh and unpolluted. There, draw on the ground a "Battle Chart of the Eight Trigrams" or Ba Zhen Tu, as in figure 1 below. The battle chart is drawn by pacing off sixty-four steps in a circle, one for each trigram in the *Book of Changes*. Next, go to the very center of the circle and set up an altar in honor of the Pole Star (Ziwei Tan 紫薇坛). One table is needed for an altar, and there should be a second table, such as a bench used for a chariot rest, on which to lay the incense and other ritual objects. On the main altar are to be laid out the sacrificial objects. Enclose the whole area in a tent made of blue-green cloth. The area is thus protected from the elements and casual onlookers. On the table in the center of the sacred area are to be arranged the following items:

1. A stone rubbing block for making ink.
2. Two earthenware candleholders.
3. Two stone flower vases.
4. Two rubbing blocks for making ink, one of red and one of black rubbing compound.
5. Two bowls of pure spring water.
6. The special seal carved from date wood as described in part 4 of this section.
7. The talismans of the six Jia spirits as described in part 4 of this section.

One tall flag pole eighteen feet in height and twenty eight smaller poles six feet in height are arranged around the sacred area according to the plan shown in figure 9 below. Next, the Daoist must prepare the following sacrificial offerings:

1. Dried deer meat.
2. The meat of an owl.
3. A rabbit's foot.
4. A fox's liver.
5. Lamb's blood.
6. Pure white rice wine.
7. Deep breathing incense.
8. Cedar wood incense.
9. An unlacquered wooden basket.
10. An antique ritual sword.
11. A yellow mulberry candle.
12. Paper for drawing talismans in five colors.
13. An oil lamp blue-green in color.
14. Red dates.
15. Roasted chestnuts.
16. A purple crab.
17. A white chicken.

The care of the master's vestments and the bringing of his food must be entrusted to two youths who have not yet reached puberty. The idle, the riffraff, and the impure must not be allowed to enter the sacred area. No one may approach the central altar but the Daoist and the two acolytes.

The rite for enfeoffing the Six Jia spirits must begin on a Jiazi day and end on a Genghai day, that is, it must cover a full sixty-day cycle. The Daoist must perform the ritual every day for sixty days, calling down one spirit each day, except on the fourth day when two spirits are enfeoffed, one in the morning and one in the afternoon. Thus the six spirits are summoned every five days. Each spirit, over a period of sixty days, is summoned a total of twelve times. By the end of the period, the Daoist will have completely familiarized himself with the rubrics, so that he may perform it at will without referring to the manuals or forgetting any of the minute details.

2. Constructing the Battle Chart of the Eight Trigrams.[12]

First, go to a spot by the river, which is not frequented, and select sixty-four clean stones. These will be used to set up a battle chart of the eight trigrams around the interior of the sacred area. Next, go into the sacred area and locate the northeast direction, which is called the "Gate of Life" in the battle chart, or the trigram Gen in the eight trigrams. This is the most important of the eight gates, around which the ritual of enfeoffment revolves. Do not let anyone see how the arrangement is done, or the method of setting up the trigrams. The eight trigrams are given the following names:

1. The trigram Kan in the north is called Xiu, or rest.
2. The trigram Gen in the northeast is called Sheng, or life.
3. The trigram Chen in the east is called Shang, or injury.
4. The trigram Xun in the southeast is called Du, or blockade.
5. The trigram Li in the south is called Jing, or vantage point.
6. The trigram Kun in the southwest is called Si or death.
7. The trigram Dui in the west is called Jing, or alarm.
8. The trigram Qian in the northwest is called Kai, or opening.

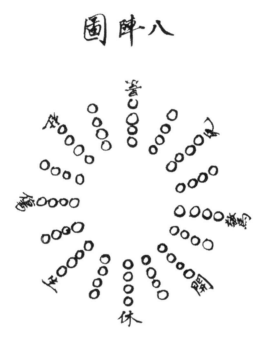

Figure 1. The Battle Chart of the Eight Trigrams, showing how the sixty-four stones are laid out in sixteen rows, four stones to each row, around the sacred area.

Four of the clean stones taken out of the river are to be laid out in a straight line behind each of these gates, and four stones in a line at a point halfway between the gates, so that there are a total of sixteen lines of stones stretching out, four to a line, around the circle. The manner of arranging the stones is seen in figure 1.

The Battle Chart of the Eight Trigrams in figure 1 relates directly to the Ba Gua, or the prognostic chart of the eight trigrams. The significance of the illustration is, however, wholly military. Behind each of the "gates an attacking army of demons" lies hidden. By the marvelous Dun Jia method

Figure 2. The eight trigrams arranged in the order of the Posterior Heavens—that
        is, with the trigram Li in the south, or top of the chart, and the trigram
        Kan in the north, at the bottom of the chart. The Daoist envisions the
        chart on the floor of the sacred area.

explained here in the manual, the Daoist learns how to envision the harmful
demon and render him or her subservient to his commands. In the method
to be taught below, the Daoist will learn how to envision each of the spirits
and how to form the proper mudra and mantra to enfief or bring the spirits
under his power. To do this he must have memorized the battle chart and its
relationship to the eight trigrams, as illustrated in figure 2. The Daoist can
thereupon summon the spirits at any time by constructing the battle chart,
either by dancing the magic "Steps of Yu" illustrated in figure 3 or by trac-
ing the chart in the left hand in figure 4.

   The Daoist paces or dances around the battle chart according to the footsteps enumerated in figure 3. That is, he starts in the north, the trigram
Kan (figure 2), and dances through the nine positions, 1 through 9, until
he reaches the trigram Li in the south. It must be noted that the numbers

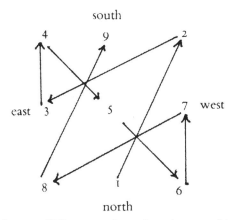

Figure 3. The sacred steps of Yü arranged as a "magic square" in ritual dance.

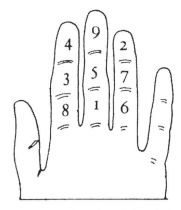

Figure 4. The magic square envisioned on the left hand of the Daoist.

in figure 3 are in fact the mystic enumeration of the magic square. No matter in which direction the numbers are added—vertically, horizontally, or diagonally—a row of three numbers will always add up to fifteen. As the Daoist paces around the sacred area according to the enumeration of the magic square, he summons, commands, or envisions the demonic spirits at the various gates. It must also be noted that the magic square can also be depicted on the left hand and the same sequence traced out by pressing the tip of the thumb to the proper joints (figure 4). The system is used not only in a sacred dance, but as a key to understanding the structure of the heavens. The spirits whom the Daoist calls under his command are thought to reside in the Pole Star of the the seven stars of Ursa Major, plus two other stars in the northern heavens. In the next step, the disciples learn the magic square as it is found in the heavens.

3. THE POSITION OF THE NINE STARS IN THE HEAVENS[13]

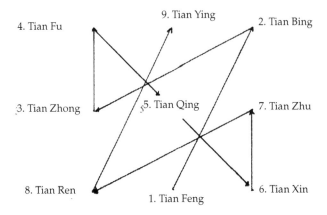

Figure 5. The nine stars in the heavens, seen as a magic square

Each of the nine stars has a secret style name and corresponds to one of the trigrams in figure 2. Furthermore, the Daoist must learn which of the five cosmic elements -wood, fire, metal, water, or earth-the star is subordinate to, at any given moment, in order to marshal all possible spiritual forces to the task of subordinating the power of the spirit to his command:

Star	Secret Name	Trigram	Position	Element
Tian Feng	Zi chin	Gan	1	Water
Tian Ren	Zi chang	Gen	8	Earth
Tian Zhong	Zi qiao	Chen	3	Wood
Tian Fu	Zi xiang	Xun	4	Wood
Tian Ying	Zi cheng	Li	9	Fire
Tian Bing	Zi xü	Kun	2	Earth
Tian Zhu	Zi hong	Dui	7	Metal
Tian Xin	Zi jiang	Qian	6	Metal
Tian Qing	Zi qin	Kun (bis)	5	Earth

Each of the nine stars has a special talismanic charm and a mantric spell, which will be given in part 7 below. The nature of the Six Jia spirits is such that only the most powerful magic invoked by the Daoist will make them obey his orders; the power of the nine stars is necessary to bring them under the Daoist's control. But before accomplishing any of the commands, the Daoist must first see to the carving of a special seal, which is used to stamp all the talismans and documents intended to summon the spirits.

4. MAKING THE SPECIAL RITUAL SEAL.[14]

Select a piece of fragrant datewood without flaw. Cut from this a 2.8-inch block, a perfect cube. On a propitious day, begin woodcarving by meditating and building the mandala as described in chapter 4; that is, command the pure spirits to guard the doors and windows of the room in which the carving is to take place. One must circulate the breath after the Thunder Method as described in chapter 6 and then begin to carve the seal. First draw the outline of the seal on the bottom of the woodblock, and then carve out the figures according to the illustration in figure 6. When done, the talismans of the nine stars are drawn on a piece of yellow paper described in part 5 below, which in turn is used to wrap the seal. The seal, wrapped in yellow paper, is then enclosed in a stone case.

Figure 6. The Qi Yi Zong seal.

The stone case is then sealed with wax and cannot be opened until the Daoist is ready to use it for summoning the Six Jia spirits. The special wooden seal is thus guarded by the spirits of the polar stars, and is always kept in a stone case when not in use. It is strictly forbidden to let it be seen by menstruating women or by the ritually impure. Ink for the seal is made from pure spring water and red powder mixed in such a way that the seal prints clearly and legibly. The seal may never be used negligently. When putting it back into the case after use, always recite the following incantation:

> The command of the Heavenly Emperor!
> Who dares to wait for a moment!
> The Emperor's seal!   ·
> Quickly, quickly, obey his will!

When using the seal it is not allowed to talk, least of all to laugh or act frivolously. If used without due respect and seriousness, it will lose its power and the Yin-bing spirits of the netherworld will lose their trust in it.[15]

5. LEARNING TO DRAW THE TALISMANS OF THE SIX JIA SPIRITS.[16]

The next step in learning to summon and command the Six Jia spirits is most difficult for the novice to accomplish since it requires a smooth and rhythmic flow of the writing brush. Each of the Six Jia spirits has its own talismanic charm, which must be committed to memory in every detail. The Daoist may not carry along his prompt book or have recourse to a library when called upon to exorcise a demon or turn away some evil force that is threatening the community. The charms of the Six Jia spirits are particularly difficult to execute, making it all the more obligatory that the disciples who would learn the method commit the talismans to memory at this point. The talismans are shown in figure 7.

Each of the talismans is drawn on a separate piece of yellow paper in black ink. When completed, the talisman is stamped with the special Chi yi zong seal and burned in order to summon the spirit.

6. THE TALISMANS AND MANTRAS OF THE NINE STARS.[17]

As mentioned above, the nine stars of the northern heavens must be especially invoked in order to win power over the Six Jia spirits. That is to say, each of the Six Jia spirits is a general leading an army of spiritual soldiers. All are ready to leap forth at the summons and call of the Daoist, provided that he has gained power over them, by a mastery of the talismanic charms and mantric incantations of the nine polar stars, i.e., the seven stars of Ursa

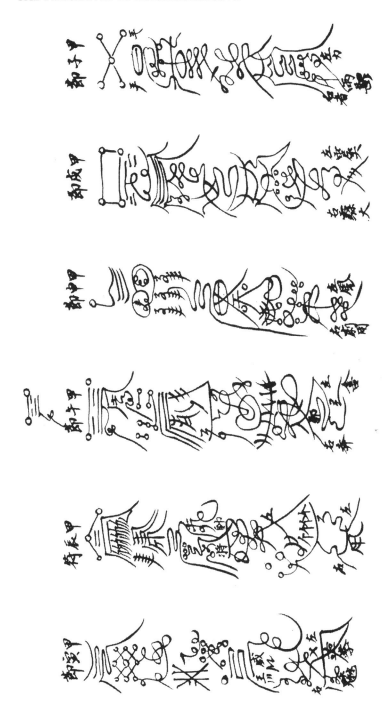

Figure 7. The talismans of the Six Jia spirits. The charms reading from right to left are: Jia-zi, Jia-xu, Jia Shen, Jia Wu, Jia-chen, and Jia Yan, respectively.

major plus two hidden stars. The next step in mastering the Dun Jia method is therefore to memorize and master the use of the talismans and mantras of the nine stars. The manner of using the star spirits is this.

First, determine the direction in the heavens in which the handle or tail of the constellation Ursa Major is pointing. The method will be more completely described in chapter 6 below. Next, draw whichever of the Six Jia talismans one wishes to use as a summons on a piece of yellow paper, and seal it with the special seal.

Second, when the talisman has been drawn and sealed, recite the following spell:

> Honor to the heavens. Let the Dao be followed.
> Succor to the nation, peace to the people!
> The spirits have bequeathed a heavenly book,
> Used now to summon the Six Jia spirits!
> Come forward, and hear my commands!
> The talisman is sent off, burned in the fire!
> Ji-ji Ru Lü ling 急急如律令!

Third, when the talisman has been burned, then take another piece of paper and quickly write down the name of the star to be invoked, according to the direction in which the constellation ursa major points. Draw the talisman for the star, stamp it with the seal, and recite the following:

> In the ___ year, ___ month, ___ day, ___ hour,
> I (Daoist title) affix the seal.
> Carry out my orders, Ji-ji Ru Lü ling!

The mantras of the nine stars and their talismans follow.

Figure 8.
The talismans of
the nine stars.

SPELL OF THE TIAN FENG STAR

> Deep and dark, black and murky,
> Armored hero of the mystic north,
> Broad and vast, leave no traces,
> Riding on the violent winds.
> Great thy strife, power for sorrow,
> Rout the enemy in deep confusion.
> join your army to my forces,
> All pervading demon vapors!
> Ji-ji Ru Lü ling!

TIAN FENG

SPELL OF THE TIAN XIN STAR

Out of chaos came the first gestation.
Floating above, pure and clean.
Yang, like a diamond, moved and created.
Yilan-hsiang Li-chen! (The trigram Ch'ien)
The four seasons were put in order,
The myriad creatures brought forth
by transformation!
Six dragons await your majesties!
Used to transport precious gems!
Beautiful, resplendent, awesome, dreadful!
Generals leading a multitude
of the realized immortals
In front of and behind the Six Jia spirits,
A hundred million fighting troops!
I do here and now command you,
Together assemble, in purity and quiet.
Ji-ji Ru Lü ling!

TIAN XIN

SPELL OF THE TIAN REN STAR

High mountains piled up,
Reaching to Mount Kun Lun,
Precipitous, steep, dangerous, lofty,
Clouds of vapor to the horizon's limit,
Mountain gullies hide the immortals;
Birds and beasts learn from them.
Grass and trees flourish and grow.
Shen cha and Yu luei,
Elves' and goblins' heroic essences,
Cause stones to fly and boulders to walk,
Spew forth fog and move the clouds,
Bind and fetter heaven and earth.
Ji-ji Ru Lü ling!

TIAN REN

SPELL OF THE TIAN BING STAR

Most heavily sullied of the spirits,
Thou whose ability to bear suffering is limitless,
Rivers from thy depths are carved
and mountains born,
The myriad nations' boundaries cut.
The breadth and length is measured out,
Soil piled up and mountain ranges shaped.
The five elements exhaust the infinite visible forms;
Fire smolders, wood grows stronger,
Water held in lakes and rivers,
Metal treasures buried,
Stretching in space across nations,
and downward in time
Through generations,
Here to this military camp in the wilds,
Within the eight trigrams and nine squares,
Which are indeed but tiny boundaries,
I command you, now today,
Crowd in about me, all ye spirits!
Ji-ji Ru Lü ling!

TIAN BING

SPELL OF THE TIAN YING STAR

Essence of the fiery star Ying Huo,
Green-faced great spirit,
Fiercely, mightily, your anger flares.
Parching red searing light!
Scorch the heavens, dry the seas,
Burning rocks and melting metal.
The skies fall and the earth collapses!
All due to thee (Xing) star.
Splendid, brilliant, shining, glittering,
Your light breaks the gathering dusk.
With your great drum you control the winds,
Burn up what has been hoarded and amassed.
The Chi, Pi, Vi, and Ch'en stars,
All are famed for their power over fire.
Today I call you under my command,
right-spirited striding soldiers.
Ji-ji Ru Lü ling!

TIAN YING

SPELL OF THE TIAN FU STAR

A deep mist, hovering, threatening;
Heaven and earth exhale, inhale.
East is turbid, west is murky.
The four seasons' strength exhausted,
The power to give life used to depletion.
The heavens shake, the earth trembles,
Waves dash up and touch the skies.
Blowing sands blind the vision!
Fire, with your overwhelming majesty,
With your overflowing power,
Help me carry out the role of master,
Bring your flags, your drums and standards.
Here today I now command thee!
Bring to me your awesome power!
Ji Ji ru lü ling!

TIAN FU

SPELL OF THE TIAN CHONG STAR

Chong-chong, the sound of thunder!
The nine heavens assemble together;
From the trigram Qian 三 going forth,
They enter by the trigram Chen (east, thunder)
A sudden shower, followed by a rainbow,
A single thunder clap!
From the depths arises a rain dragon,
Evil forces' courage buried,
Demonic spirits' traces obliterated!
Thunder shakes a hundred Li!
A shattering fist, crushing, booming.
With your sound of thunder crashing,

TIAN CHONG

Help me, send a fearful wind,
Here and now I command thee, assemble,
Drumming, dancing hordes attend!
Ji Ji ru lü ling!

SPELL OF THE TIAN ZHU STAR

Awesome, baleful, hard as steel,
Cold, sharp, glistening, gleaming,
Points and edges sheathed in cloth.
Spears and halberds numerous as clouds,
Touching the heavens and dragged in the earth,
Majestically gushing forth like a spring.
No way to prevent its forward progress.
His name is famous, his power inherited,
Assisting the White Emperor of the West.
Fire comes quickly obeying his commands.
I, now, summon thee to assemble,
Awesome, courageous, rank after rank.
Ji Ji ru lü ling!

TIAN ZHU

SPELL OF THE TIAN QIN STAR

Oh thou god who rules in the center,
Sitting, you govern the eight directions.
The Yellow Emperor has a command:
Let the four quarters praise you!
The Qi Men (Dun Jia) gates respond to you;
Your going forth is from the gate of earth.
Dwelling in the center you rule the outer,
Helping the weak, controlling the strong.
Proclaim the magic words Om-na-ta!
Left and right, strike and scatter.
Those who lose him wither,
Those who would grasp him die.
With fire he purges the deceitful!
The eight trigrams acclaim him!
I now summon thee hither.
Thou who's simplicity is good and wise.*
Ji Ji ru lü ling!

TIAN QIN

*Variant readings: thou who choose goodness and wisdom
choosing (only) the good and wise

The nine talismans with their accompanying mantric spells must all be memorized before the next step in the instructions for summoning the Six Jia spirits. The day on which a particular charm or spell is used must be determined by looking at the almanac which the Daoist master keeps in his own possession. Thus, the nine stars are arranged as in figure 5, in such a fashion that the eight points of the compass and the center each receive one of the stars. The direction in which the handle of Ursa Major points in the northern heavens indicates the mudra and mantra that the Daoist is to use at any given time during the day or night. The method is explained in chapter 6, and can be seen illustrated in figure 21. The Six Jia spirits and the nine talismans are therefore used according to the month, day, and hour, the cycle of summoning the spirits changing with the rotation of the heavens. Rather than refer continually to the almanac, the Daoist master usually memorizes the chart. Thus the spirits become effective and are put into use as the Pole Star points in their direction. Since it is impossible to know or guess this direction during the day or on a cloudy evening, the Daoist has a chart worked out to which he can refer as needed.

7. How to make the standards of the twenty-eight constellations.[18]

Twenty-eight standards are to be set up inside the sacred area in a great circle. The flags are made of silk and the poles to which they are attached must be six feet tall. The silk called for in the rubrics is to be of the five basic colors of the elements-green, red, yellow, white, and black. But in fact the flags for the twenty-eight standards are made of seven colors; there are two shades of red in the south and two shades of black in the north. Thus there are four flags in each of seven colors-twenty-eight flags, one for each of the twenty-eight constellations. The flags must be woven of silk with the warp and woof both colored with the same dye. The constellation is drawn in the upper corner of each flag, and the symbolic animal is drawn in the center. The standards may be listed in the following groups.

1. The constellations subservient to wood, which are to be drawn on standards of blue-green silk:
    The Jiao constellation with a Jiao rain dragon.
    The Dou constellation with the Xie unicorn.
    The Kui constellation with the wolf
    The Jing constellation with the An (Han) wild dog.

2. The constellations subservient to metal, which are to be drawn on standards of white silk :
    The Kang constellation with a dragon.
    The Niu constellation with an ox.

The Lou constellation with a domesticated dog.
The Guei constellation with a sheep (goat).

3. The constellations subservient to earth, which are to be drawn on standards of yellow silk:
The Di constellation with a badger.
The Nü constellation with a bat.
The Wei constellation with a ring-necked pheasant.
The Liu constellation with a roebuck.

4. The constellations subservient to the sun, which are to be drawn on standards of red (hung) silk:
The Fang constellation with a rabbit.
The Xü constellation with a rat.
The Mao constellation with a cock.
The Xing constellation with a horse.

5. The constellations subservient to the moon, which are to be drawn on standards of azure (deep blue) silk:
The Xin constellation with a fox.
The Wei constellation with a swallow.
The Bi constellation with a crow.
The Zhang constellation with a stag.

6. The constellations subservient to fire, which are to be drawn on standards of crimson (ch'ih) silk:
The Wei constellation with a tiger.
The Shi constellation with a pig.
The Zui constellation with a monkey.
The Yi constellation with a snake.

7. The constellations subservient to water, which are to be drawn on standards of black silk:
The Ji constellation with a leopard.
The Bi constellation with a snail.
The Shen constellation with an ape.
The Zhen constellation with an earthworm.

For all of the standards, use hand-rubbed ink made on the stone rubbing-block, as in the directions in part I above. When the pole and pennant are completed, insert a pheasant's feather in the head of each standard, being sure that the pole itself is six feet tall. Each flagstaff with standard and feather must then be set up, as can be seen in figure 9.

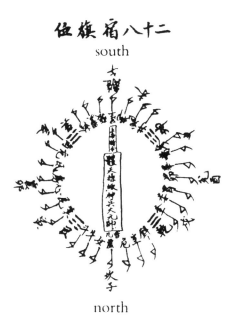

Figure 9. Arranging the standards of the twenty-eight constellations.

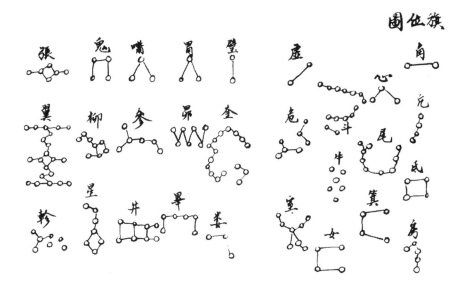

Figure 10. The twenty-eight constellations.

8. SUMMONING THE SPIRITS TO THE CENTER OF THE SACRED AREA.

The Six Jia spirits are summoned from behind a standard according to the time of the year, month, day, and hour, as computed in the method shown in chapter 6, figure 21. Each of the spirits has his or her own post, unit, and garrison name, as will be explained below. In the middle of the circle of twenty-eight standards is to be placed the great standard, which acts as coordinating general for all of the spirits summoned. Thus the spirit soldiers will not dare to leave until they hear their unit called. They can be commanded to go forth to overpower the enemy when summoned by the mudras formed on the Daoist's left hand, combined with the recitation of the mantric spells and the drawing of the talismanic charms. The standard for the large pole in the center is to be made of yellow silk, in the center of which is written, "Lian Zhen Bing Da Yuanshuai" or Commander General for Drilling the Realized Spirit Soldiers.[19]

The incense table and the altar of sacrifice are set at the base of the great standard in the center. The pole is to be twelve feet high. The writing and sending off of talismans, the use of the special seal, and the rite for swearing in the spirit generals are all to be done at the foot of the great standard. On the very top of the pole is affixed a wooden block or tablet on which the following warnings are inscribed in gold: on the front side, "Jin shu" (Imperial Decree); on the back side, "Shang Di Te Ling Zi Yang" (By special decree of the Heavenly Emperor, Talismanic writing!).

The twenty-eight standards and the central pole are set up inside the Battle Chart of the Eight Trigrams, which was described in part 2 above. Each of the poles must be set up in the proper place with reference to the eight trigrams, that is, the eight gates of the battle chart. At each of the gates, the Jade Lady or Yü Nü 玉女 spirits are to be appointed as guards of the entrance, according to the method for building the mandala described in chapter 5. The Six Jia spirit generals can now be "refined," or brought under the Daoist's control. It is necessary to envision the appearance of each spirit, and to execute the mantric summons, mudra, and talisman, to enfeoff them under the Daoist's power. Once completed, the ritual can be repeated at will. The spirits will be always ready to obey the Daoist's wish and order.

9. HOW TO SET UP THE TAN SACRED AREA.

Set up the altar so that its back is to the north. That is to say, when the Daoist faces the altar he should be looking north, while the altar faces south. The Tan or sacred area should be twenty-four feet square and eighteen feet high. There are four entrances, the four "gates" of the trigrams. Do not let anyone approach the area or look down from the surrounding mountaintops. No impure thing must be allowed near. If the rite is to be effective, and the Daoist to gain power over the spirits, only the morally and ritually pure can be allowed near the area. Youths who have not yet reached puberty should be used as acolytes, and all implements brought within the sacred area should be new and clean. When leaving the sacred area upon the completion of each rite, straighten up the mats, realign the stones, and see that the poles are all in order. The Daoist must determine ahead of time the direction from which the particular spirit is to be summoned. Thus the three directions which the Daoist faces during the rites are either Kai (the Gate of Heaven, or the trigram Qian); Xiu (the north, or the trigram Kan); and Sheng (the northeast, or the trigram Gen). Only when the altar has been set up with every detail accounted for should the ritual begin. Whenever sleeping, eating, or drinking, always leave the sacred area. The Daoist should choose the ground directly to the north of the Tan altar for his own resting place. It is forbidden to eat the five grains or the three noxious meats—dog, eel, and goose—during the sixty days of the ritual. One must also bathe before entering, and see that every rubrical detail is perfectly fulfilled.

10. THE TIME OF DAY AND DIRECTION FOR INTERNALIZING THE JIA SPIRITS.

The rite is to begin on the Jia Zi day closest to the summer solstice, and should be carried out in the following order:

1. On the Jia Zi day, at the mao hour (6 A.M.) face the trigram Chen (east) and dose the entrances to the sacred area. The spirit Jia Zi is then refined according to the rubrics described below.
2. On the Yi Qiu day (second day) ... [missing from the text].
3. On the Bing Yan day (third day) at the Mao hour, face the trigram Qian, and from the gate called Sheng (NE) summon forth the Jia Shen spirit.
4. On the Ding Mao day (the fourth day) ... [missing from the text].
5. On the Ding Mao day (the fourth day)two spirits are internalized. At the Shen hour (3-5 P.M.) internalize the Jia Chen spirit from the gate called Sheng, using the proper talisman and rubrics.
6. On the Wu Chen day (fifth day) at the Mao hour face the trigram Kan and from the gate called Sheng internalize the Jia Yen spirit, using the proper talisman and observing all the rubrics.

The Jia Xu spirit, who is enfeoffed on the second day, and the Jia Wu spirit, who is refined in the morning of the fourth day, are not included in the list here, but are included in the rubrics written below. Thus the Six Jia spirits are brought under the Daoist's power over a period of five days, two spirits always being enfeoffed on the fourth day, thus making six spirits each five days. The rite is repeated twelve times over a period of sixty days, until the Daoist is thoroughly familiar with the process.

11. THE ESOTERIC RITUAL NAMES OF THE SIX JIA SPIRITS.

During the performance of the various rites, which summon and "swear in" the different Six Jia generals, the spirits are addressed according to their secret Daoist names. The following list gives the ritual name, the Zi or style name, and the Hao or title by which the spirits are summoned. It is necessary to remember the names of the spirits in order to understand the text of the ritual in the next section.

1. The Jia zi spitit's ritual name is Yuan De; his style name is Jing Gong; his title is General Huangzhen.
2. The Jia Xu spirit's ritual name is Ling Yi; his style name is Lin Ji; his title is General Zhong Zhi.
3. The Jia Shen spirit's ritual name is Shen Quan; her style name is Jie Lüe; her title is General Ganxian.
4. The Jia Wu spirit's ritual name is Chan Ren; her style name is Zi Qing; her title is General Xiaolie.
5. The Jia Chen spirit's ritual name is Tong Yuan; his style name is Zhang Chang; his title is General Dangdi.
6. The Jia Yan spirit's ritual name is Hua Shi; his style name is Zi Fei; his title is General Jisha.

12. A DESCRIPTION OF THE APPEARANCE OF THE SIX SPIRITS.

The most jealously guarded secret of the Daoist master is the "register" or lists of the spirits' names, titles, and appearances, without which the performance of liturgy is a hollow shell, a weak imitation of the orthodox, classical tradition passed down from antiquity. The most critical part of a Daoist master's instructions is the description of the esoteric spirits' countenances, clothes, weapons, or other accouterments, which the Daoist novice who presents himself for a grade at ordination must account for. Disciples wait years at a master's feet to learn the secret names and the descriptions such as those here revealed in the text of the Mao Shan manual of military magic. The text reveals the heavenly stem, and therefore the element (direction) to which the spirit is subservient, the appearance of his or her face, clothes, weapons, and supernatural powers. A learned master can draw a picture of the spirit from memory, so well are the following passages kept in mind.

1. The Jia Zi spirit's heavenly stem is Wu. He is twelve feet tall, with two horns on his head, the face of a rat, and the body of a man. His mouth is tapered and pointed like a knife. He has a yellow beard and yellow hair, and his eyes protrude. He wears the Yuan Pao imperial robe, with a gold belt around the waist. In his hands he carries a Jiangmuo staff for controlling demons. From his belt hang a long bow, a sword, and a beaded pearl shield. The mantric cry which is used to summon him and his troops is "Xi-ta!" His lieutenant general is the Ding Mao spirit, and he leads an army of a hundred thousand soldiers. Such is his power that he can move mountains and plug up the sea, make the ground shrink or stretch, cause rocks to move and sand to fly. His spiritual strength is great indeed, and he always works barefoot.

2. The Jia Xu spirit's heavenly stem is Qi. He is nine feet tall, with the face of a man and the body of a snake. His countenance is purple, and on his head he has a golden crown. He wears a yellow robe with a golden belt, from which hangs a golden shield. Around his shoulders is coiled a snake, and in his hands he grasps a spear made of eight snakes. Hanging from his belt is a gold sack filled with stones and arrows without feathers. His mantric summons is "Zi-zhong!" Under his command is the lieutenant general Ding Qiu, and a hundred thousand spirit soldiers. Such is his power that by drawing a line on the ground he causes a river to appear; by forming a small mound of earth with the hands, he can change it into a massive cliff; with his power one can drill a well, fill up trenches, attack and invade a city, hurl stones and scatter sands. The god is violent and merciless. There is nothing that he fears.

3. The Jia Shen spirit's heavenly stem is Geng. She is ten feet tall, with the face of an ugly woman, yellow hair, and large protruding white teeth. On her head is a crown made of pearls. She wears a purple robe fastened with a jade belt, with scarlet sandals on her feet. In her hands she grasps a huge sword capable of splitting mountains. Over her breasts she wears chain-mail armor. Her mantric summons is "Zheng-ran!" Under her command is the lieutenant general Ding Hai and a hundred thousand spirit troops. By her power one can make swords fly and knives shoot out, break the enemy's ranks with self-propelling spears. Those who approach the camp (Battle Chart of the Eight Trigrams) will be cut down like blades of mown grass. Mounted cavalry troops or bandits, there are none that do not bow and fear her orders. By nature she loves to kill, and no one who meets her lives to tell.

4. The Jia Wu spirit's heavenly stem is Xin. She is eight feet tall, and her face is white and clear complexioned, with pretty features and delicate eyes. Her hair is done up on top of her head in a bun, and her robe is made of silver armor with a silver belt. She rides an excellent horse with red spots, and in each of her hands she carries a double-edged sword. Her mantric summons is "Qing-xiang!" which is intoned like singing a song. Under her command are the lieutenant general Ding Yu and a hundred thousand spirit troops. By her power, one can summon a fog and make clouds arise, befuddling the enemy so they lose their way. She can also cause gold and silver to come into one's hands, but only for the sake of good, or for helping the cause of the Dao. When the enemy approaches the camp, whistle, and she will send flying spears forth. By performing her rite, her unbounded courage will be turned against the enemy who will flee in terror. It cannot be determined ahead of time whether or not she will sally forth riding her red horse.

5. The Jia Chen spirit's heavenly stem is Ren. He is twelve feet tall with an ugly, frightful face like a Vajra (Kongo) spirit, with a three-peaked crown on his head. On his body he wears golden armor and in his right hand he carries a halberd, while standing atop a black dragon. His mantric summons is "Po-lie!" The Ding Wei spirit is his subordinate, with a hundred thousand spirit troops under his command. With his power one can dry the rivers and empty out the sea, walk on water as if it were earth, level city walls, wipe out the enemy, and ride on mists and clouds. By blowing on paper cutouts, one can change them into an army, and call a legion of soldiers out of the skies to destroy the enemy. The Jia Chen spirit's character is sharp and hard as steel.

6. The Jia Yen spirit's heavenly stem is Gui. His face is the color of black millet, and his head is shaped like a leopard's. Around his forehead is wrapped a red cloth, and around his waist is belted armor. On his feet are high boots, and in his hands, a whip made of steel. His mantric cry is "Kong!" Under his command is the lieutenant general Ding Yi, with a hundred thousand troops. By his power one can summon a great wind, shake mountains, burn fields, cut down enemy soldiers, uproot trees, cause sand to fiy, and make men lose their senses. By invoking him, one can create the image of false forests and conceal one's body so that attackers can do no harm. The Jia Yan spirit's temperament is dark and foreboding.

Figure 11. The arrangement of the altar for sacrifice.

13. On the sacrificial offerings to be laid out during the ritual.[20]

A table for holding the offerings must be set up at the Gate of Life, or at the base of the standard used during the ritual. The altar is always set up so that it faces the south, that is, the Daoist faces the north when standing in front of the altar. The offerings are laid out in the following order: in the first row, put the cups of wine; in the second row, the dried fruit; in the third row, the uncooked meat; in the fourth row, the cooked meat; and in the fifth row, the candles, vases, and so forth. The layout of the altar and the position of the Daoist with his acolytes are shown in figure 11.

With the above prescriptions, the first instruction of Master Zhuang regarding the internalization of the Six Jia spirits came to an end, with the assignment that each of us was to read the manual of instructions and come to the following day's lesson ready to draw the talismans and form the mudras as illustrated in the following pages. Since the description is meticulous and dry, it is recommended to read only one spirit's ritual at a time. The English text is complete and can be used as described in the text.

III. Performing the Dun Jia Rituals

With the sacred area now ready, and the seal, talismans, and other implements prepared, the Daoist master may now begin to refine, or bring under
control, the Six Jia spirits. At the proper time indicated for each ritual, the
Daoist goes to the incense table at the foot of the central pole and there
draws the talismans to be used for the day, sealing each one with the special seal. He then goes to the gate in the Battle Chart of the Eight Trigrams,
indicated as the proper gate for the ritual, and there lays out the sacrificial
offerings. The ritual of enfoeffment takes place at the gate, facing the direction indicated in the rubrics. The various mantric spells are then recited, the
mudras formed, and the Cui talismans drawn in the air, according to the
directions written below.[21]

1. The Ritual for Refining the Jia Zi spirit.

On the Jia Zi day, at the Ding Mao hour (6 A.M.) the Daoist master goes
first to the central flagpole and there performs obeisance. He draws the
proper talismans for the day and stamps them with the seal. When done, he
proceeds to the position on the battle chart marked Kai, the Gate of Opening, where he faces the east. There, he lays out again the sacrificial offerings,
lights incense, and bows in worship, while reciting:

> To the central, flowery land of China,
> The gods have given a heavenly book.
> The substance of heaven, the path to the Dao!
> Now drill and enfoeff the spirit armies;
> Honor to thee, General—.
> The Daoist master then recites the conjuration:
> Shang di has given his command!
> Hold the talismans on high, grasp the seal,
> Command and enfoeff the Six Jia spirits;
> Uphold the orthodox, dispel the heterodox,
> Protect the nation, bring peace to the people;
> Totally eradicate all falsities and lies.
> Grant the petition we make with this offering.
> Let us successfully carry out the ritual,
> To master the marvelous Dun Jia method.
> Bearing the Jia Zi talisman,
> I stand at the Tian-chung position;

Figure 12. The Huang Zhen talisman and left-handed mudra.

> Here I pitch my camp, delighting
> To be at this marvelous gate;
> From afar I summon the spirits,
> None dare delay to fulfill my commands,
> Once seeing the power of the talisman I hold.
> Wind and fire come at my summons!

At this point the Daoist stands still, bows, and then performs the nine-step dance of Yü as shown in figure 4. While performing the dance he recites the Tian Zhong mantric spell as in section 2, part 7 and burns the Tian Zhong talisman. When the conjuration is finished, the Daoist stands very still, closes his eyes, and meditates, envisioning the spirit as described above. The meditation lasts for a half hour. When done, he takes the sword, looks upward toward the sky, and draws in the air the "appearing" talisman (Cui fu, as in figure 12) with a single stroke. Thereupon he forms the Huang Zhen mudra (figure 12) and recites the Huang Zhen mantric spell below.

The Huang Zhen mudra is performed by first opening the left hand so that the nails of the index finger and the ring finger are stretched out parallel to each other, with the middle finger stretched slightly above. Next, bend the middle finger down and press the index finger and the ring finger over the nail of the middle finger, so that the nail cannot be seen. Finally, press the little finger and the thumb over the nails of all three fingers. Use the sleeve to cover the mudra so that it cannot be seen. The talisman for making the Huang Zhen spirit appear must be practised by the Daoist in the air many times before he actually uses it ritually, so that it can be completed smoothly and perfectly without faltering, or cutting off the action before completion.

The following is the mantric spell for summoning the Huang Zhen spirit:

O thou commander of heaven and earth,
General Huang Zhen!
Yellow beard and yellow hair,
Rat face and man's body,
Yuan robe and golden belt,
Staff of steel and engraven fan,
With your lieutenant general Wen Ba [Ding Mao],
Red-faced, towering in stature.
From Xu and Wei and the Pole Star
Call forth your heroic troops!
Level mountains and shrink the earth!
Stones fly and dust fills the air.

Thereupon the Daoist recites the mantra of Shang Di:

Ga! Cha! Gon! Om!
Quickly come and assemble here!
Receive my commands, carry them out!
Ji, ji ru lü ling!

When finished chanting the mantra, the Daoist closes his eyes and meditates, holding his breath until he hears a humming in his ears. Then he takes the great sword again and repeats the talisman for making the spirit appear, drawing it quickly in a single stroke. Then forming the mudra on his left hand, he repeats the above mantric spell, this time substituting two new lines for the original beginning:

You alone are the purest of lords,
General Huang Zhen!
Yellow beard and yellow hair . . .

When he reaches the ending, "Receive my commands, carry them out," he adds the magic words in a scolding voice:

Khat-chhit is thy name!
Ji ji ru lü ling!

With the mudra still formed on the left hand, he closes his eyes and meditates again until he perceives a red light and then a yellow light on his forehead directly above the eyes, . He immediately takes the sword again and draws the appearing talisman in the air for a third time. The mantric spell is repeated a third time, substituting for the first two lines:

> The Wu ritual for summoning Yüan-te
> General Huang Zhen
> Yellow beard and yellow hair . . .

Reaching the next to last line " . . . carry them out," he adds:

> No terror that you cannot suppress,
> Appearing in a wraith of fire,
> Quickly, upon seeing our needs,
> Send down lightning and thunder!
> Ji, ji ru lü ling!

When the Daoist has finished the mudra and mantra a third time, he again closes his eyes and meditates until he sees a red light in a purple fog before him, like the coming of an army all in dark uniforms. When he hears the angry sound of a violent wind and the clapping of a thunderbolt, then the spirit has arrived. Taking the seal in his left hand and the sword in his right he cries out:

> Now you may hide!
> Five days hence come back again,
> And show your true form!

Having finished the rite, he returns to the altar by the central pole, bows for a moment in worship, and retires from the area.

2. THE RITUAL FOR REFINING THE JIA XU SPIRIT.

On an Yi Qiu day (the second day), likewise at the Mao hour (6 A.M.), the Daoist master goes to the main standard and lights incense, performing obeisance, and writing the talismans for the day as before, stamping them with the seal. When he has finished, he goes to the gate marked Sheng in the Battle Chart of the Eight Trigrams (the northeast) and faces east. There again he arranges the sacrificial items and offers worship at the standard marking the gate, bowing with lighted incense in his hands. He then begins the incantation as follows:

> To the central flowery kingdom of China,
> The gods have given a heavenly book.
> The substance of heaven, the path of the Dao!
> I now summon and enfoeff the spirit armies.
> Honor to thee, General—.

The Daoist master then begins to recite the following conjuration:

> Shang Di has given his secret command.
> Hold up the talisman, grasp the seal!
> Command and enfoeff the Six Jia spirits!
> Stand by the orthodox, dispel all evil,
> Protect the nation, bring peace to the people.
> Completely eradicate all cunning deceits.
> Help us successfully to carry out the rites,
> For investing and commanding the Jia spirits.
> On this day, at this hour,
> I take the Jia Xu spirit's true talisman,
> And stand at the Tian Ren position.
> Here I establish my residence,
> Delighting to be at the gate of life!
> From afar answer my summons.
> Do not for a moment wait to come.
> Once having known the power of the talisman,
> Wind and fire come at my command.

The Daoist then paces the sacred dance steps (Steps of Yü) while reciting the Tian Ren mantra and burning the Tian Ren talisman. When done he stands very still and erect, closes his eyes, and meditates for a period, envisioning the spirit of Jia Xu. He then takes the great sword and in the air draws the Cui talisman for making the spirit appear. When the talisman has been drawn, he forms the mudra on his left hand and recites the mantric spell, as below.

To form the mudra, use the left hand, bend the thumb, and bring down the index, ring, and little fingers so that the nails are parallel with the top of the thumbnail. Stretch the middle finger straight upward. The mudra must be covered with the sleeve so that no one can see how it is formed. The talisman must be practiced until it is perfectly mastered. One should try to write it as if drawing on a piece of paper held in mid-air. There must not be the slightest deviation or faking on the part of the Daoist. Only when the form is perfected can it be used in the ritual.

When the talisman has been drawn in the air, the Daoist forms the mudra and recites the following mantric spell of the Jia Xu spirit Zhong Chi:

Come down from your position in the Lou star,
O thou spirit Zhong Chi!
Giant body, coarse and ugly,
Man's face and serpent's body,
Clothed in the yellow color of center,
Armor and helmet made of gold,
Snake spear eight feet in length (eight-pronged snake spear)
Serpents coiled around your body.
In your satchel arrows and stones,
Innumerable your magical changes.
With your lieutenant Ting Qiu,
Holding an axe and ringing a bell,
Under your control a hundred thousand soldiers,
Like a forest of wolves and tigers.
Cause a river to gush forth!
Seal the mountain passes! Level cliffs,
Scatter sand, make rocks fly,
Piling up to become a mountain!

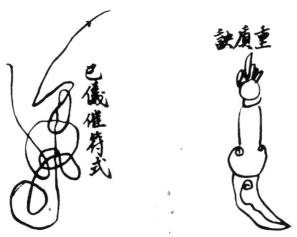

Figure 13. The talisman and mudra of the Jia Xu spirit.

To this is added the secret mantra of Shang Di:

Om! Gu! Xi! Gen!
I command thee approach the Xü position!
Hear my orders, carry them out!
Ji ji ru lü ling!

When finished with the mudra and the mantra, the Daoist closes his eyes and concentrates until he senses a wind blowing from behind on his ears. He then takes the sword and draws the appearing talisman in the air for a second time, being sure to complete the character without once breaking the smooth flow of the stroke. The talisman is drawn in the air twice, without pause. He then repeats the mantric spell and the mudra, changing the first two lines to read:

All hail to thee! With ranks of soldiers,
Numerous as a forest, General Zhong Zhi . . .

After the words "Hear my orders, carry them out" in the next to last line, he adds:

Has my second summons reached you,
As I shout out your name?
Ji ji ru lü ling!

When the mantra and the mudra have been repeated for a second time, the Daoist again closes his eyes and concentrates for a short time. When he sees a yellow mist arising before his eyes, he then takes the sword and writes the appearing talisman in the air a third time. The talisman must now be drawn in the air a total of three continuous times, after which the mudra is again formed and the mantric spell recited. The first line of the mantra is changed to read:

God of the Chi rite, hidden spirit,
O thou General Zhong Zhi . . .

Again at the next to last line the words are added:

Carry out my commands, do not hide yourself,
From afar come and show your true form.

> Put your perverse obstinacy to use,
> Mercilessly wield your cruel sword.
> Ji ji ru lü ling!

Having finished the mantra, the Daoist again closes his eyes and concentrates, envisioning a yellow light directly before him, like a wall cutting off everything that is in front. Then the sound of a bell ringing in the ears will be heard. This is the sign that the god is coming. Immediately as the god comes, take the sword in the right hand and sing in a loud voice:

> Now go back whence you came,
> To come again five days hence,
> Showing your true appeance.

With the spirit sent back, the ritual is completed. The Daoist master then returns to the central standard and replaces the seal and the sword on the table. He bows deeply in obeisance and leaves the ritual area.

3. THE RITUAL FOR REFINING THE JIA SHEN SPIRIT.

On a Bing Yen day (the third day) at the Ding Mao hour (6 A.M.), the Daoist master goes to the central standard, lights incense, and bows in obeisance. He then draws the talismans proper for the day and signs them with the special seal. He goes to the gate marked Sheng in the Battle Chart of the Eight Trigrams (Gate of Life, same position as on the preceding day) and faces the northwest. The sacrificial objects are laid out on a mat in front of the gate and the Daoist lights incense, bowing in obeisance. He thereupon recites the incantation:

> The secret orders of Shang Di!
> Hold on high the talismans, grasp the seal!
> Command and drill the Six Jia spirits.
> Support the orthodox, suppress the false.
> Protect the nation, bring peace to the people.
> Put an end to all evil deceits.
> Help us successfully to complete the Dun Jia rites.
> On this day, at this hout,
> I take the Jia Shen spirit's true talisman,
> And stand at the Tian Xin position.

Here I establish my residence,
Delighting to be at the Gate of Life.
From afar answer my summons,
Do not for a moment wait to come.
By using your talisman as proof,
Wind and fire obey my command.

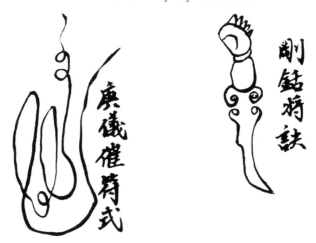

Figure 14. The talisman and mudra of the Jia Shen spirit.

The Daoist then bows in worship, rises, and performs the steps of Yü, as before. While dancing the sacred dance steps, he chants the mantric spell of the Tian Xin star and burns the Tian Xin talisman. When finished, he closes his eyes and meditates for a time. When done, he takes the sword in his right hand and draws the appearing talisman in the air with a single stroke, while forming the mudra on his left hand, and recites the mantric spell.

When drawing the talisman in the air, it must be remembered that the Daoist is to use strength on the downward movements and on the curves. The final stroke is made from left to right across the base of the character, then rises swiftly on the right side, finishing with a final flourish off to the right. As with all of the Cui or "appearing" talismans, the Daoist must practice the stroke until it is perfect and smooth, finished in a single flowing motion. In the mudra pictured in figure 14, press the nails of the index, fourth, and fifth fingers into the palm of the left hand. Meanwhile, use the tip of the nail of the middle finger to press hard against the bent thumb, so that the tip of the finger touches the line where the nail and the cuticle meet on the thumb. The following is the mantric spell of Gang Xian, the Jia shen spirit:

Thou fierce general,
Suppress and bind heaven's changes!
White teeth and gold hair,
Steel armor and woven pearl helmet,
Embroidered robe and jade belt,
Steel axe and carved bow,
With your lieutenant general Ding Hai.
Black-faced, covered with wrinkles,
With your spirit troops of a hundred thousand soldiers;
Your flying sword tossed into the air,
Slay the enemy! A mountain of corpses!

To this is added the secret mantra of Shang Di:

Shan! Shuo! Hong! Bing!
I command thee, approach the Battle Chart!
I summon your awesome wind,
To come and obey my battle orders.
Put on display your mighty power! (military merits.)
Ji ji ru lü ling!.

When done, the Daoist master closes his eyes and meditates until he hears in his ears the sound of a hollow shell. He then immediately takes the sword and draws the talisman in the air twice, followed by the talisman used by the preceding Jia-hsü rite, which is also drawn twice. The mantric spell is repeated with the first two lines changed to read:

O Gang Xian, ferocious general,
Jie Lie thy style name,
White teeth and golden hair . . .

Immediately after the next to last line, "Put on display your mighty power," the following lines are added:

If at once you do not come,
I shall shout aloud your name,
Ji ji ru lü ling!

When the mudra has been formed and the mantric spell recited a second time, the Daoist closes his eyes and meditates again for a moment, until he sees a white vapor stretching up into the heavens to the Milky Way. Then he immediately takes the sword and draws the talisman in the air three times. The talisman of the Jia Xu spirit is also drawn three times, following which the mantra is read a third time saying:

> O spirit of the Geng rite, Shen Quan,
> Thou here, Gang Xian,
> White teeth and golden hair . . .

After the next to last line, "Put on display your mighty power," the Daoist adds the conclusion:

> It is not allowed to delay for a moment;
> Come at once to the battle chart's center!
> The seal and the sword have cut away our sins,
> Preventing and covering all lack of respect!
> Ji ji ru lü ling!

When finished, the Daoist closes his eyes and meditates until he hears the sounds of swords and spears assembling on both sides. This is the sign that the god has arrived. The Daoist then takes the sword in the right hand and the seal in the left and shouts in a loud voice:

> We pray thee, be indulgent,
> Return whence thou hast come;
> Come again five days hence,
> Showing thy true form!

The Daoist then returns to the base of the central standard, replaces the seal and the sword and, after offering incense and bowing in obeisance, retires from the sacred area.

4. The ritual for refining the Jia Wu spirit.

On a Ding Mao day (the fourth day) at the Gui Mao hour (6 A.M.), the master dons his sacred vestments and goes first to the ritual table at the base of the central standard. There he offers incense and bows in obeisance

Figure 15. The talisman and mudra of the Jia Wu spirit.

three times. He then draws the talismans to be used for the ritual of the Xin spirit, Jia Wu, and signs them with the seal. He thereupon proceeds to the gate marked Sheng in the Battle Chart of the Eight Trigrams, and faces the northeast. There he lays out the sacrificial offerings, offers incense before the Gate of Life (the gate marked Sheng), and bows three times. The conjuration is then recited:

> To the central, flowery land of China,
> The gods have given a heavenly book.
> The substance of heaven, the path to the Dao.
> I hereby command and enfoeff the spirit soldiers.
> Hail to thee General—.

The Daoist then recites the following conjuration:

> The secret orders of Shang Di!
> Hold high the talismans, grasp the seal!
> Command and drill the Six Jia spirits.
> Uphold the orthodox, suppress all evil,
> Protect the nation, bring peace to the people,
> Put an end to all deceitful lies.
> Help us successfully complete the Dun Jia rites.
> On this day, at this hour,

I take the Jia Wu spirit's true talisman,
And stand at the Tian Fu star's position.
Here I establish my dwelling,
Delighting to reside at the Gate of Life.
From afar answer my summons,
Do not for a moment wait to come.
By using the power of your talisman as proof,
Wind and fire come at my command!

The Daoist then bows in worship, rises, and dances the sacred steps of Yü During the ritual dance he recites the Tian Fu mantric spell and burns the Tian Fu talisman. When the dance is completed, the Daoist slumps back on the ground, sitting with closed eyes. Before his eyes he sees a thick blue vapor, quiet and dense. He immediately arises and paces (the steps of Yü) to the south position. Taking the sword, he then traces in the air the appearing talisman of the Jia Wu spirit, General Xiao Lie, while forming the mudra on the left hand and reciting the mantric spell.

For drawing the talisman, first grasp the sword firmly in both hands and use force to form the first four loops. Then, in the second series of loops and curves, release the left hand and use the right hand only to form the strokes. Finally in the third stage, raise the sword and in a single stroke, rising outward to the right, finish off the tail of the talisman. It is necessary to practice the character until fluent. For forming the mudra, first press the nails of the middle, ring, and little fingers against the upper part of the bent thumb. Press the thumb down into the palm of the hand, so that the tips of the fingers touch the palm, while the nails touch the top of the thumb. The index finger is pointed straight upward. Always remember to cover the mudra with the sleeve so that it cannot be seen. The following is the mantric spell of the Jia Wu spirit Xiao Lie:

O thou spirit Jia Wu,
Commander Xiao Lie!
Lovely countenance, powdered face,
Delicate eyebrows, light and lustrous.
Hair bound up, golden crown on the head,
Armor made entirely of silver,
Mounted on a heron-winged horse,
Again sallying forth on foot,
With a pair of precious swords,
Joyfully singing ballads and songs.

> With your lieutenant general Ding Yu,
> Of the pearl crown called De Ren,
> Leading a hundred thousand troops,
> Summon the rain and call up the clouds!
> Cause sun and moon to disappear!
> Move them as you wish, up or down,
> Enemy lances totally beaten,
> Their courage deadened, their spirits lost.

To this is added the secret mantra of Shang Di:

> Chü! Cho! Ling! Ding!
> From afar I summon thee to come!
> When you hear my command, come at once,
> Ji ji ru lü ling!

When finished, the Daoist closes his eyes and meditates for a while, until he hears approaching the sound of beautiful music being plucked on strings. Thereupon he takes the sword and draws the appearing talisman in the air twice, following which he also draws the talisman of the preceding Jia Shen spirit twice. The mantric spell is then repeated a second time, changing the first two lines to read:

> O thou General Xiao Lie,
> Clever, nimble, quick and bright,
> Lovely countenance . . .

The next to last line is also changed to read:

> If I call again and you do not come,
> Punishment will be thy lot!
> Ji ji ru lü ling!

When done, the Daoist closes his eyes firmly and meditates until he senses before him an auspicious cloud with a wondrous fragrance. Thereupon he takes the sword and draws the talisman three times and repeats the mantric spell, changing the first two lines to read:

O spirit of the Xin ritual, Chan Ren!
General Xiao Lie . . .

Upon reaching the next to last line, "When you hear my command, come at once," he adds:

I fear that my prayer is late,
Commanding the sword to make your form take shape!
Ji ji ru lü ling!

When finished he closes his eyes for a time, until in front of the eyes can be seen a light made of five colors and in the ears can be heard the sound of ballads being sung. This is the signal that she has come. On the first time that she appears before the Daoist, be warned that she is frivolous and fickle and must not be abruptly ordered about. On the very first encounter, her attitude is often one of flirtatious laughter. In such a case, address her with a stern countenance, saying:

I command thee to go back whence thou came!
Five days hence come once again.
Bring your troops with disciplined control!
Come here to my altar and hear my commands!

If the Daoist does not actually see her face, he must add the following harsh order:

Five days hence come again,
Showing your true form!

In a few moments the light will disappear completely. Then, very slowly, retreat to the original position in front of the standard in the center of the area, replace the seal and the sword, bow in obeisance, and leave the area.

5. THE RITUAL FOR REFINING THE JIA-CH'EN SPIRIT.

On the Ding Mao day (also the fourth day) at the Jia xü hour (gloss: read between the Shen and Xü hour, or 6 P.M.), the Daoist master dons his sacred vestments and goes to the central standard to burn incense and bow

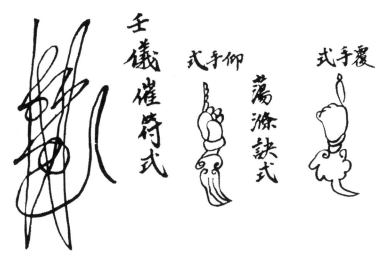

Figure 16. The talisman and mudra of the Jia Chen spirit.

in obeisance. There he draws the talismans for the Jia Shen rite and stamps them with the seal. When completed, he proceeds to the position in the battle chart marked Sheng, that is, the Gate of Life, as in the preceding ritual meditations. At the Gate of Life he faces the south and lays out the sacrificial offerings. He thereupon lights incense, bows three times, and begins the recital of the conjuration:

> To the central, flowery land of China,
> The gods have given a heavenly book.
> The substance of heaven, the path to the Dao;
> With it I command and enfoeff the spirit soldiers.
> Hail to thee General—.

The Daoist then goes on to recite the following:

> Shang Di gives an order (secret order),
> Hold high the talisman, grasp the seal!
> Command and drill the Six Jia spirits.
> Uphold the orthodox, suppress all evil.
> Protect the nation, bring peace to the people,
> Put an end to all deceitful lies.
> Help us successfully to complete the Dun Jia rites.
> On this day, at this hour,

> I take the Jia Chen spirit's true talisman,
> And stand at the Tian Ying position.
> Here I establish my dwelling,
> Delighting to dwell at the Gate of Life.
> From afar answer my summons,
> Do not for a moment wait to come.
> By using your efficacious talisman,
> Wind and fire come at my command.

When done, he bows in obeisance. Then rising, he dances the sacred steps of Yü. During the sacred dance, he recites the Tian Ying mantric spell and burns the Tian Ying talisman. When done, he stands still, closes his eyes, and concentrates on seeing the spirit. He meditates until he hears in his ears the sound of violent waves crashing. He immediately takes the sword and with violent strokes cuts the appearing talisman in the air. Though very complicated, the talisman must be drawn in a single stroke. While drawing the strokes, he forms the Dang Di mudra on his left hand and recites the Dang-di mantric spell.

For drawing the talisman in the air, begin by holding the sword straight up and let it fall in a downward stroke. Then lift the blade in the various convolutions, putting strength on each of the curves, and slashing downward in quick motions. The last stroke moves outward and upward to the right, then slashes downward, curving slightly outward. Be sure to coordinate the reciting of the mantra with the forming of the talisman. The mudra is formed in three stages. First, press the middle finger and the ring finger together firmly, then press them down to touch the print of the thumb. The pressure is then released, the thumb bent further downward, and the nails of the middle and fourth fingers are then pressed against the nail of the thumb. In the third step, the little finger is also bent downward and pushes the middle and ring fingers off the nail, so that the nails of all three fingers now touch the top of the thumb, the little finger itself resting on the thumbnail. The index finger is pointed straight upward, and the hand turned so that the palm faces outward. The following is the mantric spell:

> O thou spirit Jia Chen,
> General Dang Di,
> Highest leader of the heavenly forces!
> Protector of the stars of the northern skies!
> Prepared to destroy all wily deceivers!
> Crab-faced, hideous, repulsive, ugly,
> All thy apparel made of scaly armor,

Halberd sending forth rays of light,
Riding on a black dragon!
You come floating on a turbulent mist!
With your lieutenant general Ding Wei,
Tu Dui her secret name,
Leading a hundred thousand spirit soldiers.
Mists arise and clouds assemble,
Mountains rise up and seas tumble.
Demons wail and spirits tremble.
Riding through the skies on spirit tigers,
Vapor turns into teeming soldiers!

To this is added the secret mantra of Shang Di:

Hou! Ho! Meng! Ming!
I call thy name! O come quickly!
Hear my commands! Carry them out!
Ji ji ru lü ling!

When finished, the Daoist meditates for awhile with closed eyes. He sees before his eyes a black vapor seething and curling. Then he takes up the sword and draws the appearing talisman in the air twice, and adds to it the talisman of the preceding Jia Wu spirit which is also drawn twice. He then recites the mantric spell a second time, changing the first two lines to read:

O thou General Dang Di,
Do I hear the sound of brawling?

The next to last line is also changed to read:

A second time I call you, but you do not come!
With a loud shout I call your name!
Ji ji ru lü ling!

When the mantra has been recited and the mudra formed a second time, the Daoist again closes his eyes and meditates. When he hears in his ears the sounds of whistling, brawling, and swaggering as in a military camp, he again takes the sword and draws the appearing talisman in the air, this time repeating the strokes three times. Following this the talisman of the preceding Jia Wu spirit is also drawn three times. The mantra is repeated with the first two lines changed to read:

O thou who penetrates to the primordial northern heavens!
General Dang Di . . .

The last two lines are also changed to read:

<blockquote>
If you still refuse to obey my commands,
You will be punished by the strictest rules!
Ji ji ru lü ling!
</blockquote>

When the mudra has been formed and the mantric spell recited, the Daoist meditates a third time with closed eyes. He sees a black vapor arise like a protective wall. In his ears he hears the sounds of a myriad horses prancing and snorting, with spirited neighing. This is the sign that the spirit has come. Immediately he takes the seal in the left hand and the sword in the right and sings out in a loud voice:

<blockquote>
Hear thee, go back whence thou came!
Come again five days hence,
Showing your true form!
</blockquote>

When finished with the recitation, the Daoist returns to the standard in the center of the sacred area, replaces the seal and the sword and, after performing the usual obeisance, retires.

6. THE RITUAL FOR REFINING THE JIA YAN SPIRIT

On a Wu Chen day (the fifth day) at the Yi Mao hour (6 A.M.) the Daoist master dons his ritual vestments and goes to the standard in the center of the sacred area. There he lights incense and bows in obeisance three times. He then writes out the talismans to be used in the ritual for enfeoffmg the Jia Yan spirit and stamps them with the seal. When done, he proceeds to the Gate of Life in the Battle Chart of the Eight Trigrams and faces the north. There he lays out the sacrificial offerings, lights the incense, and bows in obeisance. The following conjuration is recited:

<blockquote>
To the central, flowery land of China,
The gods have given a heavenly book,
</blockquote>

The substance of heaven, the path of the Dao.
With it I drill and enfoeff spirit soldiers.
Hail to thee great General—.

The Daoist then continues with the following recitation:

Shang Di has given a (secret) order!
Hold high the talisman, grasp the seal,
Command and drill the Six Jia spirits.
Uphold the orthodox, suppress all evil.
Protect the nation, bring peace to the people.
Put an end to all deceitful lies.
Help us successfully to complete the Dun Jia rites,
On this day, at this hour,
I take the Jia Yan spirit's true talisman,
And stand at the Tian Ping position.
Here I make my dwelling,
Delighting to live at the Gate of Life.
From afar, answer my summons,
Do not for a moment wait to come.
By the efficacious use of your talismans,
Wind and fire come at my command.

When done, the Daoist bows, rises, and performs the sacred steps of Yü. During the dance, he recites the Tian Peng star's mantric spell and burns the Tian Peng talisman. When the dance and recitation are finished, he stands still, closes his eyes, and meditates, concentrating on seeing the spirit. When he hears in his ears a sound as of a mosquito humming, he immediately grasps the sword and draws the appearing talisman of the Jia Yan spirit in the air with a single stroke. During the writing of the talisman, he forms the mudra on his left hand and recites the mantric spell of Ji Sha.

To draw the above talisman in the air, hold the sword by the handle and raise the sword forward and upward. Use force to form the first stroke downward, slanting crosswise and then upward. In the next stroke, the sword is turned to form the four circular figures, as illustrated. Finally, the sword is lifted and the four slanting strokes formed with great power, moving backward and forward in an upward motion, applying pressure at the points. A forward and upward stroke, forming the tail of the figure, brings the talisman to a conclusion. To form the mudra, bend down the index finger of the left hand so that it touches the nail of the little finger. Then press the thumb against the nail of the little finger with some pressure, holding all three fingers down close to the palm. Then extend the middle finger and the ring finger straight upward, pressed against each other with the nails parallel. Cover the entire mudra with the left sleeve so that it cannot be seen. The following mantric spell is recited:

Ji Sha, Ji Sha!
Black killer from the Niu and Nü stars,
Leopard's face and tiger's whiskers!
Hat of red and face of black!
In your hands a whip of steel,
Violent, oppressing, killing, punishing.
With your subordinate general Ping Nan (Ting Yi)
Hideous teeth, beard of red,
Leading a hundred thousand spirit soldiers,
Like a pack of bears or wild dogs!
Secretly hiding your oppressive form!
When an enemy approaches, shoot out spears,
Summon forth a violent wind!
Shake down the mountains, level forests,
A sheet of flame crosses the heavens!
Spears fall like clouds, killing all!

Figure 16. The talisman and mudra of the Jia Yan spirit.

To this is added the secret mantra of Shang Di:

> Zu-hu! Hung pa ha!
> From afar I summon thee to come.
> Hear my orders, commanding the troops!
> Ji ji ru lü ling!

When the master has finished, he closes his eyes and meditates, standing very still for some time. All will be quiet and still, as if there were no results. Then the Daoist takes the sword again and draws the appearing talisman twice without pause while reciting the mantric spell. The first two lines are changed to read:

> O thou General Zi Fei,
> I pronounce thy secret name Ji Sha!

The last two lines are also changed to read:

> If called again thou dost not come
> I'll call in thy stead the spirit Xi-ta!
> Ji ji ru lü ling!

When the mantra is completed a second time, close the eyes and meditate until in front of the eyes a thin fog is envisioned. Then immediately take the sword and draw the talisman in the air three times, while reciting the mantric spell and forming the mudra with the left hand. The first two lines of the spell are changed to read:

> By performing thy rite, rocks are melted;
> With thy soldiers in ranks, Qi Sha!

The last two lines are also changed to read:

> Dallying stubbornly more and more!
> Hold the weapons to the fore!
> Courage flashing like bolts of lightning!
> Ji ji ru lü ling!

When finished, the Daoist must close his eyes and meditate again, until before his eyes there appears a strange pure, clear mist. Since the spirit is by nature deep and foreboding, it is not easy to arouse or envision him. If this is the case, repeat the talisman, mudra, and mantra again three times, thus bringing the repetitions to a total of six. After the sixth time, wait until there appears a light, like a ray of fire in front of the eyes, and in the ears there is an angry roar. When this happens, take the seal in the left hand and the sword in the right and shout in a loud voice:

> Never again dare to dally in coming!
> Now you may go back whence you have come!
> Five days hence come back again,
> Showing your true form!

The Daoist then returns to the table at the central standard, replaces the seal and the sword, and bows in obeisance. With this he retires, having completed the first cycle of five days in refining the method for summoning and hiding the Six Jia spirits.

On the second series of five days, the Daoist repeats the meditations, continuing to summon the Six Jia spirits according to the directions given above. The spirits are each summoned twelve times over a period of sixty days. During the total time of the ritual, the Daoist must always keep the sword and the seal near to himself, replacing them in their respective cases after each use and putting them under his pillow when he sleeps at night. At the end of the sixty-day period, all the temporary items used in the rites— the flag poles, standards, wooden tablets, and the like—are to be destroyed by burning. The Daoist digs a hole, builds a fire inside, and, after burning all of the materials, covers the ashes with rock and the rock with dirt so that no trace is left. The spirit generals, once brought under the Daoist's command, will come at his summons to obey whatever orders he may give them. The following books of the manual (parts three and four of the Dun Jia manual) list sixty or more uses to which the spirits can be put. Though the spirits are mainly used to combat one's enemies in battle, they can also be used to cure illness, exorcise, and protect the Daoist from black magic used against him by a rival practitioner.

Whether from the very beginning the practice of esoteric Daoist ritual was made extremely complicated simply to preserve its proper use for the truly devoted follower, or whether the progress of time increased the exacerbating details necessary to perform the rituals properly, is difficult to determine, especially in the instance of a text such as Qi Men Dun Jia, the military manual from Mao Shan quoted above. The text is only partially canonical, in that the Six Jia spirits are summoned and used in many orthodox rituals. The rite for internalizing the spirits is not found in such detail in the canon, nor are the terrifying uses to which it is supposed to be put, such as slaying one's enemies, moving mountains, or causing a shower of spears to fall from the heavens. These are not in any sense a part of orthodox, state-approved, and acceptable ritual. Two K'ou-chüeh or oral secrets are transmitted with the text of the Dun Jia rites, which identify the Daoist who knows the method and can be seen in use among the more knowledgeable masters of Taiwan. The Six Jia spirits are truly terrifying demons and their control is not a matter for the weak-hearted or the pretender among the Daoists. This is especially true of two of the spirits, the Jia Wu spirit of the fourth day and the Jia Yan spirit of the sixth day. To control these two demons, and any other spirit who refuses at first to obey the Daoist's commands, a special series of techniques must be used, ones that have become a part of the orthodox Daoist's repertoire.

In the case of the Jia Wu spirit, who appears as a beautiful woman but who is in fact a demon fond of killing, the Daoist must be immensely cautious. For the Jia Yan spirit, who is a brawler and a very recalcitrant servant, the Daoist must learn to use the following rubrics. If the spirit comes in a terrifying shape, eighty feet in height or in the form of a monstrous demon, so hideous that the Daoist is tempted to run in terror or "hide himself in the earth" as the text reads, it is absolutely necessary to show no sign of alarm, but to open the eyes wide so that they bulge and look straight at the misshapen demon. He then must say:

> I have here thy registers, O general,
> How dare you use a false shape!
> Hiding your true appearance!
> Now be sworn in by my feudal treaty![22]

The Daoist then takes a mirror, which was made of polished metal in earlier times but now can be a simple looking glass, and draws on both sides. On the reverse side, the Daoist writes all the esoteric names of the spirit, names not usually written out. The writing is done with red ink so that it can be rubbed out easily. On the front side is then drawn the appearing talisman-again, a form usually never drawn except in the air so that the ordinary human and spirit may not see how it is written. The reverse side of the mirror is held up facing the demon, while the Daoist is writing the talisman. When the talisman is finished, the mirror is then turned and held straight towards the demon so that the talisman can be clearly seen. The spirit will then very clearly say the words:

> My master summons me here.
> What wishes do you have for me to carry out?

With a serious voice and a stern countenance the Daoist answers:

> By the secret orders of Shang Di,
> An order has come down commanding thee,
> —of the Six Jia spirits,
> Perform the rites of the eight trigrams chart,
> Exhaust all manner of magical changes,
> Bring aid to the nation, peace to the people,
> Fulfill the heavenly Dao!
> Respectfully respond to your taboo names!
> Cautiously follow heaven's will!

The mirror is then turned so that the taboo names face the spirit. The Daoist must then see the spirit fall to its knees in respect and say to the Daoist:

> I swear to be under your command.
> Whatever your orders, I will obey.

The Daoist master then answers:

> I mutually promise, with thy taboo talisman,
> To live up to the duties incumbent on your vows.

The Daoist then goes with elation to the standard in the center of the sacred area and, after bowing in obeisance, announces to heaven:

> By imperial decree we have fulfilled and accomplished.
> The enfoeffment of the spirit —.
> (repeat all of the taboo names.)
> Together let us carry out the heavenly law!
> I swear there will never be any deceit between us!

When the recital is finished, the Daoist takes a white cock, cuts the comb with the sword, and lets some of the blood fall into a bowl. Taking the bowl in his hands, he first presses it to his own mouth, tasting the blood. Thereupon he offers it to the spirit. The spirit, too, imbibes of the blood. The Daoist then proceeds to the table and takes the talisman of the spirit, which was previously written of a piece of yellow paper, and holds up the talisman in the air. Then while holding the talisman in the left hand and the sword in the right, he cuts down the center of the talisman so that it is cut into two pieces. The left half is kept for the Daoist himself and the right half is given to the spirit by burning. Finally, the Daoist recites the mantric spell commanding the spirit to return, reminding him or her, meanwhile, to come back again in five days, as in the directions above.[23]

The ceremony of cutting the cock's comb and swearing in the spirit general must be performed at least once for each of the Six Jia spirits. If the spirit appears regularly on the second summoning-that is, during the second period of five days-it is performed on that occasion. Otherwise the Daoist must go through the above special rite to make the spirit appear in its true shape and then continue the swearing-in ceremony. Although the rite of cutting a cock's comb is very ancient and is accepted as a part of the orthodox Daoist's repertoire of ritual activities, it is very different from the stately classical liturgies of the Dao of the Right to be discussed in the next chapter. The violent, military rituals of the Dao of the Left are indeed suspect of being tainted with sectarianism, though the greatest effort is made by the Daoist to remain pure and virtuous and to use the rites only "for the good of the nation, and peaceful life of the people." There is no doubt however, that the magic of the Six Jia spirits has been used to man's detriment, and the "Left Dao" from very early times came to mean a kind of black magic that was punishable as an offense against the imperial authority.[24] Practitioners of the Dao of the Left were considered to be sectarian and punished throughout different periods of Chinese history. The manual itself, therefore, warns that the method is only to be used to help a Chinese emperor restore the throne, or to come to the aid of a person who is being attacked by black magic. The Daoist who practices this method is thought to use his own vital forces to exhaustion and to die young, because of the great effort required to command and control the terrifying Jia demons. Though a good master will learn the method, he will seldom put it to use and then only to come to the aid of a man or woman in distress. Zhuang's use of the method, described in chapter 3, was confined to exorcistic retaliation.

Whatever the power ascribed to the strange Dun Jia rites, there is no question that the style of liturgy must be categorized as heterodox, or at least outside the accepted orthodox style of meditation. The classical Thunder magic of chapter 6 is invoked to counteract its harmful effects. It is possible that Lin Chan Mei invoked Dun Jia magic in his battles to pacify north Taiwan. The manual was at least in the Lin family library by the first lunar month of 1851 and was used by the Daoists of Hsinchu as late as 1970 (chapter 3 above). The difference in heterodox Mao Shan magic and the classical, stately Dao of the Right will become evident as we consider Zhuang's teachings in the next chapter. The spirits of orthodox Daoism are bearers of peace, blessing, and contemplation, the ultimate effect of which is meditation in the presence of the eternal Dao of Transcendance. The Dao of the Left is, indeed, a polar opposite of its classical orthodox counterpart.

5. ORTHODOX RITUAL: THE DAO OF THE RIGHT

INTRODUCTION

Orthodox Daoist ritual has traditionally been distinguished from the popular village "Fa Shi," i.e, local Daoist practices, by a special meditation of "internal alchemy" leading to union with the Dao. This meditation is based on a passage from the fourth chapter of the Zhuangzi, "Heart fasting, sitting in forgetfulness," 心斋坐忘. The purpose of classical, orthodox ritual is threefold. For the adept, it leads to mystical union with the Transcendent Wu Wei Dao. For the men and women of the villages, it brings blessing and renewal. For the souls of the departed in the underworld, it brings "salvation and release" from the punishments of Buddhist-Daoist conceived nine-stage hell-purgatory. Though innumerable local variations and styles of Daoist ritual have evolved over the past two millennia, the basic structure and purpose of orthodox ritual has remained surprisingly stable. After a brief meditative hymn and entrance rite, the Daoist always begins orthodox ritual with a meditation called Fa Lu, 发炉 for "lighting the internal meditation area" and expelling all spirits from the body, after which the encounter with the Wu Wei Dao is possible. The ritual meditation, in which the Daoist master ascends to the heavens and presents a memorial or grand written document before the Transcendent Dao, is also a constant. Finally, Orthodox ritual always concludes with the Fu Lu, or the restoration of the spirits to their places inside the microcosm, once the Audience with the Dao is over.

1. KINDS OF ORTHODOX RITUAL

The earliest passages in the canon, which treat of Daoist ritual, show an amazing continuity with the liturgies of renewal and burial, up until modern times. The sixth century Wu Shang Biyao text contains the same basic structure of modern Jiao liturgies of renewal (Su Qi, Morning, Noon, and Night Audiences, and Dao Chang-Zheng Jiao; see below). Prayers are directed to the Three Realms—heaven, earth, and the underworld—to win blessing for the villagers, renew the cosmos, and free souls in hell.[2] In the Ming dynasty Canon, Gold Register (Jin Lu) rituals of Renewal and Yellow Register (Huang Lu) liturgies of burial are also found present in modern ritual.[3] Only one ancient ritual, "casting of dust and ashes on the heads of penitents," no longer occurs.[4] The word Zhai, taken from the court ritual of feudal China and the Han dynasty, was commonly used to name the meditative rituals of early Daoism. Zhai 齋 meant, according to the early Shuo Wen dictionary, a period of fasting and purification preceding a sacrifice. The term "xin zhai," or fasting of the heart described by Zhuangzi, became a form of explicit Daoist meditation and is listed in Tang dynasty sources as a commonly known Daoist practice.[5]

The word Jiao 醮 was used interchangeably with Zhai to describe Daoist ritual. Whereas in the Daoist Canon Zhai appears more frequently in the sixth-century Wushang Pi Yao, the word Jiao, or sacrifice, is found in later dynastic records to describe the rituals offered by Daoists at the court of the emperor.[6] During the Tang period, the two words, Jiao, which meant literally the pouring out of wine and the offering of incense in sacrifice, and Zhai, were often used synonymously. In later sources, a clear distinction is made between ritual offered for the living, which came exclusively to be called Gold Register Jiao (Jin Lu Jiao), and rituals for the dead, called Yellow Register Zhai (Huang Lu Zhai). This later distinction is used by Master Zhuang, and the Daoists of north Taiwan. As early as the Song dynasty (960-1280), the grand festivals of village renewal had been developed into a set formula, the structure of which is still observed in Taiwan.[7]

Following the custom established in the Song dynasty,[8] when a Daoist master is hired to perform his ritual in modern Taiwan, the people of the village ordinarily call the entire festival a Jiao, that is, a pure sacrifice. But concurrently with the Jiao, a Zhai or set of ceremonies for freeing all the souls from hell is also celebrated. Thus the modern village festivals include both a Jiao and a Zhai. Like a great symphony in which two melodic themes are developed, the Daoist performs a set of rituals whose purpose is to win blessing from heaven and union with the transcendent Dao, and at the same time celebrates another set of ceremonies whose purpose is to free the souls from hell. In the first set of rituals, which are properly called Jiao, the meditations of union are performed. These meditations invariably begin with the Fa Lu rite for emptying the microcosm and end with the Fu Lu for restoring the spirits to their proper place. In these rituals, wine, incense, flowers, and tea are offered to the heavenly spirits, hence the word Jiao used to describe them.[9] In the second set of rituals, the Daoist reads lengthy canons of merit and litanies of repentance, in a formula which does not make use of the classical Fa Lu rite of emptying.[10] The Zhai ceremonies for freeing the souls end with a great sacrifice called the Pu Du in which raw meat is used as an offering (signifying to go elsewhere to consume it), to feed the souls in hell.[11] The word Zhai is now used to describe these latter ceremonies, a change from the more general sense in which the word was used in the past.[12]

2. Ritual Meditatio Leading to Union with the Dao

According to the teachings of Master Zhuang, orthodox Jiao ritual is solidly based on the Yin-yang Five Element theory of the cosmos. In a strictly religious interpretation of chapter 42 of the Laozi, the Daoist reverses the process whereby the "Dao gave birth to the One; the One gave birth to the Two; the Two gave birth to the Three; the Three gave birth to the myriad creatures."[13] In orthodox ritual, the Daoist "returns to the roots," that is"returns" to cosmic origins, by refining the 5 elements into the 3 cosmic principles (Qi, Shen, Jing), to the state of primordial simplicity, Hun Dun, in order to be united with the eternally gestating, transcendent Dao of Wu Wei.[14]

The Dao is a nameless, unmoved first mover, as described in the first chapters of the Laozi. In the phrase "The Dao gives birth to the One," (chapter 42) "One" is interpreted to be the immanent Dao, that is, the moved first mover, also called Taiji—Great Principle—or Hun Dun—primordial chaos. Primordial chaos, or Taiji is euhemerized by religious Daoism, i.e., made to be the first of a Daoist Trinity, Yüan Shi Tian Zun, 原始天尊or Primordial Heavenly Worthy. Within the human body he stands as symbol of primordial breath; Qi 气, the basic life-giving substance within the microcosm. His dwelling place is within the head of man, where he resides in an esoteric place called the Ni Wan (Pineal gland) or upper cinnabar field.[15] When called forth from within the microcosm, he always appears in a purple mist. In the macrocosm, he rules the highest heavens.

"The One gives birth to the Two," the next line in Chapter 42 of the Laozi, is also personified as a spirit by the religious Daoists. The second spirit, Ling Bao Heavenly Worthy灵宝天尊, stands for the liaison spirit between heaven and earth. Thus the term ling refers to the half of a talisman kept in the heavens, and the bao to the precious half buried in the earth.[16] Ling Bao Heavenly Worthy is the symbol for the spirit or Shen 神 in humans, residing in the heart, symbol of will and compassion. His rule is in the center cinnabar field, and, when summoned forth, he appears in a yellow light.

"The Two gives birth to the Three," the next line from the verse, refers to the third of the Daoist trinity, Dao De Tian Zun, 道德天尊 who is taken to be a mystical personification of Laozi. Dao De Heavenly Worthy is symbolic of vital essence, Jing 精 or wisdom within humans, which resides in the lower abdomen, or "lower cinnabar field." When called forth, the "vital essence" spirit of wisdom always appears in a bright white light.

Thus the Dao is seen to give birth in turn to three principles—breath, spirit, and intuitive essence. These three principles are in the philosophic order expressed by the notions Taiji, yang, and yin. In the religious order they become three Heavenly Worthies, the "Three Pure Ones" or San Qing. From the Three Pure Ones are generated the five movers or the five elements: wood, fire, earth, metal, and water; and from the five movers come the myriad things of nature.[17]

The complicated process of meditatively returning from the many to the one, which the Daoist contemplatively performs during ritual, is difficult to describe in a brief lesson. Years of instruction from a master are required to perfect the method. If the purpose of orthodox ritual can be stated in a single sentence, it is perhaps this: the Daoist, by his or her ritual, attempts to progress from the myriad creatures, back through the process of gestation, to an audience with the eternal, transcendent Dao.[18] In a series of ritual meditations, the Daoist adept empties out the myriad spirits, until he or she stands in the state of Hun Dun, or primordial emptiness. At that moment, the Transcendent Dao, Wu Wei Zhi Dao, comes of itself to dwell in the emptied center of man. This process is called xin zhai, or fasting (voiding) the heart. Orthodox ritual is thus defined by "Union with the Dao." Daoists who perform their liturgies for the purpose of union are given zheng orthodox titles of ordination. Daoists who perform their liturgies for the sake of making a living, curing a cold, or simple exorcism, use other, specialized titles. The distinction is strictly observed, and the rank given to a Daoist at the time of ordination is determined by his or her ability to perform the various meditations of union.[19]

The teachings of Master Zhuang are explicit in deciding the official title given a Daoist. The criteria for ranking a Daoist are found in the ordination manual of the Heavenly Master, a copy of which was purchased in 1868 by Lin Rumei and is at present in the possession of Master Zhuang. The criteria are:[20]

| Grade one | Registers of the Yellow Court Canon, the meditative manual of the Mao Shan Shang Qing sect |
| Grade two and three | Registers of the Qing Wei sect style of Thunder Magic and the Pole Star rituals (see chapter 6) |

Grade four and five   Registers of the Meng Wei
                             school of the Heavenly Master
                             (discussed in this chapter)
Grade six and seven   Registers of the Ling Bao tradition
                             called a San Wu Du Gong
                             (Three five Surveyor of Merits)[21]

Thus the interpretation of Daoist ritual emphasizing the meditative aspects of union with the Dao is considered "orthodox" because it derives from the classical orders of the north-south period and the first Daoist Canon. To the original list of orthodox rituals are added those of the Song dynasty Qing Wei sect; the reason for the inclusion of Qing Wei Thunder rites will be studied in the next chapter. Its association with Mao Shan and the meditative tradition will be seen to be a strong factor in ranking it as one of the highest forms of Daoist ritual meditation. Yü Dao ho yi, the meditation in which the Daoist "joins himself as one with the Dao," continues to be the decisive factor in ranking the expertise of a master.[22]

The disciples of Master Zhuang were, therefore, ranked according to their ability to perform interior meditation. There were three kinds of disciples who flocked to Zhuang's ritual performances and listened to his discourses in the front room of the busy Hsinchu residence. The first group, were retainers and the musicians, who came simply to earn a few extra Taiwanese dollars as drummers, flutists, violinists, and cymbal players. These men were minor Daoists in their own right and could on occasion fill in as acolyte or even read one of the lengthy canons of merit and repentance. But they were never ordained and were not given the secrets of ritual meditation. The second group of disciples were Daoists who belonged by family descent to the Zheng Yi Ci Tan, the fraternity of Daoist brethren of Hsinchu City and other parts of north Taiwan. Descendants of the famous Daoists who had flocked to Lin Rumei's center for studies in the late Qing period, these men were professional Blackhead (Wu Tou 乌头) including Daoists ordained to the lowest San Wu Du Gong, the grade six "Surveyor of Merits." They knew and followed the meditations outlined below by Master Zhuang.

The last and highest circle of Zhuang's disciples were his sons, A-Him and A-Ga, who were destined to become masters after the retirement of their father. To this elite circle I was sometimes admitted, not as a rival in the profession of public ritual but as a scholar interested in the sources of Zhuang's teachings. My questions, as related in chapter 3, provoked A-Him and A-Ga to deeper study, a result that made Zhuang quite happy. Many of the esoteric doctrines, which Zhuang had hidden even from his sons, were required to understand my copy of the printed Daoist Canon. This made my questions at the lessons appreciated by both A-Him and A-Ga. It was clear, however, that we were given only a fraction of the total knowledge of Master Zhuang. It was required of the older son, A-Him, to study some twenty years, from his eleventh to his thirtieth birthday, before even being considered for ordination. For this event, mastery of the meditations of union with the Dao were required.[23]

3. TEACHINGS CONCERNING THE MEDITATIONS OF UNION
The Ling Bao Five Talismans

The discourses of Zhuang on the Dao of the Right always began with a lengthy lesson on "basic doctrines," the so-called Ben Wen.[24] These evening sessions were very long, and the first reaction was to try to escape them. Since there was no way of avoiding the lecture if I was to obtain the esoteric oral teachings that always came at the very end, I soon learned to take copious notes of Zhuang's discourses. My efforts were rewarded when I realized, by comparing the notes with canonical texts, that Zhuang's long monologues paralleled passages in the early Daoist Canon. I soon learned that canonical passages could be substituted for Zhuang's lessons and brought the canon for him to read instead. According to the teachings of Master Zhuang, the progress from the many spirits of the cosmos to the meditation of union with the Dao went according to well-ordered stages. Thus one began with the ritual called "Inviting the spirits," when all of the benevolent rulers of the cosmos were summoned. From the initial ritual, the adept passed through a gradual refinement, reducing the number to nine, five, and three spirits, until finally only one spirit was present in the microcosm. On the evening set aside to speak of the five spirits who rule the five elements, Zhuang commented on the following canonical passages:

Primordial Heavenly Worthy spoke,
To the five elder emperors,
The crowd of great holy ones of the ten heavens,
All of the assembled lords of the transcendent ultimate (Wu Ji),
With their wives (male and female Daoist spirits),
who were gathered together,
In the realm of crimson brightness,
Sitting in a fragrant garden,
Under a fragrant mulberry tree.[25]

The primordial cosmos was described in Zhuang's meditation as being in darkness, that is, generation was not yet accomplished. In the period before Long Han or primordial gestation, the Ling Bao Five Talismans (the same given to Yü the Great to control the floods), were described as initiating the process of light, life, and generation:

> A bright five-colored light penetrated the abyss,
> In the five directions;
> Suddenly in the heavens there appeared writings,
> In the shape of characters, each ten feet square.
> They appeared quite naturally,
> Generated by the Dao,
> Above the mysterious void.
> In the very center of the five rays of light
> Were carved Wen writings.
> These sparkled and glittered in a dazzling manner,
> Their light penetrated outwards in the eight directions;
> A subtle, vital light, spreading out like the spokes of a wheel.
> The light was so bright that one could not look directly at it.
> The mind was befuddled by the light.[26]

In the canonical text, the Ling Bao Five Talismans are described as a wheel of five lights, the source of primordial breath, hub of the eight trigrams and the eight directions.[27] They resonate through nature with a harmonious melody. Here is Zhuang's re-wording of the text:

> The heavenly writings, jade characters,
> Flew off and disappeared into the primordial breath
> Of the mysterious void,
> Where they congealed and became Ling Wen,
> "Realized Writs bringing spirit and precious life" Ling Bao Zhen Wen.
> Joined to the eight trigrams, they became harmonious tones.
> Joined to the five talismans, they became zhang writs.
> From possessing them, the primordial state
> Called Long Han was formed.[28]
> The visible world was generated.
> The workings of water and fire,
> Life and death,
> The myriad kalpas, and
> The light of primordial yang, were gestated.

The two principles, yin and yang
Used them to carve out the three realms.
The holy sages united with them,
To attain to union with the Transcendent.
The five sacred peaks hold them,
And are thereby filled with spiritual power.
All things by possessing them have life breath (Qi).
The nation which possesses them is at peace.
The Ling Bao five writs
Are the middle way of generation,[29]
The root of heaven and the way of earth,
Deriving from the (Dao) of Wu Wei.
He who holds them will not die.
He who honors them will have eternal life.
He who holds them in feudal oath[30]
Will see the realized immortals descend.
They who practice and perfect them
Become immortal spirits;
Passing over the struggle of death, they
Enter into eternal life.

The five writs are also called "great Sanskrit secret mudras," a term used since the early sixth century alluding to the fact that the five talismans were drawn in "bird-like" esoteric symbols which resembled the foreign Sanskrit words coming from India.[31] The Ling Bao Five Talismans are thus seen as five lights issuing from the eternal transcendent Dao before the gestation of Primordial Heavenly Worthy; that is, they helped to form the Immanent Dao, or Hun Dun, the stage of primordial chaos which was the beginning of cosmic gestation.[32] The five writs order all of nature (li zi ran) and are the source of life breath (Qi).[33] They allow the Daoist adept to cross over from the state of a mortal man into immortality or xian. They assist the dead to cross over from the realm of stygian darkness into eternal life. In a passage from the sixth-century Canon, intoned by Master Zhuang from my borrowed manual, the Ling Bao Five Talismans are described in their present-day role in Daoist ritual:[34] Again, in Zhuang's words:

The Ling Bao true writs
Were generated before Primordial Heavenly Worthy,
In the center of the void abyss,
Before heaven and earth's roots.

Before sun and moon gave off their light,
In the dark and murky transcendent ancestor (Dao),
They produced Hun Dun, yin and yang.
Because of them the great yang, the sun was made;
Because of them the spirit chart (Ho Tu) was formed.[35]
The primordial originator alchemically refined them
In the abyss of the yang palace;
Formed them in the palace of flowing fire.
As they were formed, they sent off rays of red light.
Thus they were called Qi Wen, bright red writs;
Again they were called (Qi shu Ling Tu)
The red script spirit charts.[36]
Thus the myriad emperors were able to have audience with the Dao,
To fly up and stride in the void of emptiness,
To travel in the heavenly realms,
While burning incense and scattering flowers,
They chanted the sacred spirit writs.
It was at this time that the heavens sent down the
Twelve mysterious regulators (twelve stems),
And the earth responded with the twenty-four rules.[37]
The heavens hold the five writs as ancient treasures,
And thereby rule all that is above.
The earth guards them as a secret,
Thereby causing peace to reign.
The five ancient emperors hold them in their hands,
Thus causing stability and proper order in nature.
The three sources (sun, moon, and stars) are sustained by them,
Thus maintaining celestial light.
The highest holy ones worship them,
And are thereby realized.[38]
The five sacred peaks obey them,
Thereby attaining spiritual power.
The emperor (son of heaven) holds them,
And thereby rules the nation.
The nation that possesses them attains the Great Peace (Tai Ping).[39]

4. Preparations for Orthodox Ritual Meditation

It was evident from the lessons of Master Zhuang that he expected his
sons and disciples to be familiar with the doctrines of the Laozi and the

Zhuangzi, and to meditate upon and familiarize themselves with the process of gestation and the functioning of the cosmos described in these works. The process of instruction was carefully planned, and I was scolded for trying to accelerate matters to the heart of Zhuang's esoteric magic ritual. The order of instruction, Zhuang told me, would take more than ten years and could not be accelerated without doing harm both to the disciple and to the doctrines.[40] The following is the traditional order of transmitting the doctrines of orthodox Daoism:

1. Profession of the ten rules or vows of the Daoist novice.
2. Reception and mastery of the Laozi Dao De Ching.
3. Meditation and ritual of the Three Pure Ones (San Qing).[41]
4. Meditation and ritual of the Five Talismans (Ling Bao Wu-fu).
5. Reception and mastery of the Yellow Court Canon.[42]

Only after receiving the above manuals and listening to the instructions of Master Zhuang concerning the process of gestation from the Dao of transcendence, and only after understanding the workings of yin and yang, the production of the five elements, and the other myriad details of Yin-Yang Five Element cosmology, was mention made of the esoteric rubrics of religious Daoism.[43]

The process of receiving the rules or vows of the Daoist novice and putting them into practice was a matter of great concern for Zhuang and a source of scolding for myself as well as for his sons. I was continually reprimanded for haste, for competitiveness with my colleagues, and for attempting to introduce Zhuang to other foreign scholars. The vows of esoteric transmission were binding on the master and on the disciple, and the response of the Daoist towards all outside inquirers was inevitably one of ignorance.[44]

When passing on the vows or rules of religious Daoism, Zhuang sat facing the west, composed himself, and addressed us only after we had settled down to listen in quiet composure. The following are the first ten meditation rules given to the novice in Zhuang's words:[45]

1. Banish all hatred from the heart. Hatred, anger, and brooding cause the powers of yin to devour the inner man.
2. Be benevolent and merciful to all living things.
3. Do good to all and avoid acts which harm others.
4. Purity of heart and mind include banishing impure thoughts.[46]
5. Both in interior thoughts and exterior acts be loyal to friends.
   Never speak badly of others, especially of a fellow Daoist.

6. The breath of life must be regulated; nothing should be taken in excess. Wine may not be drunk during ritual.
7. Do not try to win over others, but always yield and take the last place.
8. Do not argue or dispute, but behave always as if in the presence of spirits.
9. Put self-interest last, and never be critical of others. Life-breath is injured by seeking praise, or resenting blame.
10. Use the whole heart and mind to achieve equanimity, union, and peace.

For each of the books or rituals revealed by the master, there is a set of rules, or Jie, which the disciple must follow in order to walk in the way of the Dao.[47] Thus, before receiving the Ling Bao Five Talismans the following set of rules is proposed for the disciple:[48]

1. Do not kill, but respect all living things.
2. Do not lust after another man's wife, or any woman.
3. Do not steal or take unjust recompense.
4. Do not use deceit, to win one's own way.
5. Do not get drunk, and at all times act with sobriety.[49]
6. Love all relatives, with respect and harmony. Treat all men and women as relatives.
7. See the good points in all, and help their hearts to be joyful.
8. If a person is sad, help him or her to be happy and blessed.
9. Treat all others as if their desires were one's own. Never seek vengeance.
10. Work that all may attain the Dao.

The Jie or rules of the Ling Bao talismans thus teach the young disciple the attitude necessary to have in order to perform ritual for the benefit of the men and women of the community. One of the greatest fears of the masters of esoteric ritual is that the terrifying magical powers given to the novice may be used to harm and not to help men. Thus the disciple is carefully watched and tested before the secrets of esoteric ritual are revealed.[50] The rules are summarized in the simple "three commandments" given before the meditation of union.[51]

1. Don't forget the roots to seek the branches.
2. Don't benefit the self to the harm of others.
3. Don't get involved in things and lose the Dao.

In his final words before entering the sacred ritual area, the master tells the disciple, "When one performs the pure Zhai ritual, there is no need to go to the mountains. For it is not in the mountains but within the empty center of man that the Dao is found." The purpose of the Zhai, therefore, is interior union with the eternal Dao.[52]

5. THE JIAO 醮 RITES OF UNION

As the final days before the performance of a Jiao festival of renewal approach, the Daoist master's household is filled with the bustle of preparation. Typically, the household of Master Zhuang is totally mobilized for the occasion. Both the men and women of the family are asked to write the many documents to be sent off to the heavens by burning. In long night sessions, Master Zhuang gives final briefings to his sons and his closest disciples. The Daoists who will assist with the esoteric rituals of renewal and union are chosen, the footsteps rehearsed, the melodies Song, and the stage rubrics practiced. The disciples are reminded of the seriousness of the event, of the need to look neither left nor right when performing the ceremonies, to remain at all times filled with the sacredness of ritual meditation.[53] In Zhuang's words:

Man's body (microcosm) is noble.
Therefore the Dao opened a path,
Bequeathing Jie rules, Jing canons, and Wen scripts,
Whereby the bodily state can be transcended,
By a higher state of union with the Dao.
By preserving life essences,
Through performing the rituals,
And promising to fulfill the moral commandments,
The intuitive belly is quiet and contemplates darkness (yin);
The heart-will (zhi) is fixed on undivided brightness (yang);
All thought is reduced to the one (Hun Dun).
The six fu administrative centers of the microcosm 54
by centering (in the Yellow Court) are without sensation,
Inside and outside are pure and empty,
Joined as one with all of nature.
Then one offers incense, and pronounces the vows,
Causing the heart to ascend to the heavens,
And all the heavenly spirits to come down to earth,
To hear the music of the sacred liturgy, and
To answer the prayers of all men,

According to how they have kept the moral precepts,
And followed the way of the eternal Dao.

The occasions for performing a Jiao festival are many. The village and city temples of Taiwan each perform a Jiao of renewal once every certain number of years on the occasion of temple remodeling. Some villages perform the Jiao of renewal once every sixty years at the beginning of a Jia Zi 甲子 cycle.[55] Other villages perform a Jiao every twelve, five, or three years to free the souls from hell or to exorcise the evil spirits that cause sickness and misfortune.[56] On special occasions, such as the ordination of a new Daoist priest or the commemoration of a Daoist divinity, the Daoist masters perform a private Jiao of devotion. Such a Jiao is performed annually by the Zheng Yi Ci Tan of Hsinchu City on the birthday of the mother goddess of the Pole Star.[57] In bygone days on the mainland of China, the great Daoist monasteries celebrated continuous Jiao which lasted as long as 72, 81, or 108 days. On all such occasions, the format of the Jiao is basically the same. A minimum of 3 or 5 days are required to perform the rites of meditative union.[58]

The Jiao liturgies are clearly divided into three distinct kinds: (1) the exterior rites of offering, performed in the open forum for whole community to see; (2) the lengthy canons of merit and repentance, recited inside the temple to effect release of the souls in hell; and (3) the Ke Yi rites of meditative union. The Ke Yi rituals, as I have said, are easily identified by their format. Classical Ke Yi ritual always begins with the Fa Lu meditation for exteriorizing the spirits from the microcosm and ends with the Fa Lu which restores the spirits to their original places. A complete list of all the rituals offered at a Jiao festival will indicate to the reader the complexity of the modern (Song dynasty) liturgy of renewal and union, and at the same time illustrate the place of the Ke Yi rituals in the overall Jiao.[59] In the following list, the Ke Yi rituals of union are in italics and bold. The public rituals are indicated with an asterisk. The rites oriented to the freeing of the souls from hell are left unmarked.[60]

The Jiao Festival

FIRST DAY   CHINESE TERM

1. Lighting the temple lamps*   Bai Shen Deng
2. Sending off the memorial*   Fa Zou, Fa Biao
3. "Opening the Eyes"*   Kai Guang
4. Inviting the spirits*   Qing Shen, Chu Sheng
5. Purifying the sacred area *   Jin Tan

6. Jade Pivot Canon   Yü Shu Jing
7. Noon offering*   Wu Xian, Wu Hong
8. Litanies of repentance (10 vols.)   Chao Tien Bao Chan
9. Lighting lamps to the Three Pure Ones.   Fen Deng,[61] Jüan Lian,
                                                                             Ming Zhong
10. Ritual of the Ling Bao Five Talismans.   Su Qi

SECOND DAY

11. Reinvite the spirits   Chong Bai[62]
12. Morning Audience   Zao Chao
13. Three Officials Canon   San Guan Jing
14. Three Officials Litany of Repentance (3 vols.) San Guan Bao Chan
15. Noon Audience   Wu Chao
16. East Pole Star Canon   Dong Dou Jing
17. South Pole Star Canon   Nan Dou Jing
18. West Pole Star Canon   Xi Dou Jing
19. North Pole Star Canon   Bei Dou Jing
20. Central Pole Star Canon   Zhong Dou Jing
21. Pole Star Litanies of Repentance (5 vols.)   Wu Dou Bao Chan[63]
22. Jade Emperor Canon (3 vols.)   Yü Huang Ben Xing Jing[64]
23. Jade Emperor Litany of Repentance   Yü Huang Bao Chan
24. Night Audience   Wan Chao
25. Floating the Lanterns*   Fang Shui Deng

THIRD DAY

26. Reinvite the spirits*   Chong Bai
27. Sending off the Grand Memorial*   Deng Tai Jin Biao
28. Nine Hells Litany of
Repentance (10 vols.)   Jiu Yü Bao Chan
29. Audience of Union   Dao Chang, Zheng Jiao[65]
30. Feeding the hungry spirits
(2 vols.)   Pu Du

31. Thanking and seeing
off the spirits   Xie Shen, Song Shen

    The above thirty-one ceremonies are augmented by a number of dramatic
rituals of local origin, which do not belong to the orthodox or canonical
tradition and often are part of an oral tradition. That is, they are usually
memorized and not found in written form. The "noon offering" occurs each

day of the Jiao festival, and other popular dramatic rites, such as the climbing of the thirty-six sword ladder,[66] the summoning of the Jade Emperor,
expelling the Demon Kings[67] and the like, are performed at the will of the
Daoist Master or by demand of the local populace.[68] Thus there are variations found between north and south Taiwan and even between village and
nearby village in north Taiwan. The basic structure of the Jiao is not affected
by these colorful local variations. Furthermore, the order of performing the
rituals themselves is often changed by local Daoists and by certain orthodox
sects of Song dynasty origin.[69] The rituals used in the Jiao festival are therefore determined by the training of the Daoist master and the sect to which
he owes allegiance.

Thus many local Daoists of north Taiwan and of overseas Chinese communities, such as in modern Honolulu, perform a simplified version of the
Jiao in which the aspects of renewal and blessings are emphasized and the
rites of union are not performed. In a simple one or two day Jiao, the Daoists
commonly perform the following rituals:[70]

1. Fa Zou, sending off the memorial.
2. Chu sheng, inviting the spirits to be present.
3. Reading the various canons of merit, such as the Pole Star Canon,
   Three Officials Canon, etc.
4. Reading the litanies of repentance, the various Pao Chan manuals.
5. Feeding the hungry souls, in the Pu Du or Pu Shi.
6. Concluding rites for seeing off the spirits.

The blessings from such a liturgy derive from the canonical readings and
from the grand Pu Du banquet for freeing the souls from hell,[71] rather than
from the classical Ke Yi meditations of union.

The distinction between the classical orders, who call themselves "orthodox" and the popular local orders is, therefore, clearly seen in the manner in
which the Daoists perform the Jiao. Only the orthodox Daoist masters of a
Grade Six (Three-five Surveyor of Merits) or higher ordination use the classical Ke Yi rituals of union in performing a three- or five-day Jiao.[72] These
rituals, as underlined in the above list, are:

1. The Su Qi:	Meditation implanting the Ling Bao Five Talismans and Five Writs.
2. The Zhao Chao:	Meditation on the first of the Three Pure Ones, Primordial Heavenly Worthy, symbol of intellect and primordial breath.

3. The Wu Chao	Meditation on the second of the Three Pure Ones, Ling Bao Heavenly Worthy, the symbol of spirit and heart-will.
4. The Wan Chao:	Meditation on the third of the Three Pure Ones, Dao De Heavenly Worthy, symbol of intuitive essence and awareness of Dao presence.
5. The Dao Chang:	More commonly called Zheng Jiao, the meditation of union with the transcendent Dao.

The meditations are taught by Master Zhuang as a sort of ritual alchemy, progressing from the first rite of the five talismans to the final meditation of union. An ordered series of meditations leads from the many, that is, the myriad creatures of the macrocosm, through a series of refining stages, to the eternal Dao of simplicity. Thus in a first meditation, the myriad spirits are reduced to the five prime movers (the five elements). The five are reduced to the Three Pure Ones, or the three principles of life. Finally, the three are reduced to the state of simplicity, or Hun Dun. In this last state, the Daoist master attains union with the Dao. The term "xin zhai," therefore, as applied to religious Daoism and its interpretation of the Zhuangzi, refers to the above series of ritual meditations. The Dao comes to dwell in the "center," which is emptied of the myriad spirits.

My own problem, after hearing the explanation of Master Zhuang concerning the esoteric meditations of union, was a crucial one. If only a few of the higher Daoist masters knew the meditations called xin zhai, how efficacious were the many rituals and festivals celebrated by the deprived local Daoists who did not know the elite meditations? That is, if the meditations were essential to Jiao ritual, most of the Jiao celebrated throughout Taiwan by the lower Redhead Daoists of the various Shen Xiao, Lü Shan, or Ling Bao orders were ineffective. Furthermore, not only were the shorter one- and two-day Jiao totally lacking in the esoteric Ke Yi rite of union, even the orthodox masters of a lowly Grade Six rank might perform the externals of a Su Qi or a Dao Chang without knowing the higher stages of meditative union.

The answer, Master Zhuang assured me, lay in the proper understanding of Daoist ritual. The efficacy of the rite was in the exact execution of the rubrical directions, the summoning of the spirits, the sending off of the heavenly document, and the various mudras and mantras accompanying the Daoist's petitions. Even within the ranks of orthodox Daoism there were grades of esoteric teachings and spiritual perfection. The efficacy of the ritual depended on correct rubrical perfection, (this is called ex opere operato in Latin), but was vastly enhanced and elevated by the spiritual life of the master, ex opere operantis.[73] Thus in the two levels of esoteric teachings, the rituals could first be seen as a summoning of spirits, each in its proper attire and with the classical color or vapor accompanying the vision. Each of the esoteric rites had a secret liaison official, the envisioning of which made the rite efficacious. For each ritual a document was prepared and the proper liaison official summoned to carry it to the throne of the heavenly worthies. The appearance of the liaison officials, the mudras and mantras necessary to command them, and the proper spirit to whom the document is addressed, were among the most important secrets required to make the rituals effective. The following are the spirits addressed for the various rituals, with their messengers:[74]

1. Su-Qi:	Primordial breath prior heavens Tai Yi heavenly worthy, with the lightning bureau Heavenly Lord Chang and the messengers of the Shu Wen, and the piao documents.
2. Zhao Chao:	Heavenly Marshal Xie, with the green zi document official Tong zi.
3. Wu Chao:	Official of earth, Tai Sui deity with the Heavenly Marshal Yin, the mortal bearer of the Shu Wen document.
4. Wan Chao:	Official from beneath the earth, the military spirit Marshal Wen, with the immortal bearers of the shu-wen and piao documents.
5. Dao Chang:	The heavenly lord of eternal life; with the official bearers of the shu-wen document.

Each of the Ke Yi meditations thus has a special liaison official and a specific heavenly deity to whom the rite is addressed. By addressing the documents to the proper deity, in the specified formula, and with the liaison messenger appointed for the day, the ritual is effectively performed. The Jiao can be interpreted on a lower, less esoteric plane as a sending off of documents to the various deities who control the forces of nature. By the ritual of the Daoist, the spirits of the cosmos are prevailed upon to grant heavenly blessing, give abundance on earth, and free the souls from hell. But on a higher, meditative plane, the Jiao is interpreted as a ritual for bringing about union with the Dao. That is to say, the Daoist first unites himself to the Dao of transcendence, and then carries the petitions of the men and women of the community before the Dao of Wu Wei. Thus in the final definition, the highest form of esoteric Daoism is seen to be based upon the premise that the master first unites himself with the Dao and then uses his supernatural powers to save others. From his position of esoteric union, he memorializes the spirits of the three realms (heaven, earth, and underworld) to give man blessing. All his marvelous powers come to him by reason of union with the Dao.

The higher esoteric plan of the Ke Yi rituals are therefore seen to lead to a state of mystic union. The Su Qi ritual begins the alchemical process of refining the spirits of the microcosm by establishing a feudal union with the five primordial rulers of the five elements. The ritual itself enacts the ancient ceremony for enfeoffing a vassal by a feudal lord. The Daoist, who plays the role of Hun Dun or Taiji, takes five talismanic contracts, the Ling Bao Five Talismans, described in the opening pages of this chapter. These true writs, the same used by Yü the Great to control the floods, the same brought by a dragon-horse to Yao and Shun to confirm their rule over the cosmos and later buried in the spirit-cave atop Mao Shan, are now used by the Daoist to renew the life-giving power of the five elements in the cosmos. The talismans of the east, south, center, west and north one by one are used to establish a feudal contract. The talismans are ritually burned and their vapors visualized in the Daoist's meditation. The Ling half of the talisman ascends to the heavens and the Pao is buried inside the microcosm. The table below shows the order of burning.[75]

DIRECTION	COLOR	ELEMENT ORGAN	SPIRIT TABOO NAME	NUMBER
East	Green emperor	Wood-liver	Ling wei yang (Fu Xi)	9 (3)
South	Red emperor	Fire-heart	Qih piao (Shen Nong)	3 (2)
Center	Yellow emperor	Earth-spleen	Han shu niu (Huang Di)	1 (5)
West	White emperor	Metal-Lungs	Bai zhao Jü (Shao Hao)	7 (4)
North	Black emporor	Water-kidneys	Xie Guang Ji (Zhuan Xü)	5 (1)

The Ling Bao Five Talismans are identified in the heavens by the first row of numbers, representing stars surrounding the North Star. When implanted in the earth or in the microcosm, they are represented by the second set of numbers. Though the Ling Bao Wu-fu Xü in volume 183 of the Daoist Canon identifies the Five Talismans with the mythical Ho Tu from the ancient apocryphal texts, an association also made in the sixth-century Wu Shang Bi Yao,[76] and although the first set of numbers (9,3,1,7,5) is still associated with the Ling Bao Five Talismans in modern ritual, once the talismans have been "implanted" (An Zhen Wen), the second set of numbers represents their earthly activity.[77] There is perhaps no more esoteric ritual in the history of religious Daoism than the Su Qi liturgy of the Five Talismans. Many Redhead Shen Xiao Daoists of north Taiwan readily admit that they do not know how to perform the ritual and leave it out of the Jiao festivals of renewal.

Once the Ling Bao Five Talismans have been implanted in the microcosm, the process of refinement is continued in the Three Audiences, the rituals called Zhao Chao or Morning Audience (12 in the above list), Wu Chao or Noon Audience (15), and Wan Chao or Night Audience (24). Thus, in answer to my question, Zhuang proposed two interpretations. In the meditations of the Three Audiences, the rituals are understood, by the people and the lower grades of Daoists, to be ceremonies for sending off documents to the spirit rulers of the heavens. But in the esoteric sense, the Three Audiences are interpreted as an alchemical meditation in which the five elements are refined into the Three Principles of life.[78]

In the earthly manifestation of the Ling Bao Five Talismans, wood of east is given the mystical number three and fire of the south is the number two. In the Zhao Chao morning meditation, the Daoist sees the blue-green vapor of east and the bright red vapor of the south, that is, the essences of the elements wood and fire, combine in the empty center of the microcosm. The three of wood and the two of fire are fused in the alchemical furnace inside the Daoist's body. In the Three Mountain tradition, which Master Zhuang teaches, the body's empty center is the Yellow Court, Huang Ting. The elements of wood and fire are fused here, and become Yüan Qi, primordial breath, a purple vapor personified as Primordial Heavenly Worthy, within the lower cinnabar field (Xia Dan Tian, belly). Wood's three and fire's two —considered the first five—symbolizing life breath in man, are refined here.

Next, the refinement of the element earth, to which the mystical number-five is also assigned, takes place during the Wu Chao, the noon audience meditation. In the second state of meditative alchemy, the earth of center is refined into a yellow vapor, which congeals and becomes Ling Bao

Heavenly Worthy, the personification of Shen spirit in the center cinnabar field, the heart of man. Thus the second five is now refined within the Yellow Court. Last, the element metal and the element water are refined in the alchemical furnace of the Yellow Court. In the Wan Chao, the meditation of the evening audience, metal is given the symbolic number four and water the number one. The white vapors of metal and the black vapors of water congeal into a pure white aura symbolized by Dao De Heavenly Worthy, or intuitive essence, refined in the lower "cinnabar field," the body's center of gravity. The four of metal and the one of water are refined into the third five the principle of intuitive essence in the human belly. The meaning of the grade six Daoist's title, the "Three-Five Surveyor of Merit" is now made clear. The "three fives" are the three spirits, which symbolize the three life principles, primordial breath (intellect-judgment), spirit (heart-will), and the belly's intuition.

In the final stage of the Ke Yi rites of meditative union, the three principles of life are refined into the state of Hun Tun, thus emptying the Yellow Court in preparation for union with the transcendent Dao. The final meditation is called Dao Chang, the place where the Dao is present, or Zheng Jiao, the orthodox sacrifice.[79] The ritual of the "Three Audiences" consists in offering a Jiao sacrifice of wine and incense to the Three Pure Ones, Primordial Heavenly Worthy, Ling Bao Heavenly Worthy, and Dao De Heavenly Worthy, who are, one by one, made present in the center of the Yellow Court. While externally presenting an offering of incense and wine to the Three Pure Ones, the three are internally refined and "voided," that is, reduced to the state of Hun Dun or primordial simplicity. Recalling the words of the Zhuangzi, "Only the Dao dwells in the void," the final stages of the Ke Yi rites end in a state of transcendent union.

In his teachings regarding the performance of a five-day Jiao ritual of renewal and of the Zhai rites of burial, published in Chinese by the Cheng Wen press in Taipei, Zhuang presents the meditations of union, and also the external rubrics, the mudras, mantras, melodies, and sacred dances necessary for performing Daoist ritual.[80] One short excerpt from Ke Yi ritual will be chosen from the printed selections of Master Zhuang's teachings as a sample of the intricacy of detail and the perfection of style required to perform the various meditative rituals of union.

6. THE FA LU RITE FOR EXTERIORIZING THE SPIRITS

As outlined in the pages above, the Ke Yi rituals of union all begin and end in the same manner. After an introduction in which the priest lights incense, sings the "hymn of ascent," and addresses the spirits to whom the ritual is directed, the meditation for emptying the spirits out of the body is performed. The rite is called Fa Lu, literally, lighting the incense burner, a reference to the hand-held Lu (incense burner, alchemical stove) used as the focal point of the meditation.[81] But the words Fa Lu are a homonym for "exteriorizing the register," that is, sending forth all of the spirits registered as dwelling within the microcosm. The Lu, or register, is the list of spirits over which the Daoist has control. The Lu is given to him at the time of ordination, the rank and title of the Daoist determining the number of spirits in the Lu register. Thus the grade four Meng Wei Daoist such as Master Zhuang knows the twenty-four Lu of the Zheng-i sect, where as the Grade Six San Wu Du Gong Daoist knows only fourteen registers of the Ling Bao tradition.[82]

During the Fa Lu ritual the Daoist empties out all the spirits that dwell within the microcosm, according to the list (Lu) he has received at his ordination. After having exteriorized the spirits, the main body of the meditation of union takes place. That is to say, the Su Qi in which the Daoist strikes a feudal treaty with the five primordial movers, the Three Audiences in which the Three Pure Ones are refined, and the Dao Chang in which union with the Dao is obtained, are performed only after the spirits have been exteriorized. After the meditation of union is finished, the master performs the Fu Lu rite, which restores the register of spirits to their original place within the microcosm.[83]

As in all esoteric rituals, there are two levels on which the rite is explained. On the first level, the Fa Lu is a meditation in which the Daoist builds a mandala or a pure area around himself in order to perform the Jiao sacrifice and to send off the documents of petition. On the deeper esoteric level, it is interpreted as a ritual performance of the xin zhai, the emptying the heart and the mind of all spirits, self-projections, and images that impede the contemplation of union with the Dao. This is the first of three esoteric secrets told to the novice.[84]

In the second teaching, the disciples must be instructed by the master about the correspondence between the various organs of the body, and the spirits summoned forth during the ritual. As the year is divided into twelve months, so twelve organs of the body are selected as the special foci of ritual summoning, that is, as living quarters within the microcosm out of which the spirits are brought forth to bless and aid man. The twelve organs correspond to the twelve directions of the compass, and these in turn are imprinted as mudra on the joints of the left hand. Thus in order to summon a spirit, the Daoist must learn to press the proper joint on the inside of the left hand with the thumb, at the same time summoning the spirit from the internal organ. The tradition is oral (Kou Jue) rather than written, and is explained in the following table.

MONTH (stem)	SIGN	ZODIAC	ORGAN	DIRECTION
1. Zi	Rat	Aries	Gall	North
2. Qiu	Ox	Taurus	Liver	NNE by ¾ East
3.Yen	Tiger	Gemini	Lungs	ENE by ¾ North
4. Mao	Hare	Cancer	Big intestine	East
5.Chen	Dragon	Leo	Stomach	ESE by ¾ South
6.Si(Sz)	Snake	Virgo	Spleen	SSE by ¾ East
7. Wu	Horse	Libra	Heart	South
8. Wei	Sheep	Scorpio	Small intestine	SSW by ¾ West
9. Shen	Monkey	Sagitarrius	Bladder	WSW by ¾ South
10. Yu	Cock	Capriorn	Kidney	West
11. Xü	Dog	Aquarius	Bao Ke[85]	WNW by ¾ North
12.Hai	Boar	Pisces	San-Jiao	NNW by ¾ West

Chart: The twelve earthly stems, & the twelve directions, coordinated with the twelve bodily organs.

The spirits summoned during the Fa Lu ritual, which will be named below, are hidden within the Daoist's body. The Daoist master teaches the disciple how to press a joint on his left hand to summon forth a spirit. Figure 18 shows the joints on the left hand, which correspond to the organs in the microcosm and the twelve stems in the macrocosm.

The various mudras on the left hand begin at the base of the ring finger with the stem tzu and travel clockwise through Qiu, Yan, Mao, to the twelfth stem, Hai. Each corresponds to a direction of the compass and to an organ within the microcosm of the body. In the second stage of oral instructions, the master must explain which of the heavenly spirits are lodged in the various organs of the body, what their appearance is, when they are to be summoned, and so forth. By pressing a joint with the left thumb, a spirit is summoned. Thus the five emperors are enfeoffed into the five central organs of the body by the systematic preparatory meditation of the young Daoist, during the many years of his training. The Ruler of the East, with all his retainers, dwells in the liver. His is the breath of spring, the green-blue vapors that enliven nature and cause the grass and the green woods to be reborn, flowers to blossom, and life-giving rain to fall. He is summoned by pressing the Mao joint with the thumb. The Ruler of the South with his followers lives in the heart of man. He controls the bright fires of summer that redden the wheat and rice, brighten the noonday sun, and cause man to grow to

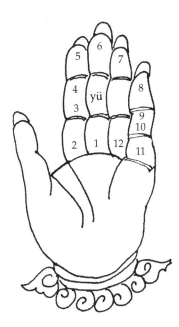

Figure 18. The left hand, showing the joints to be pressed in order to summon a
     spirit. By referring to the table above, the correspondence between the joint
     and the organ in the body, can be determined.

maturity. He is summoned by pressing the Wu joint with the thumb. The
Ruler of the West dwells in the lungs of man, a cool white breath, the spirit
of autumn. Like a sharp blade of steel he cuts the autumn harvest and, after
emptying the fields, leads the person on a spiritual path to "ku" and "xü"
emptiness. He is summoned by pressing the Yu position. The Ruler of the
North is in the kidneys, from whence he rules over water and acts as spirit
of the freezing winter. He brings rest, the stirring of rebirth in the depths of
earth's womb, the darkness of the horizon which presages dawn and new
life. He is summoned by pressing the joint marked Zi. The Ruler of the Center is in the spleen, enveloped in a rich yellow vapor, the color of the loess
soil. He is the source from which wood grows and in which metal hides,
a power which overcomes winter's damp cold and grows forth from the
ashes of fire. He is summoned by pressing the central position marked Yü.

The third secret which must be taught before the disciple is allowed to
perform the Fa Lu rite concerns the method of summoning the special liaison of the day, who acts as the messenger between the Daoist and the courts
of the heavenly bureaucracy. For each day in a cycle of sixty days, there is
a special Gong Cao messenger, whose secret name, mantric summons, and
appearance must be memorized. The teachings of Master Zhuang in this

regard are too lengthy to be repeated here.[86] The disciple is usually made
to memorize the secret name, appearance, and cyclical day on which each
Gong Cao messenger is summoned to facilitate execution of the meditation.

With the above three Kou Jue, or oral secrets, revealed by the master, the
disciple is ready to begin the Fa Lu rite for exteriorizing the spirits. The oral
secrets are not taught to the musicians or the lower members of the Daoist
entourage but are reserved for those few disciples, usually the Daoist's own
children, (men or women) destined to become Daoist masters. When done
in private to initiate a meditation of inner alchemy or to cure a sick person,
the Fa Lu is performed without musical accompaniment of any kind. But
when used during the Jiao festivals of renewal or the Zhai rites of burial, it
is always accompanied by percussion and wind instruments, the great Daoist drum being the essential signal of the inward meditations of the master.
Because the circulation of breath, swallowing of saliva, and calling forth of
the various spirits is signaled by the beat of the ritual drum, the master must
teach the external formulae of the rite to the drummer, and to the chief and
assistant cantors, the incense bearer and procession leader, who accompany
him into the ritual area and chant the rite while he is performing the meditation. The disciples perform the external rubrics of orthodox ritual, while the
master himself practices the meditations of inner alchemy.

The rubrics of the Fa Lu meditation are clearly stated in the Song dynasty *Wu Shang Huang Lu Da Zhai Li Cheng Yi*, chapters 16 and 32.[87] The
Daoist and his entourage enter the sacred Tan area, the disciples through
the Gate of Earth (the southwest entrance) and the master through the Gate
of Heaven (the northwest entrance). A Bu Xü meditative hymn, the lighting of incense, encircling the altar, and the reading of the entrance incantation (one for a ritual offered during the day, another for a ritual offered at
night) precedes the actual Fa Lu meditation. The esoteric "Incantation to
the Auspicious Spirits," which acts as a prelude to the meditation, is clearly
described in chapter 32 of the above-mentioned canonical text, in which the
Daoist first envisions the five elements as primordial movers interpenetrat-
ing the macro- and microcosms. While forming the mudras on the left hand,
the master closes his eyes and sees the five internal organs, the five peaks
of the external world, and the five stars in the heavens, with his own body
as center of the cosmos. The five emperors are seen to be inside the five organs, with an army of soldiers and retainers, horses and chariots, dressed in
the colors proper to their elements and directions. Thus the Emperor of the
East has an army dressed in green-blue, the Emperor of the South leads an
army dressed in red, the west in white, the north in black, and the center in
yellow. The incantation begins with the loud command of the Chief Cantor

who sings: "Let each of the ritual masters meditate upon the law!"

With these words the master begins to see the interior of the microcosm come alive with the vapors and spirits he is about to summon forth. He sees the Primordial Heavenly Worthy dwelling in the upper cinnabar field in the head; that is, one of the nine sacred palaces in the head (heavens) for indwelling spirits. The Primordial Heavenly Worthy is enveloped in a blue-green mist and commands the highest of the Daoist heavens, with a myriad of heavenly worthies and retainers in attendance. The Ling Bao Heavenly Worthy dwells in the central cinnabar field in the chest, that is, the heart. He is enveloped in a yellow vapor, and is surrounded by a myriad realized spirits in the second highest Daoist heaven. The Dao De Heavenly Worthy is envisioned in the lower cinnabar field, in the belly. He is enveloped in a white vapor and surrounded with a myriad realized spirits in the third of the Daoist heavens. While the Daoist master envisions the Three Heavenly Worthies, the Five Emperors, and so forth, the chief cantor and the other members of the entourage are singing a description of what the master envisions. When the hymn has ended, the chief cantor intones: "Sound the Daoist drum twenty-four times!"

With these words the drummer begins to strike the great Daoist drum used during the master's celebration of liturgy. The drummer first strikes the drum with eight slow blows, at the end of which the metal gong (a brass bowl) is struck once. The master grinds his teeth on the left side of his jaw once, swallows saliva, and envisions the spirits of the eight directions in the heavens. The drummer then strikes the drum again eight blows and the metal gong is rung a second time. The master grinds his four upper and four lower front teeth and swallows saliva, while envisioning the spirits of the central regions in each of the eight directions. Finally the drummer strikes the drum a third series of blows, while the Daoist grinds his teeth on the right side of the jaw and swallows saliva, envisioning the spirits of the lower regions stretching out in eight directions. Thus the three times eight or twenty-four cosmological divisions of the world, with all their realized spirits, are alerted to the master's summons. While the drum is being sounded, the master recites inwardly a secret conjuration or spell, which has several variant readings in the canonical texts but follows the same general pattern as that used by the orthodox masters of Taiwan:

> The Nine Mansions of the Highest Heavens,
> Are guarded by the Great One,
> With hundred spirits like a forest of sentinels!
> The Hun and Po souls (in man) are united;[88]
> Blue-green its going forth, dark and mysterious its return.

Like the bright rays of the sun,
Eternal life, which does not grow senescent,
Suppress and destroy the heterodox and evil,
Quickly, quickly, like the highest heaven's life breath,
An imperial order!

The master thereupon kneels in the center of the sacred T'an area with the cantors and acolytes on his left and right. As the assembly of disciples sings the words of the Fa Lu, the master begins his meditation. The following are the words of the text and a translation:

1. Wu shang san tian	Transcendent, highest Three Heavens
2. Xüan, yün, shi, san Qi	Mysterious, primordial, original, three breaths!
3. Tai Shang Lao JunTai	Shang Lord Lao!
4. Dang zhao chu chen shen zhong	Now call forth from within my body
5. San Wu Gong Cao	The three-five Gong Cao officers,
6. Zuo Yu guan shi je	The left and right official messengers,
7. Zuo Yu feng xiang	The left and right incense bearers,
8. Yi Long Qi li	Dragon-riding dispatch officers,
9. Shi xiang jin tong	Incense-bearing golden lads,
10. Juan yen san hua Yü Nü	The jade girls who carry messages and scatter flowers,
11. Wu Di zhi fu	The Five Emperors carrying the talismans,
12. Zhi R xiang guan shi zhe	The special incense messenger of the day,
13. Ge san-shi-liu ren qu	In all, thirty-six spirits come forth!

Their coming forth is stately and elegant
Quickly they carry up the official documents
May the orthodox gods of the soil
Assemble here today to guard the altar
[variant line],
To carry out the ritual of the Dao.

While the words are being chanted, the master envisions the heavenly worthies and the spirits within his body. One by one he summons them forth to take up their positions around the sacred area, visualizing them appear as follows.[89]

1. Wu-shang san t'ien: 無上三天

The master sees the abode of the Three Pure Ones in the head, the chest, and the belly respectively. He sees the white vapor from the lower abdomen (also called the lower cinnabar field) rise up toward the occiput in his

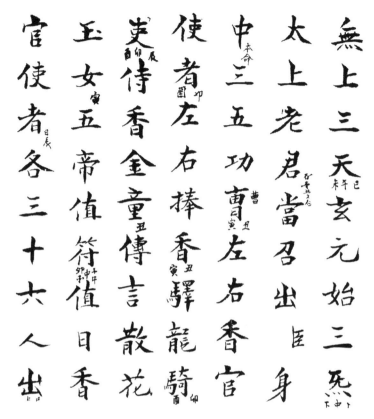

Figure 19. The Fa Lu rite for exteriorizing the spirits.

head. Next he sees the yellow vapor from the center part of his body (the central cinnabar field, abode of the Ling Bao Heavenly Worthy) also rise upward toward the occiput. Finally he envisions the blue-green breath of the Primordial Heavenly Worthy in the Ni Wan palace in the head. The three breaths come upward into the head and rest under the scalp, waiting to be summoned forth through the occiput. The Daoist presses the joints on the left hand market Wei, Wu, and Si in order to summon the Three Pure Ones.

2. Xüan, yüan, shi, san Qi 玄元始三炁

As these words are recited the Daoist presses the joint marked Qiu on his left hand and sees the Primordial Heavenly Worthy come forth from the occiput in the center of his head. The Primordial Heavenly Worthy goes to the north wall of the sacred area, where he occupies the very center throughout the ceremony. Next he presses the joint marked Yü, in the center of the middle finger, and sees the Ling Bao Heavenly Worthy come forth. The Ling

Bao Heavenly Worthy also goes to the north wall and takes up the position to the left or east of the centrally located Primordial Heavenly Worthy. Finally, he presses the joint on the left hand marked Wu and sees the Dao De Heavenly Worthy come forth. The third of the Pure Ones takes the position to the west or right of the Primordial Heavenly Worthy on the north wall.

As the Three Pure Ones come forth to take up their positions of preeminence in the ritual area, the place occupied by the emperor in court audiences, the Daoist master also envisions a splendid court of mythical animal retainers that always accompany the Three Pure Ones. In the east is the great blue dragon that represents the powers of spring. In the south is the red phoenix of summer. In the west is the white tiger of autumn. In the north is the black tortoise in its armor, the symbol of winter. The Daoist himself occupies the center, playing the role of the alchemical furnace, the central void in which the Dao of eternity is to be present. In each of the interstices—that is, on either side of the northeast, southeast, southwest, and northwest—are two lions and two herons, respectively, a total of sixteen guardian spirits. Finally over his left eye the Daoist envisions the sun with nine rays and the moon with ten rays coming forth.

3. Tai Shang Lao Jun 太上老君

The third of the Three Pure Ones is especially invoked in the third phrase of the Fa Lu meditation. The Daoist presses the joint marked Qiu on the left hand and asks the intercession of Lord Lao, or Laozi, in summoning forth the spirits before effecting the rite of union. In some rituals, the invocation to Lao Jun is changed to Dao Jun, a technical term for the second of the Three Pure Ones, Ling Bao Tian Zun. The latter invocation is found in a special version of the Fa Lu used to precede the ritual chanting of the Tu Ren Jing, the canon for helping mankind pass through the stages of hell into eternal life.[90] In the latter case, the master presses the joint on the left hand marked Yü when summoning the Ling Bao Heavenly Worthy.

4. Dang zhao chu chen shen zhong 当召出臣身中

The Daoist presses the joint on his left hand which corresponds to his Ben Ming star, that is to say, his zodiacal sign and patron spirit. At the time of his ordination, a special star, a patron spirit, and a temporal see, or place of spiritual jurisdiction (zhi), is assigned to each Daoist master, according to the year of his birth.[91] The patron spirit acts as a special liaison official for the Daoist's documents and prayers addressed to the three stages of the cosmos-heaven, earth, and watery underworld. At this point in the Fa Lu, the Daoist calls upon his private Ben Ming spirit to assist in the rite of exteriorization.

5. San Wu Gong Cao 三五攻曹

The three-five Gong Cao refers to the liaison officials of the three stages of the cosmos (heaven, earth, and water), and the five directions (five elements, five rulers). Since the numbers three and five are consistently used for three principles of life, or the Three Pure Ones, and the five movers or the five emperors, the Daoist master now establishes control over the secret messenger spirits, the Gong Cao who relay messages between the three stages of the world and the supreme heavenly worthies. In the esoteric doctrines of Master Zhuang, there are five secret Gong Cao spirits assigned to the Three Pure Ones and five assigned to the Five Emperors. The first five are summoned forth by pressing the joint marked Qiu on the left hand. The last five are summoned by pressing the joint marked Yen.

6. Zuo Yu xiang guan shi je 左右香管使者

The left and right official messengers are the spirit officials who control yin and yang. In this orthodox version of ritual meditation they are named the six Jia (left chest, yang) and the six Ding (right chest, yin) messengers. They are, however, a far cry from the violent Six Jia spirits of Chapter 4, as used in the Dao of the Left. Within the microcosm of the orthodox master, they are pure spirits who protect the emptied center or the Yellow Court from any outside distraction during the meditation of union. The Jia spirits are summoned by pressing the joint marked Mao, while the Ding spirits are called forth by pressing the joint Yu.

7. Zuo Yu feng xiang 左右捧香

The left and right incense-bearing spirits are lodged in the liver and the lungs (east and west) respectively. The left spirits are summoned by pressing the joint marked Qiu, and the right spirits by the joint marked yen. This and the following invocation are not found in the Song dynasty version of the Fa Lu, but are in the sixth-century Wu-shang Bi Yao and the various editions of Master Zhuang.

8. Yi Long Qi li 驛龍騎吏

The dragon dispatch officials are lodged in the big intestine (left, yang) and the kidneys (right, yin). They are summoned forth by pressing the joints on the left hand marked Mao and Yu (and the other joints indicted in the illustration).

9. Shih xiang Jin Tong 侍香金童

The golden lads, who act as the immediate fore runners of the Five Emperors, are housed in the liver (yang, east). They too are summoned forth by pressing the joint marked Qiu.

10. Zhuan Yen san hua Yü Nü 傳言散花玉女

Immediately after the golden lads come the jade lassies, who precede the five emperors as royal court princesses. They are seen singing hymns of praise, scattering flower petals, and burning pure incense before the sacred Five Emperors. Their residence is in the lungs (yin, west), and they are summoned forth by pressing the position marked yen.

11. Wu Di zhi fu 五帝值符

The emperors next come forth from their positions with in the five central organs. Each is seen to hold aloft the Ling Bao talisman proper to his jurisdiction. When the Daoist presses the joint marked Mao, the emperor of the east comes forth from the liver in a green vapor. The Daoist presses the joint Wu and the emperor of the south comes forth from the heart in a red vapor. The Daoist presses the central joint, Yu, and the yellow emperor comes forth from the spleen in a gold vapor. The Daoist presses the joint Yu and the emperor of the west comes forth from the lungs in a white vapor. Finally the Daoist presses the joint marked zi and the emperor of the north comes forth from the kidneys in a black-purple vapor. Each takes up his position in the sacred area, thus completing a marvelous mandala of pure spirits surrounding the Daoist in the center of the cosmos.

12. Zhi r zhi xiang guan shi je 指日香官使者

The incense-bearing messenger spirit of the day is next summoned forth. This spirit is computed daily by the Daoist master, from a list of sixty spirits, each of which successively takes up his or her duties in a sixty-day cycle. The sixty Jia Zi spirits are said to be the grandchildren of the San Huang, the Three Ancient Emperors of the San Huang Wen, and the children of the six Jia and six Ding spirits who control the powers of nature. The list of the spirits and the way of computing when each is to be summoned is one of the secrets given to the Daoist novice by his or her master sometime before ordination. Without knowing how to compute the Jia Zi spirit of the day, the performance of the Fa Lu is impossible.

13. Ge san-shih-liu ren chu 各三十六人出

In the last phrase of the rite of inner emptying, the Daoist summons forth the three times eight, or twenty-four spirits of the cosmos, eight each for the head, chest, and belly. Next he summons the three Hun souls that represent the powers of yang, and the seven Po souls that symbolize the influence of yin. Finally he calls forth the last two spirits of the microcosm, the Lord Yang and the Lady Yin. Thus thirty-six spirits are summoned forth from the body in the final invocation. With the body now emptied of all the spirits and the mind freed from any thought, even that of the highest heavenly worthies, the Daoist is ready for the meditation of transcendental union. The requirements for union, in the interpretation of Master Zhuang, are fulfilled as demanded in the Zhuangzi. The xin zhai or "fast of the heart" has been accomplished by a meditation of internal alchemy. The Daoist, at the end of the Fa Lu rite, has been reduced to a state of Hun Dun, or primordial emptiness, ready for an encounter with the Dao of transcendence.

The written instructions of Master Zhuang concerning the Fa Lu have been published in Chinese.[92] The above description provides a first glimpse of the intricacies of orthodox meditation, a technique that takes years of practice to perfect. The keynotes of the meditations of the orthodox Dao of the Right are peace, simplicity, and purity. The purpose of the Ke Yi rites of union is to win blessing for the people, as well as contemplative union for the Daoist master. They are an extreme opposite of the military Dao of the Left described in chapter 4 and quite different, in turn, from popular forms of Song dynasty Thunder ritual, described in the following chapter. The orthodoxy of a master is judged by his ability to perform meditation as described in the above pages, and to work always for the good of his fellow man, as will be seen in the final chapter.

6. Thunder and Lightning Purification: Neo-Orthodoxy of the Sung

Daoist Three Mountain Alliance 三山滴血派 Oral Teachings

INTRODUCTION

The stately Tao of the Right just described in chapter 5 has remained, from the time of the north-south period until the present day, the hallmark of orthodox religious Daoism. Daoist learning its meditations and classical rituals have been rewarded with the highest rank at ordination, and have performed Jiao 醮 liturgies of renewal for the imperial court as well as for the village temple. But the rituals of classical orthodoxy had one drawback in everyday use. Complete purification was necessary to perform the five rites of "Union with the Dao" properly. The slightest stain on the consciousness of the adept, the presence of any impure spirit, destroyed the efficacy of the meditations of union. Further, popular Daoist orders, unaware of the meditations of pure emptiness, summoned hosts of spirits and demons that could never be admitted to the pure area within the temple during the classic Jiao ritual of renewal. Orthodox Daoism therefore needed a new kind of ritual, able to purify and control the host of unorthodox spirits evolved over the ages by Daoists of sectarian affiliation.[1]

A second factor promoting the acceptance of a new kind of orthodoxy during the late Tang, through the Song and the later Yuan or Mongol dynasties was the deep and colorful influence of Tantric Buddhism. Suppressed by the Wuzong emperor in 845, Tantric Buddhism flourished throughout the Tang dynasty, from the city of Chang An in west China and Mount Tian Tai in ZheJiang (浙江天台山) to Yunnan in the southwest. The esoteric Buddhist schools brought a new kind of mudra and mantra, and a systematic mandala style of meditative ritual that resonated with the liturgies of orthodox Daoism. The use of pseudo-Sanskrit seed words and complicated two-hand mudras caught the imagination of the Tang and the early Song Daoist masters. The response of Daoism to Tantric Buddhism, especially in the proliferating local Daoist sects of the Song period, was evident in the rapidly developing Thunder-Vajra style of rituals well into the Song dynasty.[2]

As mentioned in the opening historical treatise in chapter 1, a variety of Thunder Vajra schools developed during the Song period. Almost all Daoist schools developed their own style of Thunder ritual. Of the many schools, three seemed to have been more successful and have come down in healthy and flourishing form to the present. The three schools are:[3]

1. Qing Wei Thunder Vajra rites, developed in southwest China during the early Song period.
2. Fire-master Thunder Rites, attributed to Wang Zihua during the late Tang - early Song period.
3. Shen Xiao Thunder Magic, brought to court by Lin Lingsu in 1118.

Besides these three styles, the Qing Ming sect of the southern Song period developed another form of Thunder Magic which is still found in the Canon and influential until today.[4] Some Thunder Vajra sects attribute the founding of the method to Xu Xun, a legendary Daoist said to have died in A.D. 374. Xu was wafted up to heaven in broad daylight, but left behind twelve disciples to spread his doctrines. Most Xu Xun legends seem to be Song dynasty creations; his name appears in the dynastic histories, but the legend about Thunder ritual and the slaying of a great serpent seem to be most popular in Daoist writings since the mid-Song, from about 1100, until today.

The legends told of Xu Xun describe the master as being a Confucian official as well as a Daoist expert.[5] A huge, snake-like demon was said to be attacking the people under his administrative jurisdiction. With his twelve followers he confronted the snake and destroyed it with the power of thunder. The snake, a symbol of yin, or the demonic forces of nature, is commonly used in kung-fu (gongfu) and T'ai-chi (Taiji) physical fitness demonstrations. It is seen as an attacking creature with great mobility and indomitable resolution. In the Daoist interpretation, the black magic of the "popular" Mao Shan, Lü Shan, and Shen Xiao sects make use of a snake-like spirit to harm opponents. The use of the snake chart will be demonstrated below in discussing the instructions of Master Zhuang concerning the exorcistic use of Thunder Vajra ritual.

The paraphernalia of Thunder Magic is common to all the Daoist schools that use its purifying ritual. A thunder block, or vajra, made of date wood is used to summon the spirits of thunder. Two-handed mudras described below are used to command the five orthodox thunder spirits to counteract harmful black magic.[6] Thus Thunder Vajra ritual may be seen as a form of neo-orthodoxy developed during the Song period to counteract the spread of popular sectarian Daoism, and to purify the sacred area where "Three Mountain Alliance" ritual meditation takes place.

1. Three Styles of Thunder Ritual

The three main styles of Thunder ritual—the Qing Wei, Fire Master, and Shen Xiao are distinguished by clearly identifiable styles of liturgy. Each of the schools developed its own lu, 籙 or list of spirits' names. Each proposed its own style of meditation and popular ritual and held sway in a particular region in China.[7] The style of Thunder Ritual taught by Master Zhuang is partially derived from the Qing Wei sect, from a "Hua Shan" thunder manual originally in the collection of Wu Jingchun. Besides the Hua Shan manual of Thunder Magic, a series of hand-written documents teaching *Qing Wei Wu Lei Fa* (清微五雷法 Five Thunder Method) were purchased by Lin Rumei at Lunghu Shan ca. 1868, and in common use by the Zhengyi Daoist of Hsinchu City in 1888.[8] The two sets of directions are similar but not identical. The differences in these and Shen Xiao Thunder Magic are pointed out in the *Dao Fa Hui Yuan*, the critical treatise on Thunder ritual in the Daoist Canon.

The Qing Wei style of Thunder Vajra ritual taught at Longhu Shan, Wudang Shan, and Hua Shan, give evidence of late Tang dynasty Siddham Sanskrit with Daoist affiliations. In the interpretation of the Three Mountain Alliance tradition, the power of thunder is stored in the five central organs and in the gall bladder, while using mantra similar to syllables used by Tendai Buddhism in Japan and Tantric Buddhism in Tibet. Thunder stored in the gall bladder lights the alchemical furnace within the microcosm, that is, the lower cinnabar field in the belly of man. Thus all the meditations described in the previous chapter can be initiated by summoning thunder to purify the interior and "light the alchemical furnace" in a sort of adaptation of tantric mantra into the orthodox tradition. Furthermore, the Qing Wei school claims Wei Huacun, the legendary women founder of the Mao Shan meditation school, as its own founder.[9] Thus its primary use is for inner cultivation, and considered part of the orthodox ritual described by Master Zhuang in chapter 5 above.

The Fire-master Thunder Rites of Wang Zihua, oral legend says, originated on the southern peak Heng Shan and on Mount Tian Tai in southeast China. The critical work on Wang Zihua is found in the Daoist Canon, as seen in chapter 76 of the *Dao Fa Hui Yuan*. The late Sung dynasty expert Bai Yüchan described the esoteric use of the Thunder method as an internal purifying meditation. By swallowing saliva and breathing in through the nostrils, the alchemical furnace in the lower cinnabar field (Xia Dan Tian 下丹田) is lit and the power of thunder used to cure colds, exorcise, and purify the sacred Daoist Tan 壇 altar. In the manuals brought back to Taiwan from Lung Hu Shan by Lin Rumei, Qing Wei rites are also used to heal the sick, as well as purify the adept for "union with Dao" meditation.[10] The Qing Wei style uses esoteric Sanskrit names to summon the Thunder spirits, distinguishing it from the "new" Thunder Magic of Lin Lingsu and other proliferations of Sung sectarianism.

The new Shen Xiao brand of Thunder Magic is found in volumes 881 to 883 of the Daoist Canon. The style probably is rightly attributed to Lin Lingsu, the court favorite of the Hui Zong emperor. In it, the names of the traditional spirits of the orthodox lu have been changed and the meditations of inner alchemy almost unnoticed. There are new and original sets of talismans, mudras, and mantras, oriented toward curing sickness rather than toward use in rites of renewal or union. In the later Ming period the forty-third generation master of Lunghu Shan, Zhang Yüchu, explains why the magic of Wang Zihua is to be distinguished from the popular Shen Xiao orders spreading throughout southeast China.[11] Each master, Zhang says, devises his own version of the rubrics. The talismans and mantras are multiplied so that the true doctrines are lost and false versions multiplied. For contributing to this tendency the popular Shen Xiao orders are severely criticized. Chapter 66 of the Dao Fa Hui Yuan concurs with the criticism, adding that the use of evil spirits to harm men was widespread in the popular Thunder Magic orders.[12] The orthodox orders used Thunder Ritual as the most effective means of counteracting such black or "sinister" Dao of the Left magic.

To Bai Yuchan, the great Daoist master of the late Song period, is attributed the achievement of purifying and making orthodox the rituals of the Shen Xiao order. Like Lu Xiujing in the fifth century, who edited out the forgeries of Ge Zhaofu before publishing the Lingbao Canon, so Bai Yuchan in the thirteenth century edited the Shen Xiao texts and gave them the aura of respectability. Bai was given the official title, "Official of the Shen Xiao Rubric," for his strenuous efforts to bring unity into the chaos of Sung sectarianism. Nevertheless, when signing his Daoist documents and addressing the heavenly worthies in prayer, Bai did not use a Shen Xiao title. Rather, he signed himself as a "Master of the Shang Qing meditative tradition, knowledgeable in Thunder Magic and in the military exorcisms of the Pole Star sect."[13]

Though relieved of its earlier aberrations, the new Shen Xiao sect is still considered to be the latest and least of the orders of Daoist brethren. As practiced in Taiwan today, new Shen Xiao Daoism, like the aberrant form of popular Mao Shan Daoism, makes use of evil talismans to kill, injure, or harm people in the community. For this reason, Daoists who seek to climb the various stages of perfection within the ranks of orthodox Daoism, are given Thunder Magic titles from the Qing Wei sect and draw away from the simpler forms of new Shen Xiao exorcism. The Heavenly Master at Lunghu Shan kept manuals from all three of the dominant thunder sects and taught them to the Daoist coming for a license of ordination according to the expertise and demands of the visitors.[14]

To Master Zhuang, the beginnings of Thunder Magic must be sought in the Tang dynasty, rather than in the later Song. Historians who write about Thunder Ritual confirm finding mention of Thunder rites in dated canonical texts before the Song dynasty. Others hold that Lin Lingsu was the first to practice Thunder Magic and thus won imperial approval at court.[15] Still others hold that the founders of the *Tian Xin Zheng Fa*, a branch of Thunder Ritual attributed to an offshoot of the Heavenly Master sect, brought it to court a few years before Lin Lingsu.[16] Though it would be difficult to establish the existence of officially sanctioned Thunder Vajra sects before the Song dynasty, it does seem plausible that kinds of Thunder Vajra rites were practiced on the local level before the coming of the Song dynasty innovators. Though the name "Five Thunder Method," came to typify the Thunder rites of the Song, thunder rubrics are definitely seen in the Tang dynasty canon.[17]

2. The Teachings of Master Zhuang on Thunder Ritual

The teachings of Master Zhuang regarding the rites of Thunder Ritual were inherited from the last of the men to instruct him in the esoteric rubrics of religious Daoism, Lin Xiumei. Lin gave Zhuang 23 manuals containing the instructions for meditation and the rubrical directions for performing thunder ritual. The first manual of preparatory meditation was a nineteen-page Commentary on the Yellow Court Canon. It is used in conjunction with the Yellow Court Canon itself and expresses philosophically the distinction between the Tao of transcendence and the meditations by which the body is prepared for realizing Dao presence. The second manual, called the *Huashan Qing Wei* Thunder Vajra Rubrics, was one of the manuals brought to Taiwan by Wu Jingqun in 1823 and kept in the Lin family collection until 1928 when it was given to Zhuang. Both works are in the author's microfilm collection, listed in part three of the bibliography at the end of this book. The latter manual will be used in the following pages as an illustration of the teachings of Master Zhuang on the performance of Five Thunder ritual. To introduce the meditations used by the Daoist to prepare to wield power over thunder, I shall attempt to summarize briefly the teachings of the first

manual, in keeping with the preliminary nature of this study. It would require a full-length monograph to explain the subject adequately.

The meditation in which the Daoist sees him or herself in the presence of
the transcendent Dao is prepared for in a series of alchemical-like processes
whereby the principles of life within the body are "refined" and "joined" in
the Yellow Court, which is conceived to be an empty center within the microcosm of the human body. The Daoist does not refine or summon the ultimate transcendent Dao of the Wu Wei, for a transcendent act cannot be refined or summoned. Instead the body is prepared by acts of purification and
emptying for a state in which awareness of the Transcendent Dao as present
can take place. In the commentary on the Yellow Court Canon, the disciple
is first taught that the use of, or interpretation of texts, which promote fang-
chung, (sexual hygiene) may not be used by the Daoist who hopes to learn
Qingwei Thunder Meditation, or reach the higher stages of inner cultivation. The texts of internal alchemy meditation are to be interpreted as visualizing circulation of breath, colors, and sacred images, summoning the
spirits of the Prior Heavens into specific places within the Daoist body. The
spirits of the Posterior Heavens are distinguished from the Heavenly Worthies of the eternal Prior Heavens. These latter spirits are purifying forces,
preparing the Yellow Court before the contemplation of the Transcendent
Dao. The role of Thunder ritual in the preparatory meditations is to be a
stimulus and catalyst in the alchemical process of purification.

Thus, in the explanation of the *Commentary on the Yellow Court Canon*, and
in chapter 76 of the *Dao Fa Hui Yüan*, the alchemical furnace is the lower cinnabar field within the belly of man.[18] The nose, which breathes in and expels
air during the meditation of interior alchemy, is taken to be the "male symbol" during the process of refinement, that is, the bellows which supplies
wind and breath to the fire within the furnace. The mouth, which remains
closed, is considered to be the female symbol, or the supplier of saliva to
the furnace in the belly. The saliva, however, is not ordinary material saliva
alone but a mixture of the colored vapors that contain the principles of life,
acting as fuel and ingredients for the alchemical process in the belly. Thus,
the actual refinement is seen to take place in the lower cinnabar field, quite
unlike the Indian kundalini process of interior awakening.

The various breaths of the five elements and the three principles of life are
visualized as mixed with saliva and swallowed. The alchemical furnace in
the belly, which has been lighted by the power of thunder, then refines and
joins the various breaths into the "hierophant," or the ruddy child, the pill
of longevity, or the immortal fetus, depending on the wording of the text
or the choice of the translator, the words being analogous. In no sense can

the physical or the conceptual image be taken to be the Dao of Transcendence. The ultimate Wu Ji Dao 無極 之道 (Transcendent Dao Principle) is present only during the performance of orthodox liturgy when the Daoist has the flame pin or diadem inserted in his ritual crown, or during the meditation in the private chambers of his residence while he is in the depths of contemplation, and mental imaging is stopped or contained within. At all other times, though he has indeed formed the hierophant within the Yellow Court in his own body, and though he can again join himself in union with the Transcendent, the state of union is potential and not activated. Union is therefore realized by the power of thunder, and thus the Thunder Magic ritual of the Qing Wei tradition is called a direct descendant of the Mao Shan Shang Qing school of Lady Wei Huacun and the Inner Yellow Court Canon Tradition.

In the Qing Wei tradition of Thunder Ritual, the power of the thunder is first stored by a meditation which takes place each spring.[19] On the first day after the Lunar New Year in which a thunderstorm takes place, the Daoist faces the direction of the thunder and breathes in the breath of electrified atmosphere while forming mudras on both hands and reciting mantric spells. The power of the thunder is circulated throughout the organs of the body and finally stored in the gall bladder. When ready to perform the meditations of internal alchemy, the thunder is used to light the fire in the alchemical furnace in the belly. Thereupon the meditative process of refinement begins. The vapors of the elements metal and water are first joined together into seminal essence. The vapor of metal is white and is stored in the lungs. The vapor of water is black-purple and is stored in the kidneys. Both vapors are circulated upward and mixed with saliva in the mouth. By breathing in through the nose and swallowing saliva, the mixture of breath and saliva is sent to the furnace in the lower cinnabar field, the belly, and refined into vital essence. The ultimate product is seen to be a white vapor, which is personified as the third of the Daoist trinity, the Dao De Heavenly Worthy.

Next, the yellow vapor of the element earth is envisioned to come forth from the spleen and mixed with saliva in the mouth. By breathing inward through the nose and swallowing saliva, the mixture is again sent downward to the furnace and refined into a yellow-gold vapor, the symbol of primordial spirit. From the yellowish vapor is seen to congeal the Ling Bao Heavenly Worthy, the second of the Daoist trinity. Finally the vapors of the elements wood and fire are joined to form a purple image of primordial breath. The vapor of blue-green wood is drawn forth from the liver, and the breath of red fire issues forth from the heart, creating the color purple. Both are mixed with saliva and sent downward to be refined in the belly. The product is refined into a deep blue vapor, which solidifies into the Primordial Heavenly Worthy. Thus all three principles of life are seen as present within the lower cinnabar field. In the final stage of meditation, the Daoist completely stops mental imagery and heart's desiring, and sees the three primordial breaths refined into one, (hundun 混沌) in the "central void" which is taken to be a space between the kidneys and the fifth lumbar vertebrae, the "Yellow Court" center of the microcosm. The hierophant, or the "cinnabar pill" of immortality, is formed here, by joining the Three Principles—primordial breath, original spirit, and vital essence—into one. The Daoist sees him/herself as standing in the presence of the eternal transcendent Dao as long as the meditation lasts, that is, as long as Qi breath-awareness is held within and contact with the external world is shut off.

It is only after perfecting the meditations of the Yellow Court (Gold Pavilion) that the Daoist can effectively control the power of the thunder to heal illness or expel evil. The rituals for curing illness are considered to be under the patronage of the fire master, Wang Zihua, deriving from Mount Tian Tai. The rites of union are attributed to the early Han dynasty immortal, Zhu Gan, a spirit honored in one of the temples of Hua Shan in west China. The Thunder Vajra manuals in Master Zhuang's library are subdivided into manuals of healing/purification, and manuals of contemplative union. The two distinct styles of liturgy, the one oriented to meditation and the other meant for exorcisms, are each assigned a patron spirit and a ritual tradition. Both styles of Thunder Meditation are transmitted by the Heavenly Master at Lung Hu Shan and were brought back by Lin Rumei to Hsinchu City, Taiwan, and taught between 1868-88.[20] The teachings of Master Zhuang concerning both systems, meditative and healing, are described in the following pages.

3. MEDITATIONS FOR GAINING CONTROL OF THUNDER.

The very first step in the process of learning Thunder Visualization, once the meditations of the Yellow Court Canon have been perfected, is the ancient method called Yue Jian or stellar position.[21] The method is mentioned in the Zhen Gao by Tao Hongjing, thus showing that it was used at Mao Shan as early as the sixth century before the creation of Thunder Ritual.[22] The Sung dynasty work, Dao Fa Hui Yüan, in chapter 77 shows it to be an essential part of the Thunder rubric.[23] Its adoption into the Qing Wei school and the fire-master tradition of Wang Zihua, therefore, shows the influence of Mao Shan, as well as the late Song dynasty Daoist Bai Yuchan, on the two orders.

1. Finding the Gate of Life

In order to understand the method one must first recall the Battle Chart of the Eight Trigrams, described in figure 1 and 2 in chapter 4. In the battle chart, the gate of hell or the trigram *Gen* 艮 is called "Gate of Life." The reason for the two names, opposed in meaning, can be seen in the figure 20. In the ordinary eight trigrams of King Wen—that is, the trigrams arranged in the order of change in the posterior heavens, also called the *Lo Shu*, the trigram Gen is found in the northeast position. Gen is thought to be the most vulnerable position for attack, that is, the direction from which the powers of evil will attack the body and make it sick. This is because the yin lines, the i.e., the weak broken lines, are inside while the strong yang line is on the outside of the circle. If an army attacks the defender at the position *gen*, it is an easy matter to overcome the first strong yang line of defense, and pass through the two weak yin lines. No general would attack at the qian 三乾 position nor at the kun 坤 position. The qian line is invulnerable since it is three solid yang lines, while the kun line is too obvious a place. Since it is composed of six weak broken lines, the defending general is likely to hide an army in ambush at the kun position and defeat any attacking forces.

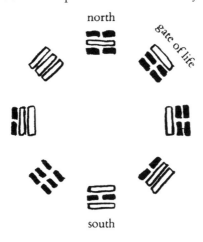

Figure 20. The eight trigrams of King Wen; the Lo Shu.

The position gen, however, seems strong but is in fact weak. For this reason the direction of the northeast is called the "gate of hell" or the "demon's entrance" in classical orthodox Daoist terms. A whole ritual of purification, the Jin Tan[24] 禁壇 liturgy, was invented to "close the devil's gate." Only after the Daoist master has sealed off the northeast position can classical liturgy be performed in the village temple. The rite of closing the "gate of hell" is therefore considered essential in the steps toward renewing the cosmos or curing sickness. Furthermore, the gen position is considered to be the direction through which the vital essences of life flow away. Within the microcosm of the body, it is the heart, the gate through which seminal essence, primordial breath, and spirit escape, leading man inevitably from life to death. The Daoist by his meditations of inner alchemy seeks to seal off the gate of escape and keep life breath, spirit, and vital essence within the microcosm. Thus gen is seen to be truly the "gate of life," the gate through which life can flow away or be preserved. It is very important to be able to locate the gate of life and guard it with great care.

Chapter 4 in which the Six Jia spirits were brought under the Daoist's control, made special use of the gate of life. Each of the rituals in which one of the terrifying Jia spirits was enfeoffed under the Daoist's control took place at the gate of life. The position from which the evil spirits were subordinated and controlled, and the subsequent position from which they were summoned to attack, was the trigram gen in the Battle Chart of the Eight Trigrams. The Daoist who uses Thunder meditation to counteract the black magic of the Dao of the Left must therefore always be aware of the location of the gate of life. Even relationships in the Chinese society may be seen in light of the "gate of life" concept. As the attacking general does not attack in the weakest position, neither does one speak against a fellow man in his weakest point. Rather, one seeks to strengthen a potential weakness.

The secret taught by Thunder meditation, borrowed from the ancient system of prognostication called Yüe Jian, is that the gate of life, or the position gen in the trigrams, changes. It is different for every month of the lunar calendar, as well as for the day and the hour. Without knowing its location, the proper performance of exorcism, blessing, or even meditation is impossible. The gate of life is at the precise position pointed to by the handle of the Pole Star constellation, Ursa Major.[25] The system is illustrated in figure 21.

Thunder must be summoned from the direction in which the Pole Star is pointing, in order to counteract the evil power of the Six Jia spirits or whatever other black magic is being used against the client of the Daoist master. Further, the gate of life indicates the directions from which prayer is to be initiated and the place through which the soul of a deceased person is to escape from the underworld. In the esoteric sense, it can be interpreted to be the gate of eternal life. The Yüe Jian method is therefore important both in performing burial ritual and in choosing the direction from which thunder is to be summoned. The Daoist master teaches a poem or conundrum to the novice to instill the method for finding the gate of life:

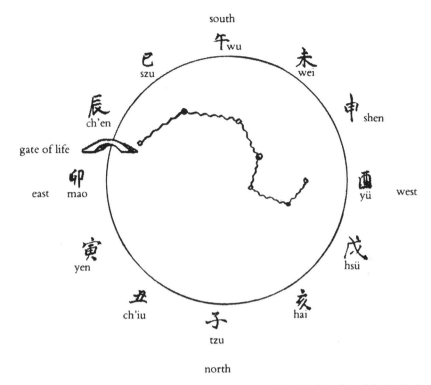

Figure 21. The gate of life is located in the direction that the handle of the Pole Star constellation, Ursa Major, is pointing.

In the shen, zi, and chen months
When the horse points to yan
The spirit passes through mao
The three noxious breaths are at si, wu, and wei.

In the yan, wu, and xü months
When the horse dwells in shen
The spirit passes through yu.
The three evil breaths are at hai, zi, and qiu.

In the si, yu, and qiu months
When the horse passes through hai
The spirit escapes through zi.
The three evil breaths are yan, mao, and chen.

In the hai, mao, and wei months,
When the horse is at si,
The star of escape is at wu.
The three evil spirits are at shen, yu, and xü.

The tip of the Pole Star handle is called "the horse" in the poem, and is commonly called Po jun 破軍in esoteric terms. The direction in which Po jun points is the gate of life, while the direction the open top of the dipper points is evil. A special chart is also made which shows the position of the Po jun star at any given time of the night and day. The novice may thus refer to the chart whenever the sky is cloudy at night or a special meditation is to be performed during the day.

The Yüe Jian method is also used in burying the dead, as mentioned above. On the evening before the interment, in the front room of the household where the coffin is kept in mourning, the Daoist prepares a special mound of rice called a Cao ren, or "grass-man." A rattan mat is laid on the ground and a bushel of pure white rice is poured on top of it. The rice is shaped to resemble a man or a woman, and eyes made of stones, ears made of pomelo leaves, and so forth, are inserted into it. Around the effigy, in a circle, are laid a series of small lamps, one series for each of the eight directions, that is, the eight trigrams. Each line in the trigram is represented by a lamp. Thus the trigram qian in the northwest, composed of three straight lines, receives three lamps. The trigram kun in the southwest, composed of six broken lines, receives six lamps. The ritual area resembles the illustration in figure 22.[26]

The Daoist performing the rite holds a paper lantern attached to a willow branch, which represents the soul of the deceased. He dances around outside the circle twelve times, and jumps into the interior of the mandala of lamps as he passes the gate of life. He then dances around the interior of the circle twelve times, and jumps out again through the gate indicated by the 7th Pole Star po jun. Finally, he steps into the interior of the circle, and draws a secret fu talisman with the willow branch, scattering the rice in the five directions. The secret talisman is in fact the character Gang 罡神, the esoteric name for the po jun tail of the pole star. The soul is thereby released and escapes outwards through the gate of life into the realm of the immortals in heaven.

The Yüe Jian must further be used to determine the direction that the master must face during thunder meditations when practicing ritual alchemy in the privacy of his own house. Thus the month, day, and hour in which a given meditation is performed is determined by the position of the Pole Star. The power of thunder is summoned forth from the organ within the Daoist's body which corresponds to the direction in which the po jun points. Thus by referring to figure 18, the direction of the thunder and the corresponding organ in the body from which it is summoned can be determined. As noted above, during the special meditation performed on the

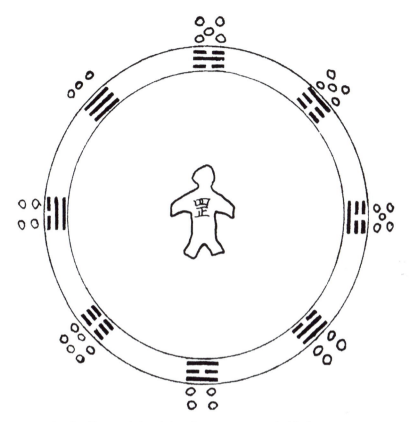

Figure 22. The Cao Ren and the eight trigrams represented in lamps.

occasion of the first thunderstorm after Chinese New Year, the thunder is stored in the gall bladder, which acts as the center for most brief rites invoking Thunder ritual.[27]

Once the power over the thunder has been obtained, the Daoist must begin to practice the use of the rubrics until he has perfected the method before attempting to use it in the public forum. Thus the thunder method makes use of mudra, mantric seed word, and circulation of breath in a meditation performed by the Daoist master in the privacy of his own quarters, in preparation for the ritual use of the Thunder Magic in cures and exorcistic battles. The manual containing the rubrics for the Thunder Magic meditations is called *Shi Zhuan Qingwei Qi Jüe* 師專清微炁決 or *The Master's Transmission of the Qingwei [school] Breath secrets.*[28]

 2. Summoning the Thunder Breath.

In the first step, preparation for drawing a talisman, one must learn to summon forth the zu qi 祖炁, the ancestral (thunder) breath from the center of the microcosm. The center is to be conceived as a void between the kidneys and the stomach in the lower regions of the body; that is to say, the secret court in which the ancestral breath dwells is the Yellow Court of the center. If one does not use the ancestral breath in writing a talisman, the charm will have no effect; that is, it will not be filled with spirit awareness ling 靈.

Form the left hand into the sword mudra: bend the little finger and the ring finger down so that they touch the palm of the hand. The thumb is then put under the two bent fingers so that the tips of the ring and little fingers press against the nail of the thumb. The index and middle fingers are extended straight upward. When formed, the master uses the left hand in the sword mudra form to hold the paper on which to draw the talisman and the right hand to hold the brush—but does not at first write with it. Instead, envision the talismanic word, seeing exactly how it will be written on the blank piece of paper, balancing it by size, position and so forth. Then pronounces the mantic seed word, xü, meanwhile seeing a gold-colored ray of light diffuse over the surface of the paper. Then breathe in the golden vapor-like light, until it reaches the very gates of the Yellow Court in the center. Next, imagine a second talismanic character on the surface of the paper and breath forth the mantic seed word, bi. Breathe in the vapor of the second character and mixes it with the first on the tip of the tongue, inside the closed mouth. Thereupon swallow saliva and circulate the mixture of the first and second breath so that it too enters from the paper; its vapor is breathed into the mouth and mixed with the saliva by the tongue, while muttering the mantic spell: "The Three Houses (Lords) have met!" As the mantra ends, see the three vapors now join together into a small bluish-black precious pearl in the center of the Yellow Court. The small round pearl begins to throw off light and gradually heats, becoming a reddish flame. The flame extends upward in a single thread, until it passes through the various organs of the body and ascends into the niwan (pineal gland) or the Ming Tang, the royal court of the brain. Then see the sun shining immediately above the left eye. The sun is round, with seven rays of light coming from it. Over the right eye also see the full moon, with ten rays of light issuing from it. The two spheres then join into a single white circle just inside the frontal lobe, between the eyebrows. A drop from the white sphere comes down into the mouth as a precious pearl. The Daoist then breathes vapor issuing from the pearl onto the tip of the writing brush and begins to write the talisman. The talisman is initiated by drawing a hollow circle, which represents the ultimate transcendent, Wu Ji 無極. Then while saying the mantic word, ka, put a dot in the center of the circle and recite the mantic spell:

The One Primordial Breath of the Prior Heavens
By ordered stages rules the myriad spirits!

Then quietly continue to oneself:

Red is so red that it seems like blood
White is so white that it looks like snow
The Path is such a path that it leads to the central void!
The dust of the world is heavy, a heavy ton of lead!

Continuing to write the talisman, draw a second circle with a dot in the center, representing the Tai Ji, the immanent Dao, and from the dot in the center of the circle see the power of the thunder issuing forth. This completes the first step.

Next the Daoist employs the thunder "breath," or the Gang star's qi energy, to complete the talisman. He begins to meditate upon the power of the thunder, recalling that it must be drawn from that direction in which the Gang star (po jun) is pointing. Unless the direction is properly ascertained, the following rubrics may not be performed.

The Daoist closes his eyes and envisions a red star as large as a bowl of rice, above the left eye. See the star as a bright sun, diffusing its rays about the body. Then he see the seven stars of Ursa Major imprinted in one's own body. The four stars of the bowl are imbedded in the toes of the left and right foot and the knees of the left and right leg. The three stars of the handle are in the belly, the heart, and the tip of the tongue. The Gang 罡 star, the star that points at the gate of life, is thus envisioned as embedded in the tongue of the Daoist. Alive with the shining rays of the Pole Star constellation the Daoist then uses the tip of the tongue as a brush and, on a yang day (an odd-numbered day), draws the character for yang on the hard palate, the roof of the mouth. With the character for yang completed, breathe out through the mouth so that the breath or vapor of yang, mixed with the light of the Pole Star, shoots out and penetrates the red sun shining above the left eye. On a yin day (an even-numbered day) draw the character yin on the hard palate and spit out the rays of yin into the red sun above the forehead. As soon as the rays from the mouth penetrate the red sun, the whole image dissolves and immediately there appears a terrifying spirit with three heads and six arms, whose esoteric name is "Gundari." The two center arms and the two right arms each hold a sword. The spirit is so high that it stretches upward into the sky. The spirit bends down and puts the Daoist on its shoulders, standing up so that the Daoist now is in the heavens.

Next, the Daoist draws the mantic word, hong, on the hard palate and breaths out into the spirit, who is now addresses as the Gang spirit, the spirit of the star that points to the gate of life. As soon as the vapor from the Daoist's mouth has touched the spirit, the following mantic spell is recited:

> The Heavenly Emperor has dispatched a command!
> Given to the Tian Gang 天罡 spirit to carry.
> How dare the evil spirits of the five directions
> Not wither away and utterly die?
> One breath of the immortal flying spirit,
> The myriad demons are killed in their lairs!

The Daoist then presses the xü, yu, wei, zui, center (yü), wu and chen joints on his left hand and recites:

> O Red Sun spirit, the Three-Five (liaison spirits)
> Come to thy aid!

The three-five liaison spirits are seen to come as supporting troops for the Tian Gang general's victory. The Daoist again forms a mantic character on the hard palate, using the tongue as a brush: the character for fire 火 and Dou 斗 (bushel) are drawn side by side and then spit out as a vapor which covers the assembling spirits. Meanwhile the Sanskrit mantra is recited three times: "Om! Gu! gun da li po ka!" The Gang 罡 spirit (whose mantic name is Gundari) is seen suddenly to turn his body and, with angry eyes opened wide, bend the tip of the Daoist's ritual sword. The Daoist chants:

> Oh ye (evil spirits) who seek to slay me!
> Now you must flee my magic powers!
> (Hua kai, that is, the Geng
> position, true north)

As soon as the recitation is finished, the Daoist breathes in through his nose the fiery vapor, which is still balanced on the end of the sword. The magical breath with its power of thundering fire is drawn down into the Yellow Court in the center of the microcosm and mixed with the vapors of the Daoist's body. The breath is then exhaled, while the Daoist draws the Gang talisman on the piece of paper on the table before him.

The Gang talisman is a basic design used by Daoists of all orthodox traditions to sign documents or to finish off the writing of a talisman with a flourish. There are other meditative methods of writing the talisman, but the above is standard for the Daoists using the thunder rubric derived from the Qingwei tradition of Hua Shan. Tantric Buddhism in Japan and Tibetan share these mantic words and images.

3. Using the thunder breath to cure a cold and perform exorcisms.

The power of thunder, once infused into the body, can be used to bless a child that has a simple cold. The Daoist presses the mao position with the thumb of the left hand and sees a reddish-purple light coming from the east. He breathes the reddish-purple vapor in through both nostrils and circulates it through the body, finally gathering it into the Yellow Court in the center of the microcosm. Then swallow saliva and mix the breath with the breath inside one's own body. Then while uttering the word, xü, breathe forth the vapor and draws the gang 罡 character on the palm of the left hand with the index and middle finger of the right hand. Finally press both hands on the head of the child, in the manner of blessing an infant or patting a child of whom one is fond. The child will quickly recover.

The thunder breath from the seven Pole Stars can be used to exorcise a demon causing a sudden disturbance or a nighttime fright in a younger member of the family. The Daoist chants the mantic words in the left column while pressing the joints on the left hand, indicated in the right column:

MANTRA	MUDRA
kuei	yan
shao	mao
quan	chen
hang	si
bi	face of the index finger
fu	central joint (yü), middle finger
piao	above the central joint

When the mantra is recited and the mudras formed, the Daoist then envisions standing with the mountain of the east, Tai Shan, directly behind his left elbow. On the mountain there is a cave. From the inner recesses of the cave a black vapor is issuing forth. The vapor is baleful, extraordinarily cold, causing the teeth to chatter when breathed in. In the following spell, sha 煞 means baleful, demonic influence. The Daoist recites the spell three times:

> Heaven sha, earth sha, year sha,
> Month sha, day sha, hour sha,
> All you evil demonic sha vapors

Do not enter (the child's) belly!
Pains in the belly will make (him or her) die!

Then draw the Gang 罡 talisman on the hard palate with the tongue and presses the mudra for overcoming the noxious black vapor; that, is, press the lower central joint on the left side of the middle finger. The directions for performing this cure are to be passed on by oral tradition; the master does not usually transmit the directions in written form. There are in all seventy-two noxious breaths, computed according to the almanac, the birth date of the possessed child, or the baleful directions of the Yue Jian method explained in figure 22.

The Daoist can use Thunder Medtation to control the rays of the sun in order to effect a cure or exorcise an evil spirit. In this method, the Daoist first presses the mao position on the left hand and meditates, seeing just above the corner of the left eye a round, red sun with seven rays of light emanating from the center. Then recite the following mantra: "Om kuo gi lai/kun da li /po ka!" The mantra must be recited continuously seven times without taking a breath. Thereupon breath in the seven rays of vaporous light, circulating them through the body until they reach the Yellow Court and are drawn within. In the Yellow Court they are mixed with the Daoist's vital breath and the stored breath of the thunder; finally they are breathed forth while exhaling through pursed lips, so as to form the mantic word, Xü. As the breath is slowly exhaled, draw the Gang talisman on the roof of the mouth and direct the vapor to the body of the possessed person.

On a day which falls under the influence of yin (even numbered days), the Daoist changes the rubrics in the following manner: Press the yu joint on the left hand and see just above the corner of the right eye a full, bright moon. From the moon issues ten rays of light. Then recite the following mantic spell ten consecutive times without taking a breath: "Om kuo ke lai ha/lai po li po ka!" When finished reciting the mantra, breath in the ten rays of vaporous light and circulate them through the body until they enter the Yellow Court. Finally breath forth the vapor in the direction of the person to be exorcised while pronouncing the mantic word, Xi; then draw the talisman of the Gang spirit.

Zhuang taught that Thunder Meditation is required, before performing the Fa Lu (mandala building) ritual described in chapter 5. It is never allowed, he insisted, to use the popular Shen Xiao or Redhead forms of thunder ritual described in Gaoshang Shen Xiao Yü Qing Zhen Wang Zi Shu Da Fa (Shen Xiao Da Fa) recorded in volumes 881 to 883 of the Daoist Canon. The difference between the two styles is in the meditative use of the Yellow

Court Canon in the Qing Wei Thunder Magic sect, versus the popular spirit summoning, curing, and blessing oriented rituals of the Shen Xiao Redhead orders. The Five Thunder Rites of Master Zhuang derive from the former source, and the rituals of the Redheads of Hsinchu City, as seen in the teachings of the Zhang and Qian clans, from the latter work.[29] It is important to note that externally the rituals appear to be almost identical. The Redhead Daoists also make use of the datewood thunder block, the talismans and mudras, and the mantric seed words. The distinction is to be found, first, in the quality of the interior meditation and, second, in the spirits summoned to Redhead ritual. In the case of the Redhead Daoists, the spirits and immortals of the popular religion and local beliefs play a central role. The devout laymen who attend the services can identify the spirits summoned by the Redheads and offer private worship, often in their own homes to the pantheon of the Shen Xiao and Lü Shan 閭山 popular folk religion gods. The spirits that the Qing Wei Daoists summon, on the other hand, are esoteric and their appearance, apparel, and summons are hidden from all but the Daoist master's sons and closest disciples. The meditative use of Thunder-vajra ritual is attributed to the woman Daoist Zu Shu, in the Qingwei oral tradition.

4. The Practice of Thunder Ritual

Perhaps the most perplexing enigma in the study of Daoist schools and ritual practices is the professional rivalry between the orthodox sects of antiquity and the more recent orders which originated during and after the Song period. The rivalry is not only in the external forum where Daoist compete for the patronage of the pious faithful; it is in internal forum as well, where great magical battles are fought between competing Daoist masters. The very meditations of the various sects are subjected to the scrutiny of the opposing orders and declared to be zheng 正 orthodox, or xie 邪 heterodox, according to the conformity of the color of the vapors to the classical texts of antiquity. Thus the late Sung Daoist, Jin Yünjong, accused the popular Shen Xiao order of being wu fa, or without real power, because the color red is substituted for the dark-blue vapor used when summoning the Primordial Heavenly Worthy. Professor Noritada Kubo describes the Quan Zhen school as "reformation" Daoism in his *Chugoku no Shukyo Kakumei* because the religious discipline, as well as the aura of internal meditation, differed somewhat from the classical orthodox style.

It is therefore most interesting to read in the texts of the Celestial Masters from Lung Hu Shan in Jiangxi province that the Qing Wei style of Thunder ritual is used to oppose the magic of various heterodox styles of ritual.

The Five Thunder rubrics of the Redhead Shen Xiao order are diametrically opposed to the Thunder rituals of the orthodox Zheng Yi tradition. Three Mountain Alliance masters teach that the Qing Wei Thunder rites in the Dao Fa Hui Yüan differ from the Thunder Magic of Lin Lingsu and the local Shen Xiao orders. The spells found in the esoteric texts of the Heavenly Masters say specifically: "Bind the heterodox spirits and send them back to Lü Shan and Mao Shan!"[30]

The biography of Lin Lingsu indicates, as mentioned above, that Lin Lingsu and his style of Shen Xiao rubrics were introduced to the court of Hui Zong by the twenty fifth master of Mao Shan, Liu Hunkang. It seems reasonable to surmise that Mao Shan had adapted the new forms of ritual introduced by Lin Lingsu. But the opposition of the Heavenly Master sect to populart (vs. Yellow Court Canon) Mao Shan seems to have derived from another heterodox source as well. The Tao of the Left was attributed, at least from the early Ming period, to Mao Shan popular Daoists. In the nineteenth and early twentieth centuries the popular local Daoists operating in JeJiang, Jiangsu, and FuJian provinces were very often called simply "Mao Shan Daoist Masters," a term used in some parts of modern Taiwan as well. The rites of Dun Jia black magic, as well as Redhead styles of popular sword-ladder climbing, trumpet-blowing exorcisms, and other such dramatic exhibitionism, became popular throughout southeast China. The Heavenly Master not only opposed these forms of popular liturgy by invoking the exorcisms of Thunder ritual, but invented grades of ordination and Daoist perfection for the Shen Xiao orders as well, which led them upward into the ranks of orthodoxy. Thus, the higher stages of Shen Xiao ordination, as administered by the Heavenly Master at Lung Hu Shan, included the titles and the registers of orthodoxy. There was no grade one Shen Xiao ordination. Grades two and three already introduced the Redhead Daoist to monastic meditation. Instead of grade one, the aspiring master was elevated out of the ranks of heterodoxy into the more profoundly meditative orders of antiquity.[31]

The opposition between the classical sects and the modern regional orders is well illustrated by the magical battles and jousts which take place between the masters of Taiwan, using a kind of black magic known as Mao Shan snake magic. It is of course far removed from the classical Shang Qing school and the Yellow Court Canon. The term "Mao Shan Daoist" refers to a form of local Daoist black magic found in the southeastern provinces of China and the countryside of Taiwan. Popular Mao Shan magic employs the Six Jia spirits to attack an opposing Daoist or to cause bad weather, sickness or even death to an opponent. In order to understand the principle on which the snake magic works, it is necessary to recall the Battle Chart of the Eight Trigrams, as seen in figure 20.

In the explanation of the eight trigrams of change given at the beginning of chapter 6, the trigram gen was shown to be the position of greatest weakness, while the trigram qian was the source of the greatest strength. An army is invincible, and the magic of a Daoist master all powerful, which begins from the northwest position, that is, the trigram Qian. The peculiar rubric of Mao Shan black magic is that the circle of the eight trigrams is opened up into the form of a snake. Starting from the trigram Qian in the northwest position, the eight trigrams are unwound to resemble a writhing serpent. The effectiveness of the serpentine figure is seen in the mobility of the trigram qian which becomes an invincible army of spirits in the hands of the Mao Shan master. The head of the attacking snake is seen to be the trigram qian, which can be moved hither and thither to find the vulnerable spot in an opponent's circle of magic. The snake chart resembles the diagram in figure 23.[32]

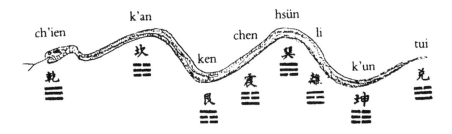

Figure 23. The Battle Chart of the Eight Trigrams unwound into the form of a serpent. The diagram also represents hills in which defending armies are hidden in ambush.

In applying the magic of the Mao Shan snake chart, the Jia spirit proper to the day, with its army of spirit soldiers, is put at the trigram qian and used to attack an enemy Daoist master. It can also be used to defend the orthodox master, in which case the chart is seen as a series of rising mountains in which armies have been hidden in ambush. The kou jüe 口訣 oral secrets explaining the method are as follows:

Qian:	Experienced battle trained soldiers. Attack!	(Wood conquers).
Kan:	Hidden soldiers. Ambush.	(Water conquers).

Gen: Gate of demon/gate of life.   (Thunder purifies)

Chen: Reserve army.   (Fire and earth conquer).

Xün: Reinforcements.   (Wood conquers).

Li: Thunder brigade.
              Penetrate deeply.   (Metal conquers).

Kun: Defensive army.
              Protect and defend.   (Water and earth conquer).

Dui: An army of heroes.
              Protect and defend.   (Water and earth conquer).

The Daoist who uses either the popular Mao Shan method of black magic to harm a person, or a combination of the Mao Shan method with the Six Jia spirits of chapter 4, is not allowed to learn the inner alchemy meditations of the orthodox Tao of the Right of chapter 5. That is, the meditative ritual of orthodox Cheng-i Daoism must cast out all impure spirits before the meditations of internal alchemy are effective. When the terrifying Six Jia are purified spirits by Thunder Ritual, they can be used to protect the sacred area where an orthodox ritual is taking place. The power of the evil "Dao of the Left" is effectively destroyed. Thus the conflict between the orthodox orders and the popular local sects is a spiritual antagonism of a very basic nature. The evil spirits are indeed xie, in that their very presence renders orthodox ritual ineffective. The master must expel all but the highest spirits of the ultimate heavens from the sacred area and from the microcosm of his own body in order to perform orthodox ritual. The fa lu meditation of chapter 5 is not only a pious entrance into orthodox ritual, it is absolute essential if one hopes to practice internal alchemical meditation. It is obvious that Qing Wei Thunder ritual is a powerful way to overcome the Tao of the Left, as well as to defend oneself against all sorts of impure spirits encountered at provincial and local levels of religious practice.

The Five Thunder Method can, therefore, be better understood in the role assigned to it by the Heavenly Masters of Lung Hu Shan. "Bind the evil spirits and send them back to Mao Shan and Lü Shan" is one of the most important adaptations of Thunder Magic to the needs of the older classical orders. That is, the rubrics of the Five Thunder Method were invoked to protect the orthodox master against the powers of magic that the classical tradition could not handle. Thunder Magic is a necessary ingredient in the fa biao 發表 rites of announcing and the qing shen 請神 rites of invitation to village Jiao festivals of renewal. The spirits of the highest pure heavens could be invited safely to the local temple only because Thunder ritual was invoked to expel and keep out the spirits of heterodoxy. Thunder rites are used to oppose Mao Shan black magic and the Dun Jia Tao of the Left in an ingenious rite of defensive purification.

5. THE DANCE OF THE HO-T'U.[33]

At the end of a Jiao festival of temple renewal, as described in the previous chapter, the Daoist master performs the ritual called Zheng Jiao 正醮 (orthodox sacrifice) or Dao Chang 道場, the rite of union with the eternal Tao. The rite is the culmination of the three- or five-day Jiao festival and, by attending or simply watching the performance, the bystanders are granted immortality. At the very end of the rite, the Daoist master receives back from the heavenly emperors a shu wen 梳文 or Imperial Rescript, in which the prayers of the whole community are granted, the souls released from hell in a general amnesty, and Xian-hood or immortality awarded to the village members who supported the Jiao and whose names appear on the Rescript. But the gift of immortality and blessing once awarded can again be lost. The powers of darkness and evil, the very serpent that is the symbol of yin, can act to destroy the blessing and pull the members of the once renewed community back into the cycle of change. Yang can be worn away by the powers of yin, and death must inevitably conquer. The spirits that have been expelled can come back and cause ill fortune in the newly renewed cosmos.

As Xu Xun once killed the serpent during the third century Jin 晉 period, so the Daoist master of the present attempts to slay the evil Mao Shan snake demon. The Shu wen memorial is carried into the sacred area by the chief cantor, who dances into the center of the temple using the Lo shu 落書, that is, the eight trigrams arranged as the principle of change-the pattern from life to death-as he approaches the Daoist master. The chief cantor represents the power of yin, which works inexorably to drain away yang and cause cyclic change in the world of nature. The high priest, or Master of Exalted Merit, receives the Rescript in an attitude of profound reverence. He then kneels and summons forth the power of the thunder, as described above. Thereupon he stands, and begins to dance the steps of the Ho tu 河圖, the eight trigrams arranged in the pattern of the Dao of Transcendent immortality.

In order to understand the significance of the eight trigrams arranged in the order of the Ho tu, compare figure 24 with figure 20.[34] In the Ho tu arrangement of the trigrams, the trigram qian appears in the south, and the trigram kun in the north.

Figure 24. The arrangement of the eight trigrams in the order of the Ho tu. In this
arrangement the trigram qian, or the position of greatest strength, is in the
south, the ninth and last position of the sacred dance of Yü.

The Daoist master receives the Shu wen heavenly rescript, and begins to
dance the Ho tu, or the magical steps of Yü the Great that the ancient ruler
originally used, according to legend, to stop the floods. The sacred steps
begin at the trigram kun, marked 1 in the diagram, and continue through to
the trigram qian, marked 9. The master must dance the steps of Yü twelve
times, one for each month in the year, and one for each of the earthly stems.
As he finishes each series, he moves over thirty degrees in the circle so that
all twelve directions of the cosmos are effectively sealed off with the trigram
qian; the ninth step of the sacred dance seals off each of the twelve directions from the attack of the serpent yin. As he seals off each direction, the
Daoist master through the power of the thunder rubric assigns a spirit to
guard the entrance. Thus the Mao Shan Daoist's black magic and the heterodox spirits of the provincial orders find the sacred area effectively sealed
to entry. The Mao Shan serpent's magic is negated by the opposing power
of the trigram qian.

To insure the further safety of the shu-wen rescript and the preservation
of the blessings it promises, the Daoist master, in the most esoteric of mudras and mantras at his command, appoints the six jia and the six ding spirits (chapter 4) to guard the twelve entrances of the sacred area. Thus the
very spirits commanded by the power of the Mao Shan Tao of the Left are
now turned around and put to work for the Tao of the Right by the power

of Thunder Magic. The Daoist invokes the mighty spirit of the Pole Star handle, the Gang Shen, to subdue and command the terrifying jia spirits. As he dances around the positions in the Ho tu, he encounters the chia spirits one by one. In front of the violent and untrustworthy Jia wu spirit he falls back to the ground, visibly moved by her beauty. In front of the qi sha general, Jia Yen, he stares in a haughty and forceful manner. By the end of the graceful dance steps the six jia spirits are subdued and obedient to the Daoist's commands. Such is the power of the Thunder rubric that the evil spirits invoked by the Mao Shan Tao of the Left now turn and attack it instead. The function of Thunder Magic as a basic tool in the rites of exorcism can thus be seen in the classical Jiao rites of cosmic renewal. It has become a tool in the hands of the orthodox masters to subdue the spirits of the heterodox gods of popular Daoism.

The cycle of ritual has now turned a full revolution. From the violent Jia spirits used in the Tao of the Left, analogous to the "Dartmapala" violent spirits of Tantric Buddhism, Master Zhuang has first turned to the classical and stately Tao of the Right, and then back again to the rites of purificatory exorcism to subdue and convert the terrifying demonic forces of heterodoxy. The spirits are indeed only projections of the master's own meditations of inner alchemy. His power over the personified forces of nature is seen to derive from a meditation in which the master has stood before the Dao of transcendence and been united, even if for a very brief moment, with the inexpressible Dao of Laozi's *Dao de Ching*. Like a Boddhisattva, the Daoist must use this power to save fellow humans from the distresses of everyday life. In so doing, the ultimate goal of Daoist ritual is immortal life for all who seek help.

Abbreviations
Pinyin followed by Wade-Giles in parenthesis

CK	*Zhen Gao (Chen Kao)*
CMTC	*Qi Men Dun Jia (Ch'i-men Tun-Jia)*
CTW	*Quan Tang Wen (Ch'üan T'ang Wen)*
HHS	*Hou Han Shu*
HS	*Han Shu*
JAOS	*Journal of the American Oriental Society*
MHCH	*Muo Hai Jin Hu (Muo-hai Chin-hu)*
T	*Taisho Tripitaku (Taisho Shinshu Daizokyo)*
TFHY	*Dao Fa Hui Yuan (Tao-fa Hui-yüan)*
TT	Daoist Canon
WSPY	*Wu Shang Bi Yao (Wu-shang Pi-yao)*
YCCC	*Yun Ji Qi Qian (Yun-chi Ch'i-ch'ien)*

Notes

INTRODUCTION

1. See chapter 5, pt. 4, for the rules of a Daoist novice.
2. Chapter 1, note 110.
3. Though I use the term "Daoist Canon" here and in chapter 1, pt. 3, it must be noted that the Chinese term Dao Zang was used to identify the lists of canonical books composed by Lu Xiu Jing and others in the Fifth and Sixth centuries, and did not refer to an actual printed canon until the reign of the emperor Tai Zong (A.D. 976-997), in the Song dynasty. The first printed Buddhist Canon was also published during emperor Tai Zong's reign. The extant version of the Daoist Canon was printed during the following Ming dynasty, as explained in the text. Before the Song and the Ming dynasties, then, the Daoist Canon was a list of books considered to be canonical, rather than a printed collection, which could be purchased, as today. Until the present century, the canonical books had to be laboriously copied out by hand, as transmitted from master to disciple.
4. Daoist Canon (TT), vols. 877, 878.
5. Chapter 1, notes 176-179; chapter 5, notes 20-21.

CHAPTER ONE

1. Pp. 1-3 represent the opinions of Master Zhuang on the history of religious Daoism. The remainder of chapter 1 will attempt to show what Zhuang held to be the historical foundations for his teachings, and to distinguish historical fact from legend.
2. The twenty-four registers or lu that distinguish the orthodox Meng Wei or the Zheng Yi Heavenly Master sect, of which Master Zhuang is a member, are found in the Daoist Canon (abbreviated TT), vol. 877, *Tai Shang San Wu Zheng Yi Meng Wei Lu*. See chapter 5 for a full discussion.
3. The Yellow Court Canon (Huang Ting Jing) is one of the basic texts of the Shang Qing Mao Shan sect, treated in chapter 1, notes 92-112. The text is found in TT, vols. 130-131, 189-190, and 679, chapters 11-12.
4. The Qing Wei school is treated in chapter 1, notes 135-139, and chapter 6, notes 12-13. The meditative and ritual practices of Qing Wei Daoism as taught by Master Zhuang are the subject of chapter 6, parts 2 and 3.
5. The Bei Ji or Pole Star sect has been studied by Isabelle Robinet, and other western historians in recent years. Its lu, or registers, are found in TT, vol. 879. The legendary founder of the order is Zhu-ge Liang; Wu Dang mountain and its martial arts form of Daoism is mentioned in the sixth century compilation Zhen Gao (TT, vols. 637-640), chapter 14. The Six Jia "Dao of the Left" as a form of spiritual martial arts is the subject of chapter 4 below. Since the style of magic that uses the Six

Jia spirits became popular at Mao Shan in the late Song and early Ming dynasties, present-day Daoists who practice the more violent forms of military black magic are often called Mao Shan Daoists. Forms of kung-fu (Gongfu) and T'ai-chi ch'üan (Taiji Quan) martial arts are said to derive from Wudang Shan.

6. The Shen Xiao order is discussed at the end of this chapter; see notes 155- 164 below. The opinions of Master Zhuang concerning the order are stated there, and in note 7.

7. The registers, or lu, of some Shen Xiao orders contain harmful talismans and forms of black magic meant to cause illness or even death. On this basis, the order is sometimes classified as heterodox. Examples of the talismans that can be used to cause as well as to cure headaches, arguments, and divorce between husband and wife, are found in the *Zhuang-lin Hsü Dao Zang* (*Zhuang Lin Xu Daozang*) Taipei: Cheng Wen Press, 1975), pt. 4, Volume 24, pp. 6931-6959.

8. Local Daoists who came to Long Hu Shan to purchase a license of ordination from the Heavenly Master were almost always given the registers of the Shen Xiao order. See John Keupers, *"Daoist Exorcism," in Buddhist and Taoist Studies* (Honolulu: University of Hawaii Press, 1977), chapter 5. The great Song dynasty Daoist Bai Yu Chan devoted much of his life to rectifying the heterodox practices of the Shen Xiao Daoists. See notes 161-173 below.

9. See chapter 2 below, notes 10 and 20.

10. The teachings of Master Zhuang are divided into three genre, or styles, of liturgy-the military Dao of the Left treated in chapter 4, the literary Dao of the Right discussed in chapter 5, and Five Thunder Ritual, which is treated in chapter 6. This later form of Song neo-orthodoxy is the classical Daoists' response to the sectarianism of the Song dynasty's popular Daoists. By learning the orthodox version of thunder ritual, the popular Daoists were led upward into the ranks of orthodoxy. See chapter 5, notes 19-22.

11. Fu Chin Jia, *Zhong Guo Dao Jiao Shi* (The History of Daoism in China) (Taipei, 1966), pp. 48-53; *Dokyo no Jittai* (Anonymous work, Kyoto, 1975), pp. 26-32. In Master Zhuang's opinion the historians who consider the possessed mediums or wu 巫 (sometimes called shamans) to be predecessors of orthodox Daoism are in error. Medium possession is allowed by local Shen Xiao orders and the Lü Shan Redhead Daoists, but not by the classical orders described in the following pages.

12. Szu-ma Ch'ien (Si-ma Qian), *Shih-chi* (Shi Ji), Chin Shi Huang Ben Ji, 37th year.

13. Si-ma Qien, Shi Ji, Xiang Yü Ben Ji, tells of Zhang Liang's part in the founding of the Han. For canonical biographies, see TT, vols. 141, 558, 992.

14. TT, vol. 142, chapter 18, p. 1a, line 5.

15. Seidel, Anna, *La Divinisation de Lao Tseu dans le Taoisme des Han* (Paris, 1969), pp. 34-50; Han Shu (HS), *Biography of Han Wu Di*, chapter 6, p. 32a; 103 B.C., 4th-5th month.

16. Master Zhuang insists on the primacy of the apocryphal Ho Tu and the Lo Shu in the transmission of the secrets of orthodox Daoism. The Ho Tu is symbolic of the chart of the Prior Heavens, the eight trigrams of Fu Hsi, and the Ling Bao Five Talismans described in chapter 5. The Lo Shu, the magic square of the Posterior Heavens, or the visible world of change, is symbolic of earth, the eight trigrams of King Wen, and rituals of purification. These two ancient charts are mentioned but not univocally defined in pre-Han sources. Thus the Ho Tu is mentioned in the *Lun Yü*, chapter 9, and the *Shu Jing*, Gu ming chapter (Legge, vol. 3, p. 12).

The Ho Tu and Lo-shu are central themes of the *Gu Wei Shu*, the ancient apocryphal texts, which probably date from the mid-Han period. *I-sho Shu-sei*, a critical work on the apocryphal texts by the Japanese scholar Yasui Kozan has been published, (vols. 2, 3, and 5 appeared in Tokyo in 1975). Citations from the *Gu Wei Shu* used in the following pages are taken from the above and from the *Muo Hai Jin Hu* (*MHCH*), a critical Qing dynasty work on the apocryphal texts. The Ho Tu is an essential part of the orthodox Master's lu, or register, appearing as the tenth in a list of twenty-four registers; see TT, vol. 877, chapter 3, p. 1, and p. 4b, line 6 to p. 7b, line 4. See also notes 123 and 128-130 for Tang dynasty ritual involving the Ho Tu. The Ho Tu is quite diverse; its various forms will be studied in notes 17-38.

17. *Han Guan Yi*, hsia, p. 1a; *Hou Han Shu* (*HHS*), vol. 112, shang, p. 2b; *HHS*, vol. 17, p. 6a.

18. *HHS*, vol. 112, shang, pp. 11b, 14b; vol. 112, xia, p. 1b; vol. 60, shang, p. 5b; vol. 109, hsia, p. 4a. Scholars are seen to study the Ho Tu and Lo-shu, in *HHS*, vol. 112, shang, pp. 1a, 1b, 11b, 14b; vol. 112, xia, p. 1b; vol. 60, shang, p. 5b.

19. The apocryphal texts were condemned during the north-south period by the emperor Wu of Jin, A.D. 267; Xiao Wu Di of the Song in 457; and Xiao Wen Di of the northern Wei. The apocrypha were destroyed during the reign of Sui Yang Di, 604-617. See an earlier work of Yasui Kozan, *I-sho* (Tokyo: Meitoku Press, 1969), pp. 49-50.

20. *MHCH*, p. 4238; *Gu Wei Shu*, chapter 13, Chun Q'iu Ming Li Xü, p. 1b, lines 3-7.

21. *Dokyo no Jittai*, p. 25; TT, vol. 575; TT, vol. 770, chapter 25, p. 1a, lines 3-10.

22. Few modern Daoist masters know of any connection between the ancient apocryphal texts and the rituals of orthodox Daoism. Yasui Kozan, *I-sho* (Tokyo, 1969), pp. 37-50, shows how the apocrypha came to be considered a source of dissent and revolt. One can surmise that the Daoists of the north-south period and the Sui were forced to disassociate such central texts as the San Huang Wen, the Ho Tu, and the Ling-pao Five Talismans from the condemned apocrypha.

23. *Li Ji*, Yüe Ling 礼记，月令 chapter; *MHCH*, pp. 4056-4058; Huai Nan Zi, vol. 3, pp. 5b-6a. The Daoist version of the ritual is the Su Qi, 宿啟 described in chapter 5 notes 81-87.

24. *Dokyo no Jittai*, p. 26; MHCH, pp. 4056-4058; TT, vol. 183, shang, pp. 15a-b.

25. *MHCH*, pp. 4599-4604; *Gu Wei Shu*, chapter 32, Ho Tu Jiang Xiang.

26. *Gu Wei Shu*, Ho Tu Jiang Xiang, chapter 32, p. 8b, line 11 to p. 9a, line 3. *MHCH*, p. 4600, line 9 to p. 4601, line 2. The preceding fragment describes the Yellow River as bending in nine places and guided by nine stars. The two descriptions are complementary: the Ho Tu described with five stars is symbolic of the five elements, while the chart with nine stars depicts the eight trigrams plus the role of emperor or ruler in the center, as in *MHCH*, p. 4286, *Gu Wei Shu*, chapter IS, p. 6b. The fragment describes Fu Xi carving the book of changes, based on the eight trigrams, and using the same with the center position to establish the nine provinces. *MHCH*, p. 4252, *Gu Wei Shu*, chapter 13, p. 8b, lines 2-4, describes the Ho Tu as being a sacred chart depicting the rivers, mountains, and provinces of China, for the use of rulers.

27. *MHCH*, p. 4093; *Gu Wei Shu*, chapter 5, *Zhuang Hou*, p. 4a, lines 3-5, describes the spirit of the Yellow River. The horse-like dragon that carries the Ho Tu out of the river is used as a motif of religious art in the much later Song period. Song and Ming dynasty commentaries on the Yi Jing often picture the dragon-horse coming out of the Yellow River with a series of fifty-five spots on its back, and the tortoise

coming out of the Lo River with forty-five lines on its carapace. The Ho Tu is taken to be a symbol of the eight trigrams of Fu Xi and the Lo Shu the symbol for the eight trigrams of King Wen. See my *Taoism and the Rite of Cosmic Renewal* (Pullman: Washington State University Press, 1972), chapter 3, which describes the commonly held teachings of the Taiwanese Daoists regarding the Ho Tu. Such systematized treatments of the two charts are also found in the popular tong shu almanacs and the manuals of feng shui geomancy. The relationship of the Ho Tu to the Ling Bao Five Talismans is known only to a few Daoist masters who have access to the Daoist Canon.

28. *MHCH*, p. 4602, lines 3-4. The gloss for the corrupt apocryphal text interprets Bao Shan to be Mao Shan.

29. *Ling Bao Zhen Wen*, see TT, vol. 191, *Lu Xiu Jing, Ling Bao Zhong Zhen Wen*, p. 1a, line 10; p. 7a, line 4, *Wu Fang Zhen Wen*; TT, vol. 183, *Ling Bao Wu-fu Xu*, p. 10a, lines 7-8. See also note 36 below.

30. *MHCH*, p. 4602; *Gu Wei Shu*, chapter 32, *Ho Tu Jiang Xiang*, p. 9b, lines 4-5.

31. Ibid., line 5, refers specifically to the chi niao, the red bird or the phoenix, a symbol of the south, seen on the temple rooftops when a Ho Tu is about to be revealed. Confucius denies any knowledge of the red bird or its significance in line 9 of the apocryphal text, thus pointing out Ho Lü's falsehood. P. 9b, lines 6-8, of *Ho Tu Jiang Xiang* contain the poem translated immediately below.

32. The modern versions of the *Yüe Jüe Shu* bear only fragmentary evidence of the above poem; the *Si Bu Cong Kan, Si Bu Bei Yao*, and *Si Bu Kan Yao* editions now have only fifteen chapters of an original sixteen. That the poem did once belong to the *Yüe Jüe Shu* is seen in the quotation taken from the *Zhen Zheng Lun*, note 33 below. The missing *Yüe Jüe Shu* text is quoted in the gloss of the *MHCH*, p. 4603, line 7 to p. 4604, line 6.

33. *Taisho ShinShu Daizokyo*, (Taisho), vol. 52, *Zhen Zheng Lun*, p. 2212a-c; TT, vol. 183, shang, p. 9b, line 9 to p. loa, line 8. *Wu Shang Pi Yao* (WSPY), TT, vol. 777, chapter 83, p. 13b, line 5. In this last text, the chart given to Yü is called the Ling Bao Five Talismans.

34. The *Zhen Zheng Lun* (Taisho, vol. 52, p. 2112) is probably a Tang dynasty text, attributed to the monk Xüan Yi. An even earlier version of the *Yüe Jüe Shu* apocryphal story is found in the fourth-century *Bao Puzi* of Ge Hong, Nei Pian, chapter 13, p. 56, lines 4-7. Ge Hong states that the Ling Bao tradition derives from the magic charts given to Yü, called Zheng Ji, ping heng, and Fei guei Shou Zhi. The first two terms refer to the Pole Star, while the latter are the "flying horse and turtle books or charts"; see the critical work of Max Kaltenmark, "*Ling Bao; note sur un terme du Daoisme religieux*," Mélange Publies par l'Institut des Hautes Etudes Chinoise, 2, 14 (Paris, 1960), pp. 559-5 88.

35. *Taisho*, vol. 52, #2112, p. 564b-c.

36. *Tai Shang Ling Bao Wu Fu Xü*, TT, vol. 183, pp. 6a-11b, line 4. The text is considered by most scholars to be one of the earliest in the Daoist Canon, dating probably from the time of Lu Xiu Jing, mid-fifth century. A lengthy version of the apocryphal story is given, linking the Ho Tu of Yü the Great with the Ling Bao Five Talismans. The words of the text are the basis for the Su Qi ritual, explained in chapter 5, notes 81-86. For a fuller treatment of the Ling Bao Wu fu Xü, see the critical treatment of Chen Guo Fu, *Dao Zang Yüan liu Kao (A Critical Study of the Origins of the Taoist Canon)* (Peking, 1963), p.64.

37. TT, vol. 183, shang, p. 11, lines 1-2. The text is similar to the reference found in the *Bao Puzi*, note 34 above.

38. *Chen Guo Fu*, pp. 62-66.

39. De Groot, J. J. M., *The Religious System of China* (Leiden, 1910), vol. 6, pp.1187-1268.

40. *Fu Jin Jia* (Taipei, 1972) suggests in the *Zhong Guo Dao Jiao Shi* (p. 57, line 8) a possible relationship between the Yellow Turbans and the later Redhead Daoists found at the local level throughout China. See note 11 above.

41. The Daoists do not distinguish themselves by the popular Redhead and Blackhead titles, but rather by the official lu or register given to each master at the time of ordination. Thus Redhead can refer to any of a number of popular Daoist schools, including the San Nai Lii Shan, the Shen Xiao, the Lord Lao, and many others. Daoists who specialize in exorcism cures, and do not know the classical registers of antiquity are called Redhead by the people of modern Taiwan. To Taiwan Daoists, the two terms Blackhead and Redhead distinguish Daoists who follow the canonical tradition from all others. In the city of Zhangzhou and elsewhere, the meanings are different.

42. It is possible to distinguish a literary theme in the early Celestial Master sect in west China, as opposed to the more military Yellow Turbans of east China. Fu Jin Jia suggests in his *Zhong Guo Dao Jiao Shi*, p. 57, line 8, that the Redheads of later times are the descendants of the Yellow Turbans of the Han.

43. Another theory holds that the *Tai Ping Jing* was given first to a late first century B.C. fang-shih, Gan Zhong Ko, from the text in chapter 75 of the *Qian Han Shu*, the biography of Li Shun Lie. The relationship between the earlier Han dynasty book, *Tian Guan Li Bao Yuan Tarping Jing*, and the later Tai Ping Canon,*Taiping Qing Ling Shu*—170 chapters, of which only 57 survive in the Daoist canon— used by Yü Chi is discussed by scholars.

44. TT, vols. 746-755, the present canonical text, has only 119 chapters. See note 46, below.

45. *HHS*, chapter 60.

46. Wang Ping, *Tai P'ing Jing Ho Xiao* (Shanghai, 1960); in this excellent work, the author attempts to restore some of the missing chapters. *Chen Guo Fu*, pp. 82-83; Fukui Kojun, *Dokyo no Kisoteki Kenkyu* (Tokyo, 1958), pp.62-86.

47. See note 113 below; the tenth master of Mao Shan, Wang Yüan Zhi, said to be a practitioner of the Tai Ping Jing style of ritual.

48. See note 44 above. Ling Bao Daoism has since the fifth-century collations of Lu Xiu Jing been considered a part of the orthodox tradition. The Tai Ping Canon, though allied with the more popular Redhead styles of Daoist ritual, seems to have had a deep influence on both orthodox and popular Daoist cults.

49. Zhang Dao Ling is canonized as a patron saint of all Daoists, whatever the sect or order to which a particular master owes allegiance. He is variously credited with writing the Ling Bao Five Talismans, as well as the twenty-four registers of the Zheng Yi Meng Wei order.

50. Wei Shu, *Lieh-chuan*, chapter 8; *HHS*, chapter 105.

51. *Chen Guo Fu*, pp. 98-100.

52. The literary documents sent off by the masters of the Zheng Yi svhool, the Ling Bao school, and the other classical orders seem to have derived from the practices of Zhang Dao Ling. For Chinese versions of these documents as used by Master

Zhuang, see *Zhuang-lin Hsü Dao Zang* (*Zhuang Lin Xu Daozang*, Taipei, 1975), vol. 19.

53. The *Shen Xian Juan* of Ge Hong in ten volumes is frequently quoted in encyclopedias such as the *Tai Ping Guang Ji* and the *Tai Ping Yü Lan*. It is found in the Han *Wei Cong Shu*, ed. by Cheng Rong, 1592 (Taipei: Xin Xing Press, 1959), vols. 38-39. The biography presented here is taken from the Ming dynasty *Li Shi Zhen Xian Ti Dao Tong Jian* (Mirror of Perfected Immortals), TT, vols. 139-149. See Chen Guo Fu, vol. 2, p. 233.

54. The term Ji Jiu 祭酒 libationer of wine, occurs five times in the Yi Li as a ceremony and later in Han times at the title of an official, appointed at the village level. The converts of the first Heavenly Master sect were most probably of the village-gentry class, and the terms Ji Jiu, Gongcao 功曹, (liaison official), Du Jiang 督讲 (chief cantor, person in charge of classic texts) were borrowed by the leaders of the sect from the language of provincial officialdom.

55. See *Taisho*, vol. 52, *Guang Hong Ming Ji*, 2103, *Er Jiao Lun*, p. 141b, line 12; the Buddhist author attributes the entire Ling Bao Canon to Zhang Dao Ling. The passage seems to be over-stated; the Ling Bao five talismans deriving from the apocryphal tradition and the yin-yang five element rituals of the Li Ji were used by the early Heavenly Masters.

56. TT, vol. 563; the *Zheng Yi Fa Wen Tian Shi Jiao Jie Ko Yi*, an early document that can probably be dated to the reign of Cao Pei, ca. 226 (p. 17a, lines (5-6), summarizes the doctrines of the first Heavenly Masters. The twenty-four zhi 治 illustrate the doctrine of the Three Pure Ones as personifications of the three principles; breath, spirit, and vital essence (p. 12a, lines 8-9) and the teachings outlined in the above paragraph are found in the earliest canonical passages.

57. TT, vol. 142, chapter 18, pp. 1-25. See p. 2a, line 1, for the influence of the Ho Tu and Lo Shu on Zhang Dao Ling.

58. See Chen Guo Fu, p. 233, and note 53 above. For other Daoist biographies, also attributed to Ge Hong, see Max Kaltenmark, *Le Lie-sien tchuan (Biographies legendaires des immortels taoiste de l'antiquite)*, (Peking, 1953).

59. *Wei Shu*, jüan 8, biography of Chang Lu.

60. Stein, Rolf, "Remarques sur les movements Daoisme Politico-religieux au IIe Siecle Ap. JC." (T'oung-pao 50, 1963), pp. 1-78.

61. Wei Shu, jüan 8; *HHS*, chapter 101.

62. Levy, Howard, "Yellow Turban Religion and Rebellion at the End of the Han," *JAOS*, 76, 4 (1956), pp. 214-227.

63. See Stein, note 60 above, for the following distinction. Henri Maspero, *Le Taoisme* (Paris, 1967), pp. 149-169, holds that the two movements were the same.

64. The Tai Ping literature influenced the literary as well as the military styles of Daoist ritual. It is used in many of the later Ling Bao rites and influences the tenth master of Mao Shan, Wang Yuan Zhi; see notes 113-114 below. Its use by the Yellow Turbans was definitely associated with the military nature of the sect. Later military Daoists did not necessarily use the Tai Ping materials in their rituals, but present-day Daoist movements continue to classify themselves as literary or military and divide the sacred Tan area used for Daoist ritual into east or literary and west or military divisions. Similarly, Zhuang's elder son A-him was taught the military Dao of the Left (chapter 4) and Tai Ji, Kung-fu, and other methods of physical self-defense. The younger son A-ga was taught to write out the docu-

ments used in the literary Dao of the Right (chapter 5). The two ministries are kept distinct, the military style being a part of the Pole Star or Wu Dang Shan registers (lu) of transmission, the literary style being a part of the orthodox Zheng Yi or Meng Wei registers. One Daoist master can learn both styles, but need not know both for a classical ordination.

65. The three colors Xuan (dark blue or purple), yellow, and white are a basic part of the transmission of the Meng Wei registers and meditations. See chapter 5, the Fa Lu meditation, notes 104-114. The colors are also used in the meditations of the Yellow Court Canon of the Mao Shan Shang Qing sect.

66. See note 56 above for an early Daoist reference to the colors. Also, *Taisho* 52, 2110, Bian Zheng Lun, p. 536c, lines 21-23, for a Buddhist discussion

67. See Chen Guo Fu, p. 88, line 2, for the Tai Ping colors.

68. TT, vol. 639, *Zhen Gao (CK)*, chapter 13, p. 6a, line 3. The masters of the Tang period were ecumenical, or open minded in their use and interpretation of the various styles of meditation, as described below. The sectarian movements of the Song period changed the colors to red, yellow, and white, as can be seen in the *YCCC*, TT, vols. 677-702, chapter 10. These latter color configurations become typical of the Redhead orders, as seen for instance in the liturgical inventions of Lin Ling Su (notes 155-156).

69. Both the orthodox Blackhead Daoists and the popular Redhead Daoists now use the two styles, military and literary, in their rituals. It would be wrong, therefore, to associate military with popular and literary with orthodox Daoist ritual. Rather, the popular Redhead orders tend to stress the exorcistic battle against the evil forces of Yin, while the orthodox Blackhead orders emphasize the meditative aspects of union with the Tao. Conflict is basically outside of the spirit of religious Daoism, and the orthodox movements of the Song dynasty will be seen below to attempt to draw the sectarian movements back into ecumenical harmony.

70. Ge Hong, *Bao Puzi*, chapter 19 lists the basic Daoist manuals known in the area of Luo Fu Shan, southeast China, of his day.

71. The Meng Wei registers and the liturgies of Ling Bao Daoism are slighted by the eccentric Ge Hong, who was more interested in methods of alchemical immortality, than in the popular rituals later propagated by his grandnephew Ko Chao Fu. Tao Hong Jing in the *Deng Zhen Yin Jüe* (TT, vol. 193, hsia, pp. 6a-23b) states that the twenty-four registers were known from the end of the Han period, having been popular in Szechuan with the first Heavenly Masters. See Fa Lu, chapter 5, sect. 6; also notes 86-88 below.

72. Chen Guo Fu, pp. 106-107. The bibliography of Lu Xiu Jing, *San Dong Jing Shu Mu-lu*, a list of books and canons in the San Dong Three Arcana, is no longer extant. References in both Buddhist and Daoist literature prove that it did exit. Thus, according to Chen (p. 106), the first Daoist Canon was in existence by the time of Lu Xiu Jing. Within the next several decades the canon had been expanded to its present seven sections; see Chen Guo Fu, pp. 107-108; Fukui Kojun (Tokyo, 1958), pp. 164-170.

73. *WSPY*, TT, vols. 768-779, published between 561 and 581, shows the basic format of Daoist liturgy to be clearly established. See the discussion of Daoist ritual in chapter 5, notes 94-97.

74. The Su Qi ritual, found in *WSPY*, is modeled after the Yüe Ling chapter of the Book of Rites. See chapter 5, notes 81-86.

75. Scholars agree that the San Dong (Three Arcana) were brought together by the time of Lu Xiu Jing, if not by the great Daoist master himself. Since Lu was a Ling Bao Daoist, the viewpoint of the Ling Bao can be seen in the naming of the three sections, a bias which has confused later scholars piecing together the elements of fourth- and fifth-century Daoist movements. In the following paragraphs I have followed the explanation of Zhuang, derived from his own collection of documents and the oral traditions of Long Hu Shan and Mao Shan which he represents. This interpretation differs from the accepted Buddhist version of the first canon; see *Guang Hong Ming Ji, Taisho*, vol. 52, 2103, *Er Jiao Lun*, p. 141b, lines 16-22. In this version the legendary Ge Xüan is made founder of the Shang Qing tradition, Zhang Dao Ling founder of the Ling Bao tradition, and Bao Jing discoverer of the San Huang texts.

76. For the foundation of the Mao Shan Shang Qing school, see notes 84-88. This paragraph reflects the teachings of Master Zhuang, and the commonly accepted canonical version of the first three Daoist orders; see Chen Guo Fu, pp.1-101.

77. The following chart differs from that of the Chen Guo Fu, p. 28 fold-out, which shows the present content of the Three Arcana as allegedly put together by the early Ling Bao Daoist masters. The Three Arcana were named after the Shang Qing texts, the Ling Bao scriptures, and the San Huang Wen. A chart made according to the names given to the Three Arcana would read:

SHANG QING CANON	LING BAO CANON	SAN HUANG WEN CANON
Yang Xi	Ge Xüan	Bao Jing
Xü Mi	Ge Chao Fu	Ge Hong
Xü Hui		

The Three Arcana canon
Lu Xiu Jing

78. The history of religious Daoism before the formation of the Ling Bao and the Heavenly Master sect is legendary. The three reputed founders, marked in section 2 of the chart with asterisks, have little foundation in historical texts.

79. Zhuang believed, as mentoned in the narration, that the San Huang Wen must have eventually been joined with the Ling Bao and Zheng Yi traditions; there was no major order separately transmitting the Lu registers of San Huang Daoism, as there was an order of Meng Wei Heavenly Master sect or Ling Bao Daoists. Rather, the San Huang Wen were one stage in a series of documents or registers given to Ling Bao and Zheng Yi Daoists, and later to all Daoists in the ecumenical period of the Tang. See chapter 5, note 42; and TT, vol. 772, *WSPY*, chapter 35, p. 2a, where the San Huang Wen is seen as one in a series of texts given to Daoist masters. Zhuang therefore listed the Meng Wei order as the third source for the San Dong Canon, the Ling Bao order in his opinion were teachers of the San Huang Wen.

80. Ge Chao Fu multiplied the Ling Bao scriptures for profit. See notes 90-91 below. Thus the popularity of the Ling Bao Jiao and zhai rituals during this period.

81. Chen Guo Fu, pp. 31-101.

82. The legendary lady Wei Hua Cun was a Meng Wei Daoist libationer (see notes 93-94).

83. Chapter 5, pt. 6.

84. Because the Tang emperors patronized Daoist liturgy, the tendency of Tang dynasty masters was definitely toward the development and propagation of the grand Jiao liturgies of renewal, and the Zhai rites for the dead. See the discussions of Wang Yuan Zhi, Chang Wan Fu, Si-ma Chen Zheng, and Du Guang Ting below. Both the stress on mystic "contemplation of union" for the highest ranks of Daoist masters, and the demands of emperors and people for the colorful rites of renewal diverted the Daoist masters from the heady dangers of metaphysical dispute, which divided the Buddhist sects of the Tang dynasty. Ritual ecumenism typified the Daoist movements of the period.

85. See Tao Hong Jing, *Zhen Gao*, chapter 19, who relates from hearsay the attempts of the elite of the southern kingdoms to acquire the Shang Qing scriptures (notes 93-108).

86. TT, vol. 193, xia, *Deng Zhen Yin Jue* (juan xia), pp. 5b-6a; p. 13a, lines 8- 10; p. 23a, lines 4-6.

87. TT, vols. 768-779. *WSPY*; all of the Jiao and Zhai rituals in this sixth century text begin with the Fa lu and end with the Fu lu, of Zheng Yi Meng Wei Daoist origin.

88. TT, vol. 193, xia, p. 6a, lines 6-9.

89. Chen Guo Fu, pp. 62-71.

90. Ibid., p. 67.

91. Ibid., pp. 68-70.

92. Chen Guo Fu, pp. 31-62; *CK*, chapter 19.

93. The existence and influence of Lady Daoist Wei Hua Cun is doubted, by some scholars who claim the events of her life in the hagiographies of the Daoist Canon are legendary. Chen Guo Fu, pp. 31-32.

94. The Yellow Court Canon is mentioned as a single volume by Ge Hong in chapter 19 of the *Bao Puzi*. It is expanded into two volumes with the revelations of Wei Hua Cun, the earlier wai chüan or "outer" text containing directions for meditation, and the later nei jüan or esoteric (inner) volume containing the new lu or list of spirits' names proper to the Shang Qing order.

95. The work of Chen Guo Fu contains all the references from the Daoist Canon for the biographies of the various Mao Shan masters discussed below. The notes will cite Chen's work alone rather than make cumbersome references to the entire Canon. See Chen, pp. 32-34, for the biography of Yang Xi.

96. Though a number of scholars hold that Yang Xi's revelations were by means of a planchette and possessed-medium visions, it seems to me that this theory must be rejected. First, the possessed medium is neither coherent nor in control during a trance, where the writings of Yang Xi were so beautiful that they aroused the admiration of the meticulous Tao Hong Jing as he collated them more than a century later. Second, the system of meditative alchemy worked out by the Mao Shan masters' is too well defined to have been composed by the random meanderings of a planchette or a medium. Either the Shang Qing scriptures were received by Yang Xi from the son of Wei Hua Cun (Chen, p. 32, line 3) or were composed by Yang and the two Xu's. Third, the masters of the Shang Qing and the Meng Wei traditions have consistently banned the rites of the possessed mediums from their liturgies and considered mediums in trance subjects for exorcism. The Mao Shan

doctrines are intended for meditations of union rather than medium possession, according to the teachings of Master Zhuang.

97. *CK*, chapter 19. The gist of the story recounted by Tao Hong Jing, here summarized, is that the esoteric doctrines of the Shang Qing sect were successfully defended from the incursions of the sixth-century literati. The Mao Shan revelations were collected and hidden in the arcanum of Daoist esoterica to become the highest and most cherished form of meditative practice reserved for the Daoist masters alone. See chapter 5, note 20.

98. TT, vol. 640; *CK*, chapter 19. Chapter 19 contains a record of a highly esoteric tradition, which was collated by Tao from oral evidence some 150 years after the dissemination of the earliest Shang Qing documents.

99. *CK*, chapter 19, p. 11a, lines 5-8.

100. *CK*, chapter 19, p. 11a, line 4.

101. *CK*, chapter 19, p. 11b, lines 5-12a, line 4.

102. *CK*, chapter 19, p. 12b, lines 9-13a, line 1.

103. *CK*, chapter 19, p. 13b, lines 6-7.

104. *CK*, chapter 19, p. 14b, lines 5-7.

105. *CK*, chapter 19, p. 15a, lines 9-15b, line 1.

106. The literati interest in the Shang Qing scriptures was not so concerned with the rituals of religious Daoism as with the new meditative manuals for attaining longevity and immortality, or with the blessing accruing from keeping sacred objects, as in the case of Ma Lang. Even Tao Hong Jing himself can be seen more as a master and scholar than as a ritual expert. The trend away from scholarly collation of canonical scriptures and toward the performance of classical ritual in the public forum can be seen in the following Sui and Tang periods.

07. Chen Guo Fu, pp. 29-30 (foldout).

108. Ibid., p. 41, lines 10-12. CK, chapter 19, p. 15a, lines 9-10.

109. *CK*, chapter 13, p. 13b, lines 2-6.

110. *CK*, chapter 19, p. 1b, lines 4-7.

111. TT, vol. 193, *Deng Zhen Yin Jue*. Only three jüan of an original twenty chapters remain to this important sixth-century work. The first chapter, shang, names the spirits of the microcosm, and the third chapter, hsia, gives a primitive version of the *Fa lu* rite for sending the spirits out of the body.

112. The purpose of the Yellow Court Canon meditations is gradually to refine the spirits within the microcosm until finally the state of void or *hun tun* is reached. See my "Buddhist and Daoist Notions of Transcendence," in *Buddhist and Taoist Studies I* (Honolulu, 1977), chapter 1.

113. Chen Guo Fu, pp. 47-50.

114. Chen Guo Fu, p. 49, lines 2-11.

115. The opinions expressed here are Zhuang's. Daoist masters were hard pressed by the Buddhist monks in the metaphysical disputes held at the imperial court. Whether from the influence of the Laozi DaoDe Jing and the Zhuangzi, which did not support philosophical debate or contention, or the immense success of Daoism in the sphere of liturgy and popular ritual, the great Daoist masters of the Tang period produced very little metaphysical disputation. The majority of Tang dynasty records in the Canon are concerned with ritual or with alchemy and hardly at all with philosophical speculation. The great debates between the Buddhists and the Daoists, the work of court Daoists, such as Kou Qian Zhi of the north-south period,

and the discussions of modern scholars have been left out of the present discussion as not germane to the teachings of Zhuang.

116. Chen Guo Fu, pp. 52-59.

117. *Quan Tang Wen (CTW)*, chapter 924, works of Si-ma Cheng Zhen. The *CTW*, a Qing dynasty compilation, is sometimes considered unreliable; some of the passages attributed to Tang authors are not authenticated. The passage quoted here is found in other canonical sources, and therefore is accepted as a Tang period document.

118. *CTW*, chapter 924, p. 13b, line 7; Zhuangzi, chapter 4, line 28. See TT, vol. 704, Zuo Wang Lun (A treatise on "Sitting in Forgetfulness").

119. TT, vol. 899, *Dao Fa Hui Yüan (TFHY)*, chapter 76, p. 3b, line 9. This Song dynasty text, attributed to Bai Yu Chan (see notes 161-173), states that the thunder rituals of the Qing Jing style involving the pole star to control thunder was taught as early as the Tang dynasty ritual expert Wang Zi Hua through the help of Si-ma Cheng Zhen. The tale is probably legendary, since there is little evidence for the actual systematization of the style before the late Tang dynasty. See notes 136-139.

120. Chen Guo Fu, p. 55, line 5.

121. Eight works are attributed to Chang Wan Fu in the Ming canon. See TT, vols. 77, 563, 990, 278-290, 198, 48, 878, and (bis) 990.

122. TT, vol. 990. Chuan shou San Dong Jing Jie Fa Lu lie shuo, shang.

123. TT, vol. 990, shang, pp. 3b-19a, for the moral precepts (jie), Zheng Yi registers, San Huang Wen, and the Ling Bao writs; TT, vol. 878 *Jiao San Tong Zhen Wen Wu Fa, Zheng Yi Meng Wei Lu Li Cheng Yi*, for the twentyfour registers, including p. 10a, line 2, Ho Tu; TT, vol. 990, *Tung-hsüan Ling Bao Tao-shih shou San-tung ching-chieh Fa-lu tse jih li*, pp. 4b-5b for the order outlined here, including "Precious Ho Tu," p. 5, line 3, and Shang Qing scriptures, p. 5b, line 7.

124. That is to say, the authentic Tang dynasty texts in the extant Daoist Canon all bear the same ritual content outlined by Zhang Wan Fu, i.e., moral precepts, Laozi Dao De Jhing, Zheng Yi Meng Wei twenty-four registers, San Huang Wen and Ling Bao scriptures including the Ho Tu register, and the Mao Shan Shang Qing scriptures. These basic documents are therefore taken to be the core of orthodox religious Daoism, as taught by Master Zhuang in modern Taiwan.

125. See Harvard-Yenching Index series, vol. 25, p. 135.

126. *CTW*, chapter 929.

127. TT, vol. 565, *Tai Shang Zheng Yi Yüe Lu Yi*.

128. TT, vol. 976-983, *Dao Men Ko Fan Da Chuan Zi*, attributed to Du Guang Ting, has passages citing and using thunder-vajra texts; by the end of the Tang period, therefore, the thunder rites were already known at least at the local level. The text was edited by disciples of Du Guang Ting, however, which put its final completion at a later date. See notes 132-139 below, on Thunder Ritual.

129. TT, vol. 565, *Tai Shang Tong Shen Tai Yüan Ho Tu San Yüan Yang Xie Yi*.

130. Chapter 5, part 6, notes 94-125.

131. The mutual influence of Chan (Zen) Buddhism and the Quan Zhen school occurred during the Song period. Vajrayana or Tantric Buddhist rites also mutually influenced the many Daoist forms of thunder ritual. With a few exceptions, the majority of the Song dynasty "reformation" movements were drawn into the ranks of Daoist orthodoxy, as will be seen below.

132. TT, vol. 324, *Tai Shang Chi Wen Tong Shen San Lu*, and TT, vols. 631-636, Jin Suo

Liu Zhu Yin, both recognized as Tang dynasty texts.

133. TT, vol. 324, ibid., Li Xiang Feng, CE 632. Wrongly attributed to Tao Hong Jing, the text shows the clear use of left-handed mudras (p. 14b, lines 2-10), pseudo-Sanskrit mantras (p. 15a, lines 2-7), and the date wood thunder-vajra blocks used to control the spirits of the pole star and of nature in general. The date wood block is later used almost exclusively for thunder magic.

134. A variety of Thunder-vajra schools were in use throughout central and southern China, from Mao Shan to the western peak Hua Shan in Shenxi. The manuals of Li Chun Feng (TT, vol. 324, p. 24b, line 4) sh are similar to the style of ritual described in the *Tai Shang Jie Wen Dong Shen San Lu*, with Hua Shan. *TFHY*, TT, vol. 883 and following, chapters 1-56 describe the registers and rubrics proper to the school. See notes 138-139 below.

135. See chapter 6, pts. 1 and 2.

136. *TFHY*, TT, vol. 899, chapter 76, p. 3b, line 9, relates the legend that Wang Zi Hua learned Qing Jing style thunder rites from Si-ma Cheng Zhen sometime before the An Lu-shan rebellion. The term Qing Jing is also used to describe some of the thunder rites taught by Bai Yu Chan in *TFHY* chapters 76 and 77. Master Zhuang insisted that these rituals are visibly different in content and manner from the "new" Shen Xiao style of the Song innovator Lin Ling Su, for which see 155-160 below. It would be technically inaccurate, therefore, to associate the Daoism of the great Song master Pai Yu Chan (associated with the semi-legendary Wang Tzu-hua) with the popular public rituals of Lin Ling-su, for which see TT, vols. 881-883, for a comparison of styles.

137. TT, vol. 899, chapter 76, p. 3a, lines 7-8.

138. Biographies of Zu Shu are in TT. vols. 75 and 149. Oral traditions still related in modern China call her a late Tang dynasty Taoist master, founder of Qingwei Daoism.

139. The closeness of Qing Wei Daoism to the masters of Zhen Yen Buddhism in west and southwest China is confirmed by the similarity in ritual texts, mudras, and mantras, shared with Buddhist tantric sects and the Daoist thunder ritual. The goddess Marishi-ten is identified in the manuals of the present Heavenly Masters with Dou Mu, the mother goddess of the pole star. The Daoist version of the Goma (Huma) ritual builds a purificatory fire dedicated to Dou Mu (Marishi-ten) and the Gang Shen (Gundari Myo-o, Gun Da Li Miao Wang).

140. Kubo, Noritada, *Chugoku no Shukyü Kaikaku* (China's Religious Reformation, Tokyo, 1967), pp. 7-8.

141. Kubo, pp. 12-13.

142. Jin Yun Zhong, *Shang Qing Ling Bao Da Fa*, chapters 4, 10.

143. Kubo, pp. 40-52.

144. Kubo, pp. 134-150.

145. Kubo, pp. 71-86.

146. The late 64th Heavenly Master granted licenses of ordination to the Daoists of the diaspora based on the manual brought back from Long Hu Shan of Zhuang, and Lin Rumei. The same Ordination manual was personally returned to the 65th Generation Celestial Master in China, per Master Zhuang's final bequest.

147. *Dokyo no Jittai*, pp. 138-139.

148. Ibid., p. 139, lines 7-8.

149. Ibid., pp. 151-154.

150. *Dokyo no Jittai*, pp. 144-151; Akizuki Kanei, "La secte de Hiu Souen et le Tsing-ming tchong-hiao tao," *Dokyo no Kenkyu*, vol. 3 (Tokyo, 1968), pp. 197-146 (article in Japanese).

151. Akizuki Kanei, p. 220, line 11.

152. *Tai Shang Zhu Guo Jiu Min Zong Zhen Mi Yao*, TT, vol. 986, xu, p. 2a, line 7.

153. *Shang Qing Tian Xin Zheng Fa*, TT, vols. 318-319. For pseudo- Sanskrit seed-word mantras, see chapter 1, p. 2a, line 10; for Pole-star exorcism using the Gang spirit (as in chapter 6), see chapter 2, lines 2- 10, et passim; Fu talismans summoning directional thunder, chapter 3, p. 11 b; the pole star is used to control the five thunder spirits, chapter 6, pp. 1a-19b; and the Six Jia and Six Ding spirits, chapter 7, pp. 3a-5a, line 6.

154. The *Tian Xin Zheng Fa* utilizes both Zheng Yi Heavenly Master materials, along with the Bei Ji Pole Star sect exorcisms, in ritual designed to cure colds and bestow popular blessings. The meditations of the Qing Wei Thunder Magic school are distinguished from this and the other popular thunder orders by contemplative style and content.

155. *Song Shi*, vol. 21, *Ben Ji*, pg. 10a, line 8; vol. 421, pp. I2b-I4a (Bo Na Ben edit.).

156. *Li Shi Zhen Xian Ti Dao Tong Jian*, TT, vol. 148, chapter 53, pp. 1a-16a, line 2; see p. 2b, lines 2-4, where Lin is said to have received five thunder magic from the Heavenly Master school. Brilliant but eclectic, he seems to have pieced together his new Shen Xiao magic from many sources, orthodox as well as popular. His colleague, the more orthodox Wang Wen Qing, is generally credited with the written materials in the Canon concerning the Shen Xiao version of ritual. TT, vol. 148, chapter 53, pp. 16a-21a. TT, vol. 900, chapter 76, p. 3a, line 7.

157. *Shang Qing Ling Bao Da Fa*, TT, vol. 963, chapter 10. In this early thirteenth-century work, the meticulous Jin Yun Zhong defends the three early orders, Mao Shan's Shang Qing sect, Long Hu Shan's Zheng Yi sect, and Ge Zao Shan's Ling Bao sect, against all newcomers to the ranks of religious Daoism in the Song. Jin seems especially upset about the Shen Xiao sect, calling its rituals wu-fa (without power, or without dharma) in chapter 10, p. 7b, line 8. He also knows Pole Star and Thunder Rites, while promoting the three ancient orders above all others (pp. 41-19b).

158. Chapter 21, p. 8b, line 3 to 22a, line 5. Jin Yun Zhong explains in this lengthy passage why the colors blue, yellow, and white are orthodox (descending from the time of Lu Xiu Jing and Du Guang Ting) and why the substitution of the color red is a mistake, or heterodox. The use of red vapor or other non-canonical or non-traditional vapors is not only a mistake but vitiates the very purpose of meditative alchemy. Not only the Shen Xiao order of Lin Ling-su was erroneous in this regard before the work of Pai Yu Chan (who corrected many of the aberrations in the Shen Xiao texts), but such texts as the Yun Ji Qi Qian (TT, vols. 677-702, chapter 10) also substituted the colors red, yellow, and white for the traditional deep blue, yellow, and white meditation of union with the Tao. Jin Yun Zhong's point is that the sequence of meditative vapors is in fact a form of reflective alchemy, bringing about union with the Tao. Those who mistake the colors are not performing meditative alchemy leading to union but making a substitute for classical liturgy, for less than orthodox motives.

159. See TT, vols. 881-883, *Gao Shang Shen Xiao Yü Qing Zhen Wang Ci Shu Da Fa*, for an account of Shen Xiao ritual. The lu or list of spirits' names, and the various

ritual formats, are quite different from the Jiao or Zhai rituals of union. For modern examples of Shen Xiao rituals after the influence of orthodoxy, see *Zhuang-lin Hsü Dao Zang* (Zhuang Li Xu Daozang, Taipei, 1975), pt. 4, vols. 21-25·

160. The great Mao Shan center descended from the heights of orthodox splendor and Shang Qing meditative ritual to the lower forms of black magic and popular exorcism sometime between Wang Yuan Zhi in the early Tang period and the popular Lin Ling Su during the Xuan Ho reign years of the Song. "Left" magic (chapter 4), climbing the "thirty-six swords" ladder, and other popular dramatic exorcism are associated with Mao Shan magicians in modern Taiwan and throughout southeast China. For an example of Mao Shan popular magic, see *Zhuang Lin Xu Dao Zang*, pt. 4, vol. 22-24 (Chinese text).

161. TT, vol. 148, chapter 48, p. 16b, line 9 to p. 18a, line 7.

162. *Bai Yu Chan Chuan Ji* (The Complete Works of Bai Yu Chan) (Taipei: Zi You Press, 1969), pp. 1-63.

163. One of Bai's three popular titles was *Shen Xiao San Shi* (Dispeller or "rectifier" of Shen Xiao Daoism); see TT, vol. 148, chapter 48, p. 17a, line 4.

164. TT, vol. 898, (*TFHY*), Chen Xiang Zhen, *Lei Ting Gang Mu Shuo* (An Outline of the Thunder Magic Sects), chapter 66, p. 1a- 10a.

165. The Qing Wei school, from its origins, seems to have mutually influenced Vajrayana style Buddhist ritual (e.g., Siddham Sanskrit). TT, vol. 898, chapter 66, p. 2a, lines 8-10 to p. 2a, line 5, identifies six kinds of Sanskritized thunder ritual, including Dong Zhen, Qing Wei, Ling Bao, and Dong Shen, an early version of which is associated with Mao Shan. See TT, vol. 884, chapter I, p. la, line 4, where Bai Yu Chan claims Ci Xu Yuan Jun (Lady Wei Hua Cun) as one of the founders of the order; see chapter 6 for meditative aspects of thunder ritual.

166. TT, vol. 898, chapter 66, p. 2b, line 6 to p. 3a, line 5.

167. Lin Ling Su is generally credited with teaching and spreading a popular form of local Shen Xiao Daoism, but the Shen Xiao style developed many other variations. See note 180.

168. The documents which Lin Ru Mei brought back from Long Hu Shan between 1868-88 (see chapter 2) indicate that Yü Fu style thunder rites are thought to be proper to the Zheng Yi Heavenly Master school. The Blackhead Daoists of north Taiwan call themselves Yü Fu Daoists. Shenxiao Daoists may receive this register.

169. See TT, vol. 879, for a complete list of the Pole Star registers.

170. TT, vol. 898, chapter 66, p. 9a, lines 4-7.

171. TT, vols. 963-972.

172. TT, vol. 900, chapter 76, p. 3a, lines 1-2.

173. The actual date of the adaptation of this practice is difficult to determine. The present system seems to have been firmly established by the late Song or early Yuan period, though the grading of Daoists by the number and kind of registers they know is seen as early as the sixth-century; *WSPY*, chapter 35.

174. Chen Guo Fu, pp. 175-179. .

175. Selections from the Dao Jiao Yuan Liu and other Mi-chueh are published in the *Dokyo Hiketsu Shusei*, Tokyo: Rukei Press, 1979.

176. See note 168 above. Yü Fu or Jade Pavilion is the esoteric title for the Zheng Yi Heavenly Master sect.

177. The grading from a lowly grade nine to a highest grade one is an obvious imitation of the imperial mandarin ranking system. It is difficult to trace the titles

of the registers as used today earlier than the Song dynasty; see note 173 above.

178. See *Dokyo no Jittai*, pp. 165-187.

179. Zhuang considers the Qing Wei sect to have flourished in Chang An city and nearby Hua Shan in the late Tang period. See notes 138-139 above.

180. TT, vol. 988, *Dao Men Shi Gui*, pp. 10-11, esp, p. 11a, lines 8-10.

181. See *Taoism and the Rite of Cosmic Renewal*, chapter 5.

182. TT, vol. 1016, *The Collected Sayings of Bai Yü Chan*, a Ming dynasty work, attributes to Bai Yu Chan derogatory statements about the popular Lü Shan order. See TT, vol. 1016, chapter 1, pp. 8b-9a.

183. The wrath of Bai Yu Chan is directed against the possessed Wu or medium rituals associated with heterodoxy and vulgar spirits by the traditional orthodox orders, as noted in note 182. The Redhead Daoists of Taiwan often act as interpreters for the possessed mediums, and thus both are often called Shen Xiao Daoists. The reason for this anomaly can be seen in note 184. The Heavenly Masters consistently gave Shen Xiao registers to all local Daoists coming for an ordination or license.

184. The Shen Xiao registers are kept in fifth place, after the four traditional orders —Mao Shan, Qing Wei, Pole Star, and Zheng Yi—as can be seen in the Dao Jiao Yuan Liu, note 175 above. Concerning the present practice in Taipei of giving Shen Xiao ordinations to all local Daoists and foreigners who ask for ordination; a common title for such licenses is Wan Fa Zong, a sort of "bringing together of all traditions" in a mid- to late twentieth-century ecumenism.

185. *Dokyo no Jittai*, p. 187.

186. Not only Taiwan, but other Chinese communities in southeast Asia, and after 1980 China itself, have experienced a renewal of festival custom in the latter half of the twentieth century despite secular industrialization. The popularity of kung-fu (Gongfu), Lion Dance and T'ai-chi (Taiji) exercises in the Chinese communities of the United States is a visible sign of a deeper movement among Asian youth to recover the festive and customary practices of their cultural roots. Chinese religious custom appears to be a means of community identification, and Daoist liturgy is a part of a deep-rooted cultural legacy.

187. See note 115 above.

CHAPTER TWO

1. *Wu Shi Jia Pu* (History of the Wu Clan), 23 folio pages, author's microfilm collection, p. 21.

2. *Hsinchu Tsong Zhi HTZ* (An Historical Gazette of Hsinchu) (Hsinchu city archives, 1946), p. 141.

3. Ibid, biography of Lin Chan-mei, p. 231.

4. *HTZ*, Cheng Huang Temple records, courtesy of Cheng Hung Yüan.

5. *HTZ*, pp. 401-402.

6. *Hsinchu Xian Zhi* (Hsinchu County Gazette) (1955), biography of Lin Ru Mei, vol. 9, pp. 9-10.

7. The Mao Shan Qi Men Dun Jia, the subject of chapter 4, bears the colophon "Lin Shih Mei, 1851, Westgate Villa," thus making Lin Ju Mei about sixteen years old when the book was brought into the family by an elder brother.

8. Field notes, November 1972. Three oral sources testified to the adoption: Chen A-Gong, the son of Chen Jie San; the funeral-wreath maker and son-in-law of Lin

Xiu Mei, Mr. Huang; and Zhuang himself.

9. *Hsinchu Xian Zhi* , vol. 9, p. 9.

10. Diary of Lin Ru Mei, Shu-wen document from the library of Zhuang Chen Deng Yun. Microfilm copy in the author's possession. The date was confirmed by the Hsinchu county archives, courtesy of Mr. Liu Jin Mei.

11. The talisman was originally kept in the red lacquer box hanging over the main altar of the Cheng Huang deity, Hsinchu city. In 1969 it was removed to the private residence of Lin Ru Mei's maternal grandson, Tung, with the datewood thunder block and other paraphernalia of Lin Ru Mei.

12. *Hsinchu Xian Zhi,* vol. 9, p. 10. 1886-1888,1906-1910.

13. The documents of Chen Jie San have been partially published in the *Zhuang Lin Xu Dao Zang* (Taipei, 1975), pt. 3, vol. 19.

14. Chen Jie San, Wen Jian (author's microfilm collection), title page. The descendant of one of the four Daoists, Chen Ding Feng, still performs in Hsinchu city today. See chapter 3.

15. Chen Jie San, *Wen-chien* (author's microfilm collection), p. 22-23, lists eight grades of perfection for women Daoists. Compare TT, vol. 989, *San Dong Xiu Dao Yi*, p. 9a, line 5 to p. I la, line 10, for canonical evidence of Daoist titles of ordination given to women.

16. The Chinese reckon a child to be already nine months old at the time of birth, and add a year to its age at the time of the Chinese New Year Festival. Thus Zhuang was sixteen in 1926.

17. Author's field notes, Nov. 6, 1972. The Cheng Huang temple committee, the funeral wreath maker Huang, and Chen A-Gong recall the event. Master Zhuang is noncommittal on the subject.

18. See Song Yin Zi Zhu, *Huang-t'ing Wai-ching* (Taipei: Zi You Press, 1959); and *Huang Ting Jing Zhu*, from the library of Lin Xiu Mei, author's microfilm collection.

19. TT, vol. 636, CK, chapter 2, p. 2b, lines 4-5.

20. The Teachings of Master Zhuang are published in the *Zhuang Lin Xu Dao Zang* (Taipei, 1975), Chinese text. This twenty-five-volume collection contains only the tradition of the Jiao festival of renewal (Jüan 1-50), the Zhai liturgies of burial (Jüan 51-71), the mi jüe 秘訣 rubrics meant for oral transmission (jüan 72-82) and the Shen Xiao and Lü Shan versions of Daoist ritual (jüan 82-103). Being prepared for publication are the teachings of Master Zhuang on Thunder and Bei Dou Ritual (chapter 6) and the military Dao of the Left (chapter 4).

CHAPTER THREE

1. Since the role of the Daoist, whether Blackhead or Redhead, is associated with sickness, death, or the rectifying of natural disaster, the very ministry of the Daoist elicits unpleasant associations. In the ministry of internal alchemy, bodily exercise, and gymnastics, however, the associations are pleasant and definitely of positive value. The taboo against mentioning the family Daoist, therefore, applies only to those masters who specialize in exorcism or burial. One of the major themes in chapter 3 is the association of the elite classes with meditative ritual, as opposed to the popular public ritual of curing, exorcism, and burial. Many Daoists in this chapter will be seen to seek enough affluence to practice private meditation and leave the ministry of public ritual.

2. The practitioners of medium possession and their interpreters are usually said to be members of the Lü Shan sect, or more exactly, the Lü Shan San-nai 閭山三奶 (Three Sisters) school. There may or may not be a relationship between the Lü Shan sect condemned by Bai Yu Chan in chapter 1 and the Fujian-based Lü Shan Three Sisters sect so popular in Taiwan. The Taiwanese Lü Shan Daoists are considered a branch of the Shen Xiao order, because they are given Shen Xiao titles of ordination when they approach the Heavenly Master for a license. See chapter 1, notes 184-185.

3. British Museum, OR/12673. This collection of Daoist ritual manuscripts was brought to London in 1872 from Fujian, and contains rituals identical to those used by the Daoists of Hsinchu, Tainan, Gaoxiung, and other cities of Taiwan.

4. The Taipei Ricci Institute copy of the Daoist Canon was kindly loaned to the project by the Rev. Yves Raguin, S. J., and was used by Zhuang during a portion of the study. The *Wu Shang Bi Yao* (TT, vols. 768-779) was the basis for much of Zhuang's instruction in chapter 5.

5. See bibliography of works in Japanese for the titles. Zhuang was delighted with the work of Maspero and amazed that a foreigner could derive so much from the Canon.

6. Oct. 16, 1972. See chapter 6, notes 46-48.

7. Oct. 15, 1972.

8. Dec. 2, 1967, field notes.

9. U.S.$12.50, in 1967-68.

10. See my "Orthodoxy and Heterodoxy in Daoist Ritual," where this rite is described in more detail. See also *Religion and Ritual in Chinese Society* (Stanford, 1974), pp. 325-336.

11. The Su Qi is described in chapter 5, notes 81-87. The text can be found in *Zhuang Lin Xu Dao Zang* (Taipei, 1975), vol. 5, pp. 1321-1379.

12. Chapter 6, note 48, and chapter I, notes 25-38.

13. See chapter 4, for the ritual of the six Jia spirits.

14. See note 13 above.

15. Dec. 5-10, 1970.

16. The rituals of renewal are performed according to the time of the day that corresponds to the purpose and title of the rite. Thus the Su Qi usually starts before midnight, the Morning Audience before dawn, the Noon Audience before noon, and the Night Audience before sunset.

17. See chapter 6, pt. I, sec. iv.

18. The mother goddess of the Pole Star, Dou Mu, is also patron of the martial arts, and under her Sanskrit name Marishi-ten she reigns as one of the patron spirits of Ninjitsu military techniques in Japan. The Heavenly Master maintains the registers of Marishi-ten and transmits the popular Rite to the Pole Star and Big Dipper, Pei Dou, in her honor.

CHAPTER FOUR

1. The Tao of the Right will be the subject of chapter 5. The Daoist master usually begins the novice's instruction with the playing of the musical instruments and by having him assist at classical ritual as an acolyte. The meditations of inner alchemy are reserved for the exclusive inner coterie, including the master's own sons, who

are to receive a title of ordination.

2. The ministry of military Daoism is divided into two separate titles: first, the spiritual ministry of exorcism and breath control; and second, the external practice of t'ai-chi ch'uan, kung-fu, ch'i-kung, and the other techniques of self-defense and bodily exercise and health. Since these latter techniques are also used in rituals of exorcism and purification, the young Daoist is required to perfect himself in military techniques.

3. The two ministries, wen 文 or literary and wu 武 or military, are preserved as distinct ritual styles by the masters of orthodox Daoism in Taiwan.

4. The mudras, mantras, and meditations are usually a part of the kou jüe 口訣 or oral secrets passed on by the master. Zhuang's library of written instructions was indeed rare among the Daoists of Taiwan. The manuals in Zhuang's collection are listed in the bibliography, and are in the author's microfilm and printed photo files.

5. As will be seen below, the title Qi Men Dun Jia (Marvelous Method for Hiding or Commanding the Six Jia Spirits), is a deliberate misnomer given to hide the actual contents of the manual. The title should read Register (lu) of the Six Jia Spirits.

6. See chapter 2, note 1.

7. The manual is named after Mao Shan in Jiangsu province, but belongs in genre or style of magic to the tradition of Wu Dang Shan; see chapter 1, note 5. The preface states clearly that legendarily the founder of this style of military magic is Zhu-ge Liang, and the area of composition is Wu Dang Shan in Hubei province. Zhuang's book is a Ming dynasty compilation from earlier sources. There are a dozen or so mentions of Dun Jia magic in the Ming dynasty canon, as in TT, vols. 576, 580, 857, 873.

8. See below, figure 1, for the Ba Zhen Tu.

9. *Qi Men Dun Jia*, Zhu Lin Press (Hsinchu, 1957); the pamphlet can be purchased at the temple.

10. This passage, including the quotes and the explanations, are taken directly from vol. 1 of the four-volume Qi Men Dun Jia register. References in the following pages will be given to specific charts or sections; *CMTC*, 3a.

11. *CMTC*, 3b-4a.

12. *CMTC*, 5a-5b, for the figures and diagrams.

13. *CMTC*, 6a-6b, for part 3. Note that figure 5 is a *Ho Tu*, as in chapter 6, note 48.

14. *CMTC*, pp. 7a-8b, including the instructions for making the seal.

15. *CMTC*, pp. 9a-10b.

16. *CMTC*, pp. 11a-15b, for the talismans and conjurations.

17. *CMTC*, pp. 16a-19b, for the twenty-eight constellations.

18. *CMTC*, pp. 9a-9b, for the great standard.

19. *CMTC*, pp. 21a-23b, for the *lu* or description of the six Jia spirits.

20. *CMTC*, pp. 23 b-24a, for the layout of the altar.

21. The following pages are a translation of the entire second volume of Zhuang's manual, with field notes taken in 1969, 1970, and again in 1972 with Zhuang in Hsinchu City. The manual is in the author's microfilm collection.

22. *CMTC*, vol. 2, 5a-5b; field notes, Oct. 12, 1972.

23. The above rubrics are used by the Redhead Daoists for the Kai Guang or "opening the eyes" ceremony to bless a new statue, or initiate a Jiao rite of renewal. The rite definitely belongs to the popular style of Daoist ritual as opposed to the stately Dao of the Right, in chapter 5.

24. See Sui Shu; Lie Juan; the fourth son of Sui Wen Di, was reduced to the state of a commoner for practising Zuo Dao, the "Dao of the Left" (or "Sinister Dao").

CHAPTER FIVE

1. Zhuangzi, chapter 4, p. 1, line 26; TT, vol. 207, Zhai jie Lu, p. 1b, line 1; p. 1b, TT, vol. 704, Zuo Wang Lun (坐忘论).

2. TT, vols. 768-779, WSPY, chapter 52.

3. WSPY, chapters 53, 54·

4. WSPY, chapter 50.

5. TT, vol. 704, Tang, Si-ma Cheng Zhen, Zuo Wang Lun; TT, vol. 641, Tao-shu, chapter 2, pp. 1a-8b.

6. See Zhong Guo Xüe Zhi (Tokyo, 1968, vol. 5), Li Xien Zhang, pp. 213-224; TT, vol. 878, Zhang Wan Fu, Jiao San Dong Zhen Wen. Also, Sui Shu, Jingji Zhi, Dao Zhing Shu Lu for an early definition of Daoist ritual and the Jiao; quoted by Li Xian Zhang, p. 214.

7. See TT, vol. 209, Ji Du Jin Shu, chapter 2, p. 2a, line 8 to p. 35a, line 4, for an exhaustive list of Jiao and Zhai liturgies, according to daily scheduling of rituals. Compare Zhuang Lin Xü Dao Zang (Taipei: Cheng-wen Press, 1975) 25 vols., pt. 1, vols. 1-50, for a modern five-day Jiao as performed by Master Zhuang in Taiwan.

8. See note 7 above. The Jiao festivals of modern Taiwan follow the general order of the classical fifth- and sixth-century Jiao, but add many of the popular and dramatic Song dynasty rituals attributed to the Shen Xiao Redhead order. For a description of Redhead ritual, see John Keupers, "Daoist Exorcism," in Buddhist and Taoist Studies (Honolulu, 1977), vol. 1, chapter 5.

9. Jiao thus retains its earliest meaning, the offering of wine and incense in a sort of "pure" sacrifice at the end of each ko yi 科仪 orthodox ritual of union.

10. Zhuang Lin Xü Dao Zang, pt. 1, chapters 32-39, for examples of jing or canonical readings; compare TT, vols. 527-529 for similar canons dedicated to the Pole Star. The formats of the canons are similar to the sutras read by Buddhist monks, and are obvious imitations of Buddhist ritual chant.

11. Zhuang Lin Xü Dao Zang, pt. 1, chapter 50.

12. Li Xian Zhang, pp. 225-231. See note 6 above.

13. Laozi, Dao De Jing, chapter 42.

14. See Saso, Michael, "Buddhist and Daoist Notions of Transcendence," Buddhist and Taoist Studies (Honolulu, 1977), chapter 1.

15. Huang Ting Jing Zhu (Taipei, 1959), vol. 2, p. 21b, line 6. There are two locations of Qi breath. The commonly accepted version locates ordinary breath in the lungs, or chest. The elite esoteric version from the Yellow Court Canon and the Mao Shan Shang Qing tradition puts the residence of Qi, life breath, seen as Primordial Heavenly Worthy, in the Ni Wan palace of the brain (the pineal gland, microcosmic equivalent of the heavens). The two breaths are complementary —that is, the purple-blue vapor of primordial breath is refined in the Yellow Court (the center of gravity in the body); to do this, the vapor of wood (blue-green, liver) and fire (red, heart) are mixed and refined in the Yellow Court, and become the deep purple-blue primordial spirit, named Yüan Shi Tian Zun, who is then sent to reside in the Ni-wan palace in the brain. In the orthodox religious interpretation taught by Master Zhuang, the principles are interpreted to be spirits. The spirits are to be refined, or exteriorized, until Hun Dun total simplicity is achieved, Hun Dun is what Zhuang-

zi called Xin zhai zuo wang 心斎坐忘，or mind and heart totally voided, which precedes union with the transcendent "Dao of Wu Wei."

16. Kaltermark, Max, "Ling Bao: Note sur, un terme du Daoisme Religieux," *Melanges Publies par l'Institut des Hautes Etudes Chinoises* 2 (Paris, 1960), pp. 559-588.

17. The above paragraphs relate the basic cosmology of religious Daoism, as taught by the Heavenly Master sect and transmitted by Master Zhuang. See TT, vol. 563, *Zheng Yi Fa Wen Tina Shih Jiao Jie ko yi*, pp. 13b-21b.

18. See Saso (Honolulu, 1977), ch. 1, p. 25, table 1.

19. See *JiLu Tan Qing Yüan Ko* (Long Hu Shan, 1868), collection of the Heavenly Master (*Dao Jiao Mi Jue Ji Cheng*, 道教秘诀集成 Tokyo: 1979), pp. 31a-33b.

20. Ibid., p. 33b. See also the Dao Jiao Yüan Liu, private Daost Master's manual, pp. 127-132.

21. Daoists lower than grade six do not know the meditations of union, and are not given the oral secrets for performing the Fa Lu (pt. 6 below).

22. Chapter 6, notes 12 and 13.

23. Field notes, Nov. 1972, (Hsinchu City, Taiwan).

24. Field notes, Oct.-Nov. 1972. The WSPY (TT, vol. 768-779) was used by Zhuang throughout the lessons, loaned by Rev. Yves Raguin, S. J., Ricci Insitute Library, Taipei.

25. *WSPY*, paraphrase of chapter 24, p. 2b.

26. *WSPY*, chapter 24, p. 3a, line 10 to p. 3b, line 6.

27. *WSPY*, chapter 24, p. 4a, lines 5-7 to p. 4b, line 6.

28. "Long Han" is the esoteric term for the state of primordial chaos, or Hun Dun; the period of gestation from the Transcendent Dao to the T'ai-chi (Taiji) is seen to be completed in five stages, presaging the Ling Bao five talismans, and ritually enacted in the Su Qi; notes 30-33 below.

29. *WSPY*, chapter 24, p. 4b, line 3.

30. *WSPY*, chapter 24, p. 4b, lines 3-4. Thus a feudal treaty is made between the Daoist and the heavenly worthies, using the five talismans as symbol of enfeoffment.

31. The talismanic writings of the fang shi seem to have preceded the coming of Buddhist sutras and Sanskrit from India; the Daoists of the north-south period claimed a Daoist origin even to the Buddhist teachings. See Fukui Kojun, *Dokyü no Kiso teki Kenkyu* (Tokyo, 1963), pp. 267-283, the Hua Hu Ching controversy; also *Dokyo no Jittai*, pp. 75-78.

32. *WSPY*, chapter 24, p. 4b, lines 7-10.

33. Ibid. The process is performed in ritual meditation during the Su Qi ritual, on the first evening of the five-day Jiao, in Zhuang's version of the liturgy. See *Zhuang Lin Xü Dao Zang*, part 1, chapter 20.

34. *WSPY*, chapter 24, pp. 7b-15a, line 6.

35. This phrase and the following (note 36) are to be identified, in Zhuang's interpretation, with the Ho Tu, in the Ling Bao Five Talisman form.

36. Another term for the Ho Tu, or the Ling Bao Five Talismans.

37. The twenty-four solar interstices, which correspond to the twenty-four registers of the Meng Wei or Zheng Yi teachings; see TT, vol. 878, *Zheng Yi Meng Wei Lu*.

38. The term means "union with the Tao." Thus the Zhen Ren真人 means the man or woman who has realized union through the Ling Bao ritual meditation.

39. The influence of the Tai Ping canon is seen in the concluding line of the *WSPY*

text. The Ling Bao Five Talismans bring the "Great Peace."

40. Field notes, Dec. 1967; Nov.-Dec. 1970; Oct.-Nov. 1972. The order of instruction is outlined in WSPY, chapter 35, p. 2a-b.

41. The *WSPY*, a Ling Bao text, puts the San Huang Wen in third place; the Meng Wei or Zheng Yi tradition of Master Zhuang puts the doctrines of the Three Pure Ones (San Qing) in this spot. Though the ritual order is the same, the colors of the vapors and the directions are different; see *WSPY*, chapter 38. The San Huang vapors are brown, white, and green, while the San Qing vapors are green, yellow, and white. The descriptions of the San huang are also significantly different (see chapter 43, pp. 7b-8a). The ritual that Zhuang calls Dao Chang or Zheng Jiao (*Zhuang Lin Xü Dao Zang*, pt. 1, chapter 48) is structurally the same as WSPY, chapter 49, San huang Zhai, with only the names of the San huang changed to the San Qing. Thus the difference in emphasis between the two orders, the Ling Bao order of *WSPY* and the Meng Wei order of Zhuang, is minimal, the emphasis shifting from the San huang Wen to the San Qing in the third stage of meditative alchemy. See notes 73-75 below.

42. The present order of the Heavenly Master school at Long Hu Shan, as can be seen in the references cited in note 19 above, uses the chart supplied here by Master Zhuang, rather than the order of *WSPY*, chapter 35. That is, the San Qing or the ritual of the Three Pure Ones supplants the San huang Wen as the third step in the order of transmission. But Zhuang was able to perform both versions, in his daily meditations, and passed on the esoteric teachings of the San Huang Wen in the last days before his death, in 1976. See notes 20 and 21, where the present practice is outlined more clearly. The Qing Wei Thunder Magic registers are inserted from the Song dynasty on, between the highest Yellow Court Canon, and the lower Meng Wei and Ling Bao registers. Thus, for Zhuang, the Yellow Court Canon is the highest, after which comes the Qing Wei Thunder Magic register, the Meng Wei registers, and finally the Ling Bao registers.

43. The esoteric secrets are technically passed on only from father to son, as can be seen in the Xüan Du Lü Wen, TT, vol. 7S. Possession of the canonical texts, however, constitutes the right of the disciple to seek a master and to receive instruction in Daoist esoteric meditation. Thus possession of the Ko Yi texts presupposes transmission, and allows the scholar-disciple access to the kou jüe oral explanations of the master.

44. Field notes, Oct.-Nov. 1972. Zhuang explicitly allowed the Zhuang Lin Xü Dao Zang to be published for the sake of preservation. The Mi jüe written transmission of oral secrets are in the author's microfilm collection and are being prepared for publication. See the bibliography for the Thunder Ritual titles and holdings of the Heavenly Master.

45. *WSPY*, chapter 35, p. 6a, line 10 to p. 8a, line 5.

46. Thus the vulgar form of fang-zhong sexual hygiene techniques are forbidden by the higher grades of esoteric Daoism.

47. *WSPY*, chapter 38, quoting the Ming Zhen Ko, p. 11b, lines 1-6.

48. *WSPY*, chapter 46, p. 7a, lines 3-6.

49. Zhuang did not observe this precept, except when performing ritual meditation.

50. Zhuang was not given a grade two ordination, but was kept at a grade four by Lin Xiu Mei; see chapter 3.

51. *WSPY*, chapter 46, p. 14b, lines 1-3.

52. *WSPY*, chapter 47, p. 3a, lines 1-8.

53. *WSPY*, chapter 47, p. 3a-3b.

54. The five organs plus the gall bladder.

55. Saso, *Taoism and the Rite of Cosmic Renewal* (1972), chapter 2.

56. Ong-ia (Amoy dialect) or Wang-yeh rite for expelling the demons of pestilence. This ritual belongs to the Shen Xiao style of liturgy, and is performed throughout Taiwan, especially in the coastal fishing villages.

57. Ninth lunar month, ninth day, in honor of Marishi-ten, or Dou Mu, mother goddess of the Pole Star. See the Bibliography, author's private collection.

58. Though some of the Daoists in southern Taiwan perform the Su Qi ritual without the Three Audiences and the Zheng Jiao, or by reversing the required order, the process of ritual alchemy requires that all five of the Ko Yi rites of union be performed in succession. Thus at least three days and nights are required to perform a Jiao.

59. See *Zhuang Lin Xu Dao Zang*, introduction, pp. 16-17, for the list of rituals. Also, TT, vol. 209, as in note 7 above.

60. The ritual items marked with an asterisk derive for the most part from the Shen Xiao style of liturgy for which Lin Ling Su was so famous. The rituals are dramatic and entertaining to watch. The unmarked rituals or "canons" do not require an ordained Daoist to perform, and can be read by lay experts or local fang-shi if a Daoist is not present.

61. The Fen Deng has been exhaustively treated by K. M. Schipper, *Le Fen-teng, Rituele Taoiste* (1975).

62. Chong Bai, re-inviting the spirits, varies with each Daoist master. For Zhuang's version, see Zhuang Lin Xu Dao Zang, pt. 1, chapter 21.

63. These texts are not included in the Ming-dynasty canon.

64. For the Buddhist influence in these texts, see Kamata, Shigeo, *Chugoku Bukyo Shiso Shi Kenkyu* (1965), pp. 53-56.

65. The version of the Zheng Jiao used by the Daoists of southern Taiwan and the Shen Xiao tradition is different from that used by Zhuang in the Meng Wei tradition. For Zhuang's version, see note 41 above.

66. The rite for climbing the "thirty-six sword ladder" is popular throughout Taiwan, and must be ascribed to the Shen Xiao dramatic tradition. Volume 50 of the *Taisho Tripitaka* shows cases of Buddhist and Daoist monks of the Tang period competing in the height of sword ladders and the sharpness of blades used in display of supernatural powers. The rite probably comes from India and is not a part of the orthodox tradition.

67. See Keupers, John, "Daoist Exorcism," *Buddhist and Taoist Studies* 1, chapter 4, for a description of this rite.

68. Even the most orthodox of Daoist masters must accede to the wishes of the local populace in performing the Jiao festivals of renewal. See Schipper, Op. Cit., p. 11.

69. The Shen Xiao order in particular was accused of changing both the content and the externals of Jiao ritual, as described in chapter 1. Aside from the usages of the Shen Xiao order, however, the program of the Jiao as performed by Zhuang has remained relatively unchanged since the Tang period.

70. The following order is used by the Daoists of Honolulu in the annual Pu Du celebrated at the Guan Yin temple, and the Lum Sai Ho Tang. 71. See Pang, Duane,

"The Pu Du ritual," *Buddhist and Taoist Studies 1*, chapter 5.

72. TT, vol. 282, *Wu Shang Huang Lu Da Zhai Li Cheng I*, chapter 17, p. 7a, line 9.

73. The Latin term is used in theology to describe the sacramental rites of Roman Catholicism. The proper execution of the words and the intention (ex opere operato) and the devotion and perfection of the priest performing the rite (ex opere operantis) are distinguished in Daoist grades of perfection.

74. *Zhuang Lin Xu Dao Zang* (1975) Pt. 3, vol. 19, pp. 5367, 5441.

75. Ibid., pt. 1, vol. 5, pp. 1355-1361; WSPY, chapter 53, pp. 1b-2b.

76. *WSPY*, chapter 83, p. 13b, line 5.

77. Thus, the numbers of the Ling Bao Five Talismans do not correspond to the equivalent symbols used in the Three Audiences. This discrepancy can only partially be accounted for by Zhuang's explanation. The following sets of numbers are used in the two systems:

Symbol	east	south	center	west	north
Su Qi	9	3	1	7	5
Audiences	3	2	5	4	1

According to Zhuang's interpretation, the numbers of the Su Qi are symbolic of the primordial gestation of the Ling Bao Five Talismans, as described in the *WSPY* at the beginning of the chapter. The numbers of the Three Audiences are symbolic of the workings of the five elements in the visible world of the "posterior heavens," that is, within the microcosm. It is also possible that the first set of numbers represents the Ling Bao tradition, while the second set derives from the Meng Wei tradition, and the Yellow Court Canon.

78. The explanation of meditative alchemy in the following paragraph can be found in the *Shang Qing Ling Bao Da Fa of Jin Yün Jing*, TT, vol. 963-972, chapter 21, pp. 5b-9b. It is also found in the *Huang Ting Jing Zhu*, chapter one and two, 8b-22b.

79. The explanation of the Dao Chang given here belongs to the Meng Wei or Zheng Yi Heavenly Master sect tradition. See note 41 above.

80. *Zhuang Lin Xu Dao Zang* (1975), 25 volumes.

81. The Fa Lu occurs throughout the *WSPY*, and in all of the early canonical passages describing the ko yi rites of union. It can thus be safely established as one of the earliest rites in orthodox Daoist liturgy. The *Deng Zhen Yin Jue of Tao Hong Jing*, an early sixth-century text (TT, vol. 193, hsia, pp. 61-pb) describes the rite and associates its use with Han Zhong, the area in Szechwan where the first Heavenly Master spread his doctrines.

82. TT, vols. 877-878 contain the various lu, or registers, used since the Tang dynasty and continuing in the oral transmission of the Daoist masters until the present. The lu transmitted by Master Zhuang is identical with the text of the *Tai Shang San Wu Zheng Yi Meng Wei Lu*, TT, vol. 877; Zhang Wan Fu, (TT, vol. 900), and Du Guang Ting, (TT, vol. 566).

83. The Fu lu is found in the passages described in note 81, and always accompanies the Ko Yi ritual meditations as the concluding rubric.

84. The three oral "secrets" listed here are not found in writing, but are included in the mi jue doctrines taught by the master in preparation for Jiao ritual. Field notes, Oct.-Nov. 1972.

85. Bao Go, and San Jiao below, are terms from Chinese medicine. In religious Daoism Bao Go refers to the shoulders, or the lymphatic glands, and San Jiao to the "three channels" in the belly.

86. For the Chinese text, see *Zhuang Lin Xu Dao Zang*, pt. 1, chapter 49, the *Chu Juan* or novice's manual used to teach the names and cyclical days for summoning the Gong Cao messengers.

87. TT, vols. 278-290, *Wu Shang Huang Lu Da Zhai Li Cheng Yi*, chapter 16, pp. 2b-5a; chapter 17, pp. 7a-8a, line 8; chapter 32, pp. 11b, line 6 to p. 12b, line 10. The text used is from *Zhuang Lin Xü Dao Zang*, pt. 1, chapter 48, *Dao Chang*, pp. 3755-3757. The explanations of Zhuang are from oral notes, Dec. 1970, Oct.-Nov. 1972, and from the written manual *Chu Juan* cited in note 86 above. Comparative notes can be found in the *Dao Zang Ji Yao*, vol. 4, *Kang*, chapter 7, pp. 27a-28b. The earliest use of left-handed mudras as indicated in the text can be found in the Song dynasty work Ling Bao Ling Jiao Ji Du Jin Shu (TT, vol. 210), chapter 9, p. 4a, line 7 to p. 4b, line 2.

88. The Six Jia spirits used by the orthodox Tao of the Right are not the same as the terrifying demons described in chapter 4.

89. The following pages are oral tradition, and are not found in written form with such clarity of detail in the published Daoist canon.

90. *Dao Zang Ji Yao*, vol. 4, chapter 7, p. 27a.

91. *Ji Lu Tan Qing Yüan Ko*, Long Hu Shan, 1868, collection of the Heavenly Master. Ordination manual, private collection of the author, pp. 39-45·

92. *Zhuang Lin Xü Dao Zang*, pt. 1, chapter 14, p. 3874.

CHAPTER SIX

1. Extreme caution must be taken not to identify with one side or the other in the controversy over the orthodoxy of the Thunder Magic orders. The teachings of Master Zhuang regarding the various expressions of tantric Daoism are based on the criteria of meditative union and observance of the lu registers of antiquity. Thus in rejecting the popular Shen Xiao style of magic attributed to Lin Ling Su, Zhuang did so simply because the rituals of the order were devoid of the meditative alchemy transmitted in the Yellow Court Canon tradition and because the registers (lu) of the Shen Xiao Daoists summoned spirits considered impure, unorthodox, or improper to the meditations of union. Qing Wei Thunder Magic will be used by Zhuang at the end of the present chapter to purify the microcosm and macrocosm in order to make orthodox ritual effective.

2. The vajrayana or tantric Buddhist sects of the Tang period had a deep influence on Shingon and Tendai Buddhism in Japan, but seemed to diminish in importance in China after the Yuan or Mongol period, when it was patronized by the Mongol emperors. The mudras and pseudo-Sanskrit mantras of Daoist Thunder Magic are obviously exchanges with the vajrayana schools of Buddhism (note 6).

3. TT, vols. 884-941, *Dao Fa Hui Yuan (TFHY)*, is the classical canonical treatise on Thunder Magic, containing descriptions of the various sects that flourished during the late Tang and the Song. The dynastic histories do not take notice of Thunder Magic sects before the Song period.

4. Akizuki Kanei, "La secte de Hiu Souen et Ie Tsing-ming tchong-hiao tao," *Dokyo no Kenkyu* (1968, article in Japanese), chapter 3, pp. 197-246.

5. TT, vol. 197, *Xü Zhen Jun Xian Juan*; and TT, vol. 200, *Xi Shan Zhen Jun Ba-shi-wu*

Hua Lu. Both are considered Song dynasty works.

6. Compare TT, vol. 900, *TFHY*, chapter 96, pp. 35a-38a, with *Taisho* 21, #1265, p. 295a and b; #1269, p. 297, et passim.

7. The Qing Wei sect, a descendant of the Mao Shan order, flourished in west China, Hua Shan, and the city of Chang-an. The "old" Shen Xiao or "fire-master" sect flourished on Heng Shan, the southern peak, and Mount Tian Tai. The popular Shen Xiao order flourished in Chekiang and Fukien and is prevalent in modern Taiwan.

8. See Bibliography, author's microfilm collection.

9. *TFHY*, TT, vol. 884, chapter 1, p. la, line 5; Ci Xu Yuan Jun is Wei Hua Cun; see TT, vol. 884, chapter 2, p. 6b, lines 7-8, Ci Xu Wei Yuan Jun, Hua Cun.

10. See Bibliography, author's microfilm collection. Chapter 1, notes 162-163.

11. See chapter 1, note 181. TT, vol. 988, *Dao Men Shi Gui,* p. 11a, lines 8-10.

12. TT, vol. 898, *TFHY*, chapter 66, p. 9a, line 4.

13. TT, vol. 900, *TFHY*, chapter 76, p. 3a, lines 1-3.

14. *Ji Lu Tan Qing Yüan Ko* (Long Hu Shan, 1868), pp. 33-39.

15. Michel Strickmann, "The Thunder Rites of the Song-Notes on the Shen Xiao Sect and the Southern School of Daoism," *Toho Shukyo*, no. 46 (1975), pp. 15-28. (Article in Japanese, tr. Abe Michiko.)

16. K. M. Schipper, *Le Fen-teng, Rituel Taoiste* (1975), p. 39, note 12.

17. TT, vol. 324, *Tai Shang Chi Wen Dong Shen San Lu, Li Chun Feng,* (colophon, A.D. 623). TT, vols. 621-635, *Jin Suo Liu Zhu Yin, Tang, Li Xiang Feng.*

18. TT, vol. 900, *TFHY*, chapter 76, p. 9a, lines 5-8.

19. *Hua Shan Mi-chüeh*, Fujian, Qing Lin Guan; author's microfilm collection, from the library of Wu Jing Chun, 1821.

20. See Bibliography, author's microfilm collection, for the titles of the Thunder Vajra manuals of the Celestial Master. For the following passage, the manual *Qing Wei Qi Jüe*, with the commentary of Master Zhuang, Oct.-Nov. 1975, is used as reference.

21. Han Shu, death of Wang Mang. Wang Mang is seen to climb the palace pavilion and face the Yüe Jian position before death. *HS*, chapter 99, p. 27a.

22. TT, vol. 638, *CK*, chapter 9, p. la, lines 5-8.

23. TT, vol. 900, *TFHY*, chapter 77, pp. 13b-14b.

24. See Saso, *Taoism and the Rite of Cosmic Renewal*, pp. 67-72.

25. See note 20 above. The following passages are taken from the manual, with Zhuang's commentary, field notes, Oct.-Nov. 1972.

26. See *Zhuang Lin Xü Dao Zang*, pt. 2, chapter 7, p. 4462, illustration.

27. Saso, "Orthodoxy and Heterodoxy in Daoist Ritual," *Religion and Ritual in Chinese Society* (Stanford, 1974), pp. 331-333.

28. See note 20 above. The following passages are taken from the manuscript, pp. 1a-10b.

29. See *Zhuang Lin Xü Dao Zang*, pt. 4, chapter 16.

30. *Tai Yi Pei Yü Kao Xie Mi*, and *Zhu Shuai Jiao Xie Fu Mi* (Long Hu Shan, 1868), collection of the Heavenly Master, author's microfilm files. Both of these texts refer to Mao Shan and the southern Lü Shan as centers for heterodox medium possession. The latter text says specifically, on p. 26a, lines 2-5, that the art of medium possession and the spirits used by the Mao Shan and Lü Shan Daoists are to be exorcised. The passage is parallel to that of Bai Yu Chan, in TT, vol. 1016, chapter 1, pp. 8b-9a,

except that the words "Lü Shan," i.e., the northern peak, are changed to "Mao Shan and Lü Shan," as centers for heterodoxy in late Qing dynasty south China.

31. *Dao Jiao Yüan Liu* (microfilm-xerox edition), p. 131.

32. Oral tradition, field notes, Oct. 3 1, 1972. Canonical tradition, TT, vol. 197, chapter shang, p. 27, woodblock print.

33. The dance of the Ho Tu described here is the rite used by Zhuang in chapter 3 note 15 to counteract Dun Jia black magic. The dance was performed by Zhuang on Oct. 16, 1972, in the Jade Emperor temple, Hsinchu City, as described in the following pages.

34. The Ho Tu dance steps, and the other variations of the "steps of Yü" (Yü Bu) are illustrated in Hua Shan Mi Jüe, author's private collection, pp. 2-13, (from the Hua Shan/Wu Dang Shan collection of Wu Jing Chun).

Select Bibliography: Daoist Sources
(Wade-Giles Romanization)

1. Citations from the *Zheng Tong Dao Zang*

The extant Daoist Canon, (*Tao-tsang*) was published during the Zheng Tong reign years of the Ming period (1436-1450) in 1,057 chüan, with a supplement of 63 chüan added in 1607, during the Wan-li reign years. The full 1,120 volumes were first published in 1924-1926 by the Commercial Press of Shanghai, and an inexpensive photo-offset edition was marketed by the I-wen Press in Taipei, 1962, & Shangwu press, Shanghai. The citations follow the numbers and order of the Harvard-Yenching Institute Sinological Index Series, No. 25:

VOLUME NUMBER	TITLE
16-17	*Shang-ch'ing Ta-tung Chen-ching.*
67	*Ling-pao Wu-liang Tu-jen Ching Fu-t'u.*
72	*Shang-ch'ing San-tsun P'u-lu.*
73	*Tung-hsüan Ling-pao Chen-ling Wei-yeh T'u.*
75	*H'ing-wei Hsien-p'u.*
77-78	*Szu-chi Ming-k'o.*
78	*Hsüan-tu Lü-wen.*
122-131	*Hsiu-chen Shih-lu.*
138	*Lieh-hsien Chuan.* (*Shen-hsien Chuan,* a text missing from the *Tao-tsang,* is found in *Han-Wei Ts'ung-shu;* see the following listing for Taoist hagiographies.)
139-148	*Li-shih Chen-hsien T'i-tao T'ung-chien.*
149	Supplement to the above.
153-158	*Mao-shan Chih.*
160	*Hsi-yü Hua-shan Chih.*
167	*Huang-t'ing Nei-ching, Huang-t'ing Wai-ching.*
183	*T'ai-shang Ling-pao Wu-fu.*
190	*Huang-t'ing Nei-ching Yü-ching Chu.*
191	*T'ai-shang Tung-hsüan Ling-pao Chung Chien-wen.* 193 *Teng-chen Yin-chüeh.*
200	*Hsü Chen-chun Hsien Chuan.*
	Hsi Shan Hsü Chen-chun Pa-shih-wu Hua Lu.
208-263	*Ling-pao Ling-chiao Chi-tu Chin-shu.*
278-290	*Wu-shang Huang-lu Ta-chai Li-ch'eng I.*
302-311	*Ling-pao Yü-chien*
318-319	*Shang-ch'ing T'ien-hsin Cheng-fa.*319
	Shang-ch'ing Pei-chi T'ien-hsin Cheng-fa.
323	*Shang-ch'ing Liu-chia Ch'i-tao Mi-fa.*
324	*T'ai-shang Ch'ih-wen Tung-shen San-lu.*
332	*T'ien-t'ai Shan Chih.*
337-339	*Kuang-ch'eng Chi.*

563	Cheng-i Fa-wen Tien-shih Chiao-chieh k'o-ching.
564	Cheng-i Ch'u-kuan Chang-i.
565	T'ai-shang San-wu Cheng-i Meng-wei Yüeh-lu Chiao-i.
	T'ai-shang Cheng-i Yüeh-lu I.
	T'ai-shang Tung-shen San-huang I.
	T'ai-shang Tung-shen T'ai-yüan Ho-t'u San-yüan Yanghsieh 566
	T'ien-shin Cheng-fa Hsiu-chen Tao-ch'ang She-chiao i.
572	Yang-sheng Yen-ming Lu.
575	T'ai-shang San-huang Pao-chai Shen-hsien Shang-lu Ching.
	San-huang Nei-mi Wen.
	San-huang Nei-wen Yi-mi.
576	Mi-tsang T'ung-hsüan Pien-hua Liu-yin Tung-wei Tun-chia Chen-ching.
579	Pei-tou Chih-fa Wu-wei Ching.
580	T'ai-shang Ch'u San-shih Chiu-ch'ung Pao-sheng Ching.
	Huang-t'ing Tun-chia Lu-shen Ching.
	T'ai-shang Lao-chun Ta Ts'un-szu T'u Chu-chüeh.
631-636	Chin-suo Liu-chu Yin.
637-640	Chen-kao.
641-648	Tao-shu.
677-702	Yun-chi Ch'i-ch'ien.
704	Tso-wang Lun.
746-755	T'ai-p'ing Ching.
760	I-ch'ieh Tao-ching Yin I Miao-men Yu-ch'i.
761	Lu Hsien-sheng Tao-men K'o-lieh.
762-763	Tao-chiao I-shu.
768-779	Wu-shang Pi-yao.
780-782	San-tung Chu-nang.
868-870	Pao-p'u-tzu Nei-p'ien.
876	T'ai-shang Cheng-i Fa-wen Ching.
	T'ai-shang San-t'ien Nei-chieh Ching.
877	T'ai-shang San-wu Cheng-i Meng-wei Lu.
878	T'ai-shang Cheng-i Meng-wei Fa-lu.
	Cheng-i Fa-wen Shih-lu Chao-i.
879	T'ai-shang Pei-chi Fu-muo Shen-chou Sha-kuei Lu.
881-883	Kao-shang Shen-hsiao Yü-ch'ing Chen-wang Tz'u-shu Ta-fa.
884-941	Tao-fa Hui-yüan.
963-972	Shang-ch'ing Ling-pao Ta-fa.
976-983	Tao-men K'o-fan Ta-ch'üan.984-985
	Tao-men T'ung-chiao Pi-yung Chi.
988	T'ai-p'ing yü-lan.
	Tao-men Shih-kuei.
	Tao-shu Yüan-shen Ch'i.
989	T'ai-shang Ch'u-chia Chuan-tu I.
	San-tung Hsiu-Tao I.
	Chuan-shou Ching-chieh I Chu-chüeh.
990	Cheng-i Hsiu-chen Lieh-i.
	Chuan-shou San-tung Ching-chieh Fa-lu Lieh-shuo.
	Cheng-i Fa-wen Fa-lu Bu-i.
1003	Cheng-i Fa-wen Hsiu-chen Yao-chih.
1004	Tung-hsüan Ling-pao Wu-kan Wen.
1005	Wu-yüeh Chen-hsing Hsü Lun.
	Kao-shang Shen-hsiao Tsung-shih Shou-ching Shih.

1016
1040

T'ai-shang Tung-shen San-huang Chuan-shou I.
Hai-ch'iung Pai Chen-jen Yü-lu.
Shang-ch'ing T'ien-kuan San-t'u Ching.
Shan-ch'ing Ho-t'u Nei-hsüan Ching.

2. OTHER WORKS IN CHINESE

Anonymous *Ku-wei Shu (The Ancient Apocryphal Texts)*. Muo-hai Chin-hu Collection, Taipei: Wen-yu Press, 1969.

——. *Tao-chiao Yüan-liu (The Origins of Religious Taoism, Yüan period manuscript)*, Oracle Bones Press: 2010.

Chang Hsin-wei. *Wei-shu T'ung-k'ao* (A Critical Study of Authentic and Unauthentic Texts), Taipei: Shang-wu Press, 1970.

Ch'en Kuo-fu. *Tao-tsang Yüan-liu K'ao* (A Critical Study of the Taoist Canon), Peking: Chung-hua, 1963. 2 vols.

Chou Chao-hsien. *Tao-chia yü Shen-hsien* (Taoism and Spiritual Perfection), Taipei: Chung-hua Press, 1970.

Zhuang-ch'en Teng-yün and Michael Saso. *Zhuang-lin Hsu Tao-tsang* (The Zhuang-lin Supplement to the Taoist Canon), Taipei: Ch'eng-wen Press, 1975. 25 vols.

Fu Ch'in-chia. *Chung-kuo Tao-chiao Shih* (The History of Taoism in China), Taipei: Shang-wu Press, 1966.

Fu Tai-yen. *Tao-chiao Yüan-liu* (The Origins of Religious Taoism), Shanghai: Chung-hua Press, 1922.

Hsiao T'ien-shih, ed. *Pai Yu-ch'an ch'uan-chi* (The Complete Works of Pai Yü-ch'an), Taipei: Tzu-yu Press, 1969.

Oyanagi, Shigeta, and Ch'en Pin-ko. *Tao-chiao Kai-shuo* (An Outline of Religious Taoism), Taipei: Shang-wu Press, 1966.

Sun K'o-kuan. *Sung-Yüan Tao-chiao chih Fa-chan* (The Developments in Religious Taoism During the Sung and Yüan periods), Taichung: Chungyang Press, 1965.

——. *Yüan-tai Tao-chiao chih Fa-chan* (The Growth of Taoism During the Yüan period), Taichung: Chung-yang Press, 1968.

Wang Ming. *T'ai-p'ing Ching Ho-hsiao* (A Reconstruction of the Full T'ai p'ing Ching), Shanghai: Chung-hua Press, 1960.

Yen I-p'ing, *Tao-chiao Yen-chiu Tz'u-liao* (Materials for the Study of Religious Taoism), Taipei: I-wen Press, 1974. 2 vols.

3. ZHUANG'S PRIVATE MANUALS FROM THE *CHENG-I TZ'U-T'AN* COLLECTION PUBLISHED BY ORACLE BONES PRESS IN 2010

Ordination manual of the Heavenly Master, Lung-hu Shan: 1868.

The above manuals contain taboo names of the Heavenly Rulers, Thunder Magic talismans, Pseudo-Sanskrit mantras and charms, Pole Star "Beidou" exorcisms, Five Thunder Vajra rites; Two-handed mudras; Talismanic aids for birth; Talismanic and Mantric Healing; Master Wang style talismanic healing; Master Wang style exorcistic healing; Ch'ing-wei Thunder transmission (from the *Lin Hsiu-mei* collection); notes for the using the Yellow Court Canon; ritual of the Yellow Court Canon, Hua Shan esoteric rubrics; and the *Mao Shan Ch'i-men Tun-chia.*

4. A BRIEF BIBLIOGRAPHY OF THE BASIC WORKS OF JAPANESE SCHOLARS ON TAOISM USED OR READ BY MASTER ZHUANG

Fukui, Kojun. *Dokyo no Kiso-teki Kenkyu (A Fundamental Research in Religious Taoism).* Tokyo: Shoseki Bunbutsu Ryutsu Kai, 1952.

Kamada, Shigeo. *Chugoku Bukkyo Shiso-shi Kenkyu (A Study of Chinese Buddhist Thought).* Tokyo: Shunshu Sha, 1969. Pt. 1, "The interaction of Buddhist and Taoist Thought," pp. 9-249.

Kubo, Noritada. *Chugoku no Shukyo Kaikaku (China's Religious Reformation, a Study of the Founding of the Ch'üan-chen Sect).* Tokyo: Hozokan, 1966.

- - -. *Dokyo to Chugoku Shakai* (Taoism and Chinese Society), Tokyo: Heibonsha, 1946.

- - -. *Dokyo Shiso no Hensen* (The Development of Taoist Thought). Tokyo: Yamagawa Shuppansham, 1965.

Obuchi, Ninji. *Dokyo Shi no Kenkyu (A History of Religious Taoism).* Okayama: Okayama University Press, 1964.

Oyanagi, Shigeta. *Ro-so no Shiso to Dokyo (The Thought of Lao-tzu and Zhuang-tzu and Religious Taoism).* Tokyo: Morikita Shoten, 1942.

Yoshioka, Yoshitoyo. *Dokyo Kyoten Shiron (A Treatise on Taoist Canonical Texts and their date of earliest citation).* Tokyo: Taisho University, 1955.

- - -. *Dokyo to Bukkyo, 1* (Buddhism and Taoism, Vol. 1),

- - -. *Nihon Gakujitsu,* 1959; Vol. 11, Tokyo: Toshima Shobo, 1970.

- - -. *Eisei e no Negai: Dokyo* (The Search for Long Life: Taoism), Kyoto: Tankosha, 1970.

- - -. *Dokyo no Jittai (Religious Taoism in Practice).* Peking: 1941. This excellent and little-known work was republished in Kyoto by Hoyü Press in 1975 in an anonymous limited edition.

5. Works Consulted

Anderson, P. *The Method of Holding the Three Ones; a Taoist Manual of Meditation.* London: Curzon Press, 1980

Bokenkamp, Stephan. *Early Daoist Scriptures.* Berkeley: UC Press, 1997

Boltz, Judith. *A Survey of Taoist Literature.* Berkeley: UC Press, 1987

Despeux, Catherine and Livia Kohn. *Women in Daoism.* Dunedin: Three Pines Press, 2003

Girardot, Norman. *Myth and Meaning in Early Taoism.* Berkeley: UC Press, 1983

Hendrische, Barbara. *The Scripture on Great Peace.* Berkeley: UC Press, 2006

Kohn, Livia. *Early Chinese Mysticism.* Princeton: Princeton University, Press, 1992

- - -. *Sitting in Oblivion,* Dunedin: Three Pines Press: 2010

Komjathy, Louis. *Handbook for Daoist Practice,* (10 volumes). Hong Kong: Yuen Yuen Institute, 2008

Lagerwey, John. *Taoist Ritual in Chinese Society.* New York: Macmillan, 1987

- - -. *China: A Religious State,* Hong Kong: Hong Kong University Press: 2010.

Mair, Victor, ed. *Experimental Essays on the Zhuang-tzu.* Honolulu: University of Hawaii Press, 1983

Mollier, Christine, *Buddhism & Taoism Face to Face,* Honolulu: University of Hawaii Press, 2008

Palmer, Martin, *Taoism,* London: Element Books, 1991

Pregadio, Fabrizio. *Great Clarity, Daoism and Alchemy in Early Medieval China.* Stanford: Stanford Univ. Press, 2006;

- - -. *A Study and Translation of the Cantongji.* Mountain View: Golden Elixir Press, 2011

- - -., *The Seal of the Unity of the Three,* Bibliographic Studies, Mountain View: Golden Elixir Press, 2011

Reiter, Florian C., *Basic Conditions of Taoist Thunder Magic.* Wiesbaden: Verlag, Harrassowitz & Co., 2007.

Robinet, Isabelle, *Taoist Meditation,* New York: SUNY Press, 1993

- - -., *Taoism, Growth of a Religion,* Stanford: Stanford University Press, 1997

Robson, James. *Power of Place, Religious Landscape of Nan Yue*. Cambridge: Harvard University Press, 2009)

Saso, Michael. *Blue Dragon White Tiger*. Honolulu: University of Hawaii Press, 1990.

- - -. "The Taoist Body and Cosmic Prayer," *Religion and the Body*. Ed. Sarah Coakley. Cambridge: Cambridge University. Press, 1997

- - -. *Gold Pavilion*, Boston: Tuttle Press, 1995.

Schipper, Kristofer. *The Taoist Body.* Berkeley: UC Press,1993.

Schipper Kristofer and Franciscus Verellen. *A Historical Companion to the Taoist Canon.* Chicago, University of Chicago Press, 2004.

Seidel, Anna. "Chronicle of Taoist Studies," *Cahier d'Extreme Asie,* 5, 1989-90.

von Glahn, Richard. The Sinister Way. Berkeley: UC Press, 2004

Wong, Eva. *Taoism*. Boston: Shambala Press, 1997

Index and Chinese Characters

INDEX OF CHINESE CHARACTERS

Well-known place names and mantic seed words ("mouth" □ radical on the left) are left out of the Chinese character index. Characters for special Daoist terms are found in the text, while the specialized titles of Daoist fascicles found in Chinese characters in the bibliography, are not repeated. The actual surnames of all but the major figures appearing in chapter three have been changed.

An 按
An Zhen wen 按真文 to plant the five talismans in 5 bushels of rice, & the five internal organs
Auspicious Alliance. *See* Mengwei 盟威, official titles of Zhengyi 正一 Daoists

Ba-zhen Tu 八陣圖 Battle Chart of the Eight Trigrams
Ba Kua 八卦 the eight trigrams,
Bai Zhao-zhü 白招秬 White Emperor of the west
Bai Shen Deng 拜神燈 ritual
Bai Yü-chan (or Po Yü-chan) 白玉蟾 Zhengyi Daoist who "rectified" *Shenxiao* rituals
Bai Yü-chan Chüan-ji 白玉蟾全集 *Complete Works of Bai Yu-chan*
Bai-yün Guan 白雲觀 White Cloud Monastery, Beijing
Bao 寶 "precious" the earthly half of a Lingbao Talisman
Bao-chan 寶懺 canonic ritual of repentance, a litany of spirits' names
Bao-ge 胞胳 one of the twelve "inner alchemy" organs
Bao Shan 包山 Daoist mountain where the Lingbao five talismans were buried
Battle Chart of the Eight Trigrams. Ba Zhen Tu 八陣圖 (see Chapter 4)
Bei-ji the North Pole star, center of the northern heavens
Bei-dou 北斗 See Big dipper Pole Star constellation
Ben-xing Jing 本行經 Buddhist in origin text in the Daoist Canon

Ben-ming 本命 Daoist spirit assigned according to year, month, day, hour of birth
Bi 壁 14th of the 28 constellations
Bi 畢 19th of the 28 constellations
Biao 表 a "memorial," Daoist ritual document sent to the spirit rulers of the heavens
Biao-zou 表奏 12th segment in each of the San Dong sections of the Daoist Canon
Bien-zheng Lun 辯正論 Buddhist work condemning (and describing) early Daoism
Bing-yin 丙寅 cyclical character for summoning the third of the Six Jia spirits.
Blackhead (orthodox) Taoist 烏頭 (正一盟威道士 "Wutou" Zhengyi Mengwei Daoshi)
Book of Changes, see *I-ching, Yijing* 易經
Book of Rites, Li Ji 禮記
Bu Xu 步虛 "Pacing the Void" sacred hymns and the dance steps
Buddhist Canon, See *Taisho daizokyo* 大正大藏經

Canon of Filial Piety, 孝經 xiaojing
Cao-ren 草人 funeral image of the deceased person's spirit, made of rice
Cao Pi 曹丕
Cao Cao 曹操
Chan (Zen) 禪 (centering meditation, in the lower cinnabar field / lower belly)
Chan ren 潺仁 secret name used to summon the fourth of the Liu Jia spirits

Chao-tian Baochan 朝天寶懺
chen (trigram) 晨
chen (stem) 辰
Chen Jiesan, 陳捷三
Chen Nai ma 陳奶媽, one of the three protective spirits for children and nursing mothers
Chen Dingfeng, 陳丁鳳
Cheng huang 城隍 City god/ruler, protector of an officially recognized city temple
Chi Biao Nu 赤熛怒 Daoist coded name for Yandi 炎帝, Red Emperor of the south
Chi-niao 赤鳥 red bird, symbol of the south, used in Daoist ritual and inner cultivation
Chi-shu Lingtu 赤書靈圖, the Ling Bao Five Talismans, see *LingBao Wufu Xü* 靈寶五符序
Chi-wen 赤文See also Ling-pao Wu-fu, used in the Su Qi 宿啟 Daoist ritual
Chong Bai 重拜 Jiao festival, second and third day invitation ritual ZLXDD, I, #21
Chou 丑 second of the 12 stems, "Ox"; joint on the left palm, used to summon spirits, when pressed with the left thumb. See ch. 5, "falu" 發爐 ritual.
Chu zhuan 初卷 beginner's manual, see *ZLXDD*
Chu Guan 出官 Zhengyi ritual for sending forth the 1200 spirit energies in the body
Chunqiu Mingli Xü 春秋命歷序
cui-fu 催符 a talisman drawn in the air, making the spirit appear

Dan-tian 丹田
Dang-di, 蕩滌 secret name and mudra of the fifth Liu Jia spirit.
Dao (Tao) 道
Dao of the Left (zuo Dao) 左道; Dao of the Right, you dao 右道)
Dao of *Wuwei* 無為之道 non-act, or transcendent act
Dao-chang 道場 Daoist ritual to attain union with the Wuwei Dao
Dao-jia 道家 "school" Daoists, from 400 BC to 145 CE
Dao-jiao 道教 Daoist systematic teachings/liturgical systems after 145 CE
Dao-jiao Yüanliu 道教源流
Dao-jun 道君 Ling-Bao Tianzun
Dao Guang 道光 Qing dynasty Emperor, 1821 to 1852
Dao-shi 道師 （道士）a Daoist master,
Dao-de Jing (Tao-te Ching) 道德經
Dao-de Heavenly Worthy 道德天尊 (Dao-de Tian Zun), See also Lao-tzu
Dao-de Tian Zun 道德天尊
Daoism: 道教 China's religion-philosophy (n.b.: religious and philosophic Daoism are only distinct in the minds of modern agnostics); the teachings of Daoist masters
De-ren 德仁 epithet for Jia-wu, fourth of the Liu Jia spirits; (also, a crown worn by Jia-wu),
Deng-tai Jin-biao 登台進表 Daoist public ritual for sending off a memorial to the Heavens
Deng Yougong 鄧有功 Daoist Master, founded of 天心正法 a Song dynasty Daoist school
Di 氐 constellation
Ding 丁, 六丁 Six Ding spirits "liu ding" called to control and subdue the Liu Jia spirits: Ding-chou 丁丑, Ding-hai 丁亥, Ding-mao 丁卯, Ding-wei 丁未, Ding-yi 丁乙 and Ding-yu 丁酉
Dragon-Tiger Mountain. See Lung hu Shan 龍虎山
du 杜 "blockade" name given to the trigram xun in the SE, in exorcist and thunder ritual
Dong-dou Jing 東斗經 Eastern Constellation Canon of Merit"
Dong-zhen Bu 洞真部 Arcanum of the Zhen "Dao-realized" first of the three Arcana of the Daoist Canon, original repository of the Shangqing (Mao Shan) scriptures
Dong-xüan Bu 洞玄部 Arcanum of

the Xuan Lingbao Scriptures second section of the Canon

Dong-shen Bu 洞神部 Arcanum of the Shen (San Huang/Zhengy) third section of the Canon. The Ming dynasty Zhengtong Canon (1435-46) does not maintain this early order.

Dou-mu 斗母 Mother Goddess of the Pole Star, Marishi, shared with Tantric Buddhism

Du Cheng Huang 都城隍 Cheng Huang temple located in a capitol city

Du Guang Ting 杜光庭 late Tang dynasty Daoist master

Du-jiang 都講 "Chief Cantor" in orthodox Daoist ritual; grade 7 ordination

Duke of the Yellow Stone Huang shi Gong 黃石公

Du-ren Jing 度人經 Lengthy canonical text, chanted for merit during Jiao ritual

Dun Jia 遁甲 esoteric Daoist rites used to control the six Jia spirits

Dzan-song 讚頌 hymns/melodies, 11th segment in each of the three Arcana Daoist Canon

Eight Trigrams; Ba Gua 八卦 of the Posterior Heavens houtianbagua 後天八卦; attributed to King Wen 文王, also called the Lo-shu 落書; distinguish from the xiantianbagua, also known as the Ho-tu 先天八卦, 河圖, attributed to Fu Xi 伏羲

Er-jiao Lun 二教論，Vol. 18, Taisho Canon

Er-pin 二品 (grade two Daoist ordination)

Er-shi-ba Su 二十八宿 (twenty-eight constellations)

Fa biao 發表 (Daoist ritual Announcing the Jiao celebration to all spirits)

Fa-lu 發爐 (rite sending all spirit images out of the Daoist's body); basic to all Taoist ritual

Fa zou 發奏 another name for the Fa biao ritual

Fang 方 13th of the 28 constellations, see chapter 4, section 7

Fang zhong 房中 sexual hygiene, forbidden by rule to all true Daoists

Fang-fa 方法 eighth of the classical Daoist Canon's twelve sections

Fang-shi 方士 term for proto, or "local" Taoists

Fang Shui-deng 放水燈 "floating the lanterns" ritual, to free souls from the underworld

Fei-hu Jun 飛虎軍 term given by Lin Janmei to his private army in chapter two

Fei-guei Shou-zhi 飛龜授袟 term from the ancient Apocrypha texts

Fen Deng 分燈 Daoist ritual, celebrating ch. 42 of Laozi, "Dao gave birth to One…"

Fire Master Thunder Magic, 火師雷法. See also Wang Zi hua

Five Bushels of Rice 五斗米道 Wu dou mi Dao

Five Elements. 五行－陰陽五行 Yin-yang Five Element cosmology

Five Emperors 五帝 Wu-di

Five Sacred Peaks 五岳真形圖 see Wu Yue Zhen Xing Tu,

Five Talismans. 五符（靈寶五符） See Lingbao Wufu

Five Thunder Vajra rites 五雷法 (Wu-Lei Fa), See also Thunder Ritual

Four supplements 四輔 See Si-fu

Fu 符 talismans: of the Six Jia spirits, chaper 4 for Thunder Vajra rites, chapter 6

Fu-do Myo-o 不動妙王 Japanese. term for an esoteric Buddhist protector deity

Fu Xi 伏羲

Fu-lu 復爐 ritual for restoring spirits to their places inside the body

Fu-shu 符書 books of talismans used to summon spirits;

Gang shen 罡神 the seventh or tail star of the Big Dipper; Gundali 軍打力 Gang Xien 剛銛 secret summons and mudra of Jia shen, third of the Six Jia spirits

Gao Gong Fa-shi 高攻法師 Master of Exalted Merit, Grade 6 Daoist ordination

Gate of Demon (Hell), 鬼門 *See also* gen 艮 (trigram), the direction NE on the compass

Gate of Life 生門 Sheng men, i.e., NE changes into a Gate of Life, in Thunder-Vajra ritual

Ge Chao fu 葛巢甫 Lingbao Daoist, multiplied and elaborated Lingbao documents

Ge Hong 葛洪 author of *Baopuzi*, early source of authentic Lingbao Daoism

Ge Xüan 葛玄 early Lingbao Daoist, uncle of Ge Hong

Ge Zao Shan 閣皂山 Daoist Mountain in Jiangxi Province, home of Lingbao Daoism

Gen 艮 trigram for Mountain, Northeast, "Gate of Demon" closed during Daoist ritual

Geng 庚 seventh of the ten Celestial Stems

Geng-hai 庚亥 last day of a sixty day cycle

Gold Register. 金籙 *See* Jin-lu, Daoist rites of cosmic renewal

Gong-fu 功夫, 20th century term for martial arts; time for meditation, or tea

Gong Cao 攻曹 Daoist messenger spirits, learned from a master at initiation

Guo Daojing 郭 道敬 Hsinchu city Zhengyi Citan Daoist, see chapter 3

Great Peace 太平 (Tai ping): Canonical title; early Daoist movement; "Way of Great Peace"

Gu Wei-shu 古緯書 early Daoist "weft" works, as distinct from "warp" 經 Confucian texts

Guan 觀 technical term for a celibate Taoist monastery or nunnery

Guang hong Ming Ji 廣弘明集 early Buddhist text describing and condemning Daoism

Guang Wu Di 光武帝 Han dynasty

emperor who restored the imperial throne in 25 CE

gui 鬼 eighth of the 28 celestial constellations, see chapter 4, Liujia ritual

gui 癸 tenth of the Celestial Stems, used to summon the sixth Liu Jia spirit, Jia Yen

Gui-mao 癸卯 6:00 am, the time for summoning the Jiawu spirit, Liu Jia rite

Hai 亥 earthly stem

Hai-kong Zhi-zang 海空智藏

Han-zhong 漢中

Han Guan yi, 漢官儀 , from the *Hou Han Shu* 後漢書, 112，上，2b

Han Shu-niu 漢樞紐 ritual name for Huangdi, Yellow Emperor of the Center

Han-Wei Cong-shu 漢魏叢書

Han Wu Di 漢武帝

He Ming Shan 鶴鳴山 mountain in Szechuan where Zhang Daoling practiced Daoism

Heavenly (Celestial) Master (天師 Tian Shi) school; 61st Celestial Master, 六十一代天師

Heng Shan 衡山, the Southern Sacred Peak, with a shrine dedicated to Wei Huacun

Heng Shan 恒山， the Sacred Peak of the North *see* Five Sacred Peaks

Hierophant 赤子 (chi zi), Dao conceived as a ruddy child in the body's center of gravity

Ho Zhen Gong 何真公 One of the founders of the Qingming Daoist school

Ho Lü 闔閭 King of the Wu Kingdom, from the Wei Shu 緯書 apocryphal texts

Ho Dao jing 何道敬 He Dao Jing, collector of Shangqing texts

Ho-zui 喝醉

Ho tu 河圖 "magic circle," Ba Gua eight Trigram chart of the Prior Heavens: the Ling-pao Five Talismans are a form of Ho tu, (He Tu); also a format for sacred liturgical dance

Ho tu Jiang-xiang 河圖絳象 Title of a

chapter in the *Gu Wei shu*, describing the Lingbao Five Writs

Hou tu 后土, title of the Spirit of the Soil, appointed to guard gravesites

Hsinchu Hsien-chih (xinzhu xianzhi) 新竹縣志 Official Hsinchu County Gazeteer

Hsinchu Ts'ung-chih (xinzhu cong-zhi) 新竹叢志 Official Hsinchu City History

Hua Shan 華山 Sacred Mountain of the West; and Qingwei Thunder rituals, chapter 6

Hua shi 化石

Huan-ti 桓帝 Han dynasty emperor

Huang 黃 the Gold-Yellow color of the microcosmic pericardial region, inner alchemy

Huang zhen 黃鎮 taboo name for summoning the Jia Zi spirit. first of the six Liu Jia spirits

Huang-lao 黃老

Huang-lu 黃籙 the Yellow Register rites used for burial, in modern Daoist usage

Huang-lu Zhai 黃籙齋 ritual oriented toward freeing souls from the underworld

Huang di 黃帝 the Yellow Emperor

Huang ting 黃庭 *See* Yellow Court," or Gold Pavilion; basic Shangqing Daoist text

Huang ting Jing 黃庭經 Yellow Court Canon

Huang ting Neijing Jing 黃庭內景經 basic meditation text of Shangqing Daoism; attributed to Lady Wei Huacun before the revelations of Yang Xi, and the Xu's

Huang ting Waijing 黃庭外經, Yellow Court, Gold Pavilion attributed to Wei Boyang

Hui Zong 徽宗 last of the northern Song dynasty emperors, 1101-1126

Hun 魂 the three yang aspects of the soul; see "bo" 魄, the seven yin aspects buried in the grave

Hun dun 混沌 state of primordial simplicity See also Taiji 太極

I-ching 易經 Wade-Giles Romanization for the *Book of Changes, Yijing* in modern Pinyin

I-sho 緯書 Japanese term for the *Gu Wei Shu*, the study of Prof. Yasui Kozan

Immanent Tao 有為之道 Yuwei zhi Dao, Hun dun, Taiji

Ji 箕 constellation

Ji 己 earthly stem

Ji-ji Ru Lü-ling, 急急如律令 ancient Daoist blessing, spirit summoning chant

Ji-jiu 祭酒 "Wine libationer," ancient title for a Zhengyi Daoist

Ji-juan 記傳 tenth biographical section of the three Arcana, the "early" Daoist Canon.

Ji-lu Tan Qing Yüanke 288n19, 給籙壇靖元科 Daoist Ordination Manual

Jia, 甲，六甲 Liu Jia, names of the Six Jia spirits: Jia-chen 甲辰, Jia-xü 甲戌, Jia-shen 甲申, Jia-zi 甲子, Jia-wu 甲午, and Jia-yen 甲寅

Jia pu 家譜 officially recognized register of clan or family names

Jia-zi 甲子, first year of the 60-year Chinese calendar cycle

Jiang muo 絳魔 staff used in the Liu Jia rites to control spirits

Jiao 醮 Daoist rites of cosmic renewal

Jiao 角 first of the 28 constellations

Jie 戒 rules, regulations, vows required to receive Daoist initiation

Jie-lü 戒律 officially recognized Daoist rules and vows

Jie-lüe 節略 style name used to summon the Jia Shen spirit

Jin 晉 dynasty

Jin Lian Zhengzong 金蓮正宗, aka "Quanzhen 全真" Daoism

Jin-lu 金籙 Gold Register, i.4., Jiao 醮 Daoist Rites of Renewal

Jin-lu Jiao, 金籙醮 Jiao rites for cosmic renewal; grand village renewal festival

Jin shi 進士 doctor of letters

Jin shu 金書 "Gold" document sent to the highest rulers of the Daoist spirit-world

Jin Tan 禁壇 Daoist ritual for purifying the sacred *Tan* area

Jin Yunzhong 金允中 late Sung dynasty Taoist; author of DZ 963-972 Shangqing Lingbao Dafa 上清靈寶大法, critic of Daoist Lin Lingsu, Shenxiao and Tiantai Daoism; see John Lagerwey's analysis, in Schipper-Verellen *The Daoist Canon*, 2003: Vol. 2, pp. 1024-28

jing 驚 alarm, frightened, a esoteric name for the "west" in the *Ba Zhen Tu*, see chapter 4

Jing 經 "warp" Confucian writings, as opposed to "weft" wei 緯 proto-Daoist texts

Jing 井 fourth of the 28 constellations, the "wild dog:"

Jing 景 vantage point, esoteric name for the trigram Li in the south of the Ba Chen Tu

Jingji zhi 經濟志 A chapter of the Sui dynasty history

Jiu Pin 九品 the nine grades of Taoist ordination; described in ch. 1 and 5

Jiu Yü Baochan 九獄寶懺 litany to free souls from the nine underworld hells

Jüan 卷 (fascicle) term use for a numbered, bound fascicle

Jüan lien 捲簾 "rolling up the screen," Fen deng ritual, audience with the Dao

Kai 開 (opening) "Gate of Heaven" *Qian* 乾 in the Ba Zhen Tu

Kai Guang 開光 ritual for "opening the eyes" or bringing a spirit into a carved statue

Kan 坎 trigram for the north, "water", the position of the North Pole Star in the cosmos

Kang 亢 fifth of the 28 constellations

King Wen 文王 Wen Wang

Ko yi 科儀 technical term for Daoist "inner alchemy" based ritual

Kou jüeh 口訣 Daoist oral teachings, not found in canonical writings

Kui 奎 third of the 28 celestial constellations; mantic word used to heal with vajra-light

Kun 坤 north in the Ho-tu eight trigrams; the southwest/earth in the Lo-shu 8 trigrams

Kundalin 軍大力 Mantic summons for the seventh star of the dipper, Gangshen, or Pojun 破軍; to use the summons correctly, Tang dynasty pronunciation "Gundali" must be used.

Lang-yeh 琅琊 name of the ancient Daoist kingdoms of Shandong and Fujian provinces

Lao Jun 老君 religious Daoist spirit's name, identified with Lao Tzu

Lao-tzu Tao te ching, 老子道德經 *(Laozi Daode Jing)* 279n115

Li 離 trigram for the south, "fire," in the *Loshu* version of the 8 trigrams

Li Ji 禮記 "New Text" Confucian Ritual classic; source of classic Daoist rituals

Li Chun Feng 李淳風 (602-670); Daoist, teacher of Bu Xu 步虛 "pacing the void" sacred dance; cited in Big Dipper, and Thunder-Vajra rites

Li Shun Lie 李尋列, qian Han Shu 75, named Gan zhong ke 甘忠可 as author of *Taiping Jing*

Li tzu-jan 理自然 the Lingbao five writs "bring order to" nature's cyclical changes

Lie Xian Zhuan 列仙傳 Biographies of the Immortals

Lin Chan (Jan) Mei 林占梅 eldest son of Hsinchu city's elite Lin clan, warrior

Lin Ji 林霽 （齋） style name of the second of the Six Jia spirits

Lin Xiu Mei 林修梅 9th adopted, "Guofangzi" son of the elite Lin family

Lin Ru Mei 林汝梅 fifth son of the elite Lin clan, founder of the Daoist Zhengi Citan

Lin Ling-su 林靈素 charismatic court Daoist, favorite of Song Emperor

Huizong

Lin Shih-mei 林士梅 one of the older Lin brothers, signed the Liu Jia manual, ch. 2, n7

Ling 靈 the upper or heavenly half of a talisman; bao 寶 is the earthly half

Ling Bao 靈寶 second of the three great Daoist orders; see Gezao Shan

Ling Bao Five Talismans 靈寶五符 (*Lingbao Wufu*), Daoist Canon, Vol. 6, #315 太上五符序

Ling Bao Zhen Wen 靈寶真文 Lingbao True Writs, basic Daoist ritual meditation

Ling Bao Tian Zun 靈寶天尊 Ling-Bao Heavenly Worthy, second of the Daoist Trinity

Ling tu 靈圖 fourth of the 12 segments in each of the Sandong (three early Daoist canons)

Ling Wei-yang 靈威仰 taboo name for summoning the Green Emperor of the east

Ling wen 靈文 name given to the five talismans in the sixth century *Wushang Biyao* text

Ling-yi 靈逸 ritual name given to the secind of the Six Jia spirits (ch. 4)

Liu 柳 12th of the 28 constellations

Liu Jia 六甲 Six Jia spirits

Liu Hun Kang 劉混康 Song dynasty Mao Shan Daoist

Liu Ding 六丁 Six Ding spirits

Lo-shu 落書 magic square, chart of the "Posterior Heavens" 8 Trigrams 後天八卦)

Lou 婁 seventh of the 28 constellations

Lou Hui-ming 樓惠明 one of the Daoist courtiers who stole Shangqing documents

Lu 籙 register; lists of Daoist titles, spirits, summons, taught by the Daoist master

Lu Xiu Jing 陸修靜 early Daoist master, compiler of the first Daoist Canon

Lu Shan 廬山 famous Buddhist-Daoist mountain

Lun-yü 論語 *The Analects of Confucius*

Long han 龍漢 primordial era of cosmic gestation, attributed to the Lingbao Five Talismans

Long Hu Shan 龍虎山 Dragon-Tiger Mountain; home of Zhengyi Mengwei Daoism

Long-men 龍門 most influential Daoist school of the modern Quanzhen monastic order

Long-wei 龍威 a Wei Shu "weft" tradition recluse, who revealed the five talismans

Lü Shan 閭山 mythical Daoist mountain, source of popular Daoism. *See also* San-nai Lü Shan

Ma Han 馬罕 protector and preserver of the Shang Qing texts

Ma Lang 馬朗 protector and preserver of the Shang Qing texts

Ma-tsu 媽祖 surnamed Lin, protectress of fishing and farming along the coast of SE China

Magic Square, 落書 also called "Magic Square of Nine," see Lo shu above

Mao 卯 fourth of the 12 earthly stems, used in Dun Jia, Zhengyi, and Qingwei ritual

Mao Shan 茅山 home of Shang Qing Daoism (ch. 1) and Dun Jia magic, ch. 4;

Marishiten, 摩利支天 *See also* Dou-mu (Tou-mu) 斗母

Maspero, Henri, "*Le Daoisme*" translated into Japanese, highly respected by Master Zhuang

Master of Exalted Merit 高攻法師 Gao-gong Fa-shi

May Fourth Movement, 五四運動

Meng-wei 盟威 Auspicious Alliance (twenty-four registers of); the Zhengyi order

Mi-jüe 秘訣 professional Taoist secrets, in hand-written manuals

Ming-zhi Xiu-yüan 明智修院 Lin family Daoist studies center, Hsinchu city, Taiwan

Ming-zhong 鳴鍾 ritual for "sounding the bell"

Ming-tang 明堂 basis for the Daoist "Planting the five true writs/five talismans"

Monthly Commands. See also Yüeh-ling 月令

Mother Goddess of the Pole Star. 斗母 Tou-mu (Dou Mu)

Nan Dou Jing 南斗經

Nei-jüan 內卷

Nei-pien 內篇 first seven chapters of the Zhuangzi

Nei-dan 內丹 meditative alchemy

Neo-confucian 新儒學 Song and Ming dynasty intellectual movement

Nine heavenly stars "九天", two + seven of the Big Dipper; nine spirits in nine palaces of the head: Tian-chin 天禽, Tian-chong 天衝, Tian-zhu 天柱, Tian-peng 天蓬, Tian-fu 天, Tian-xin 天心, Tian-ren 天任, Tian-bing 天芮, Tian-ying 天英

Ni-wan 泥丸 "upper cinnabar field", the Pineal gland in the brain's center

Niu 牛 sixth of the 28 constellations

Nü 女 tenth of the 28 constellations

Nü Gua 女媧 wife of Fu Xi, legendary founders of the Chinese family

Pan-luo Xin-jing 般羅心經 The Heart Sutra

Pei 沛 birth area of Zhang Daoling, before moving to Mt Heming

Ping-heng 平衡 ritual name given to the seven stars of the Big Dipper

Ping-nan 屏報 ritual name used to summon Dingyi, a subordinate general of Jia Yen, the violent sixth of the Liu Jia spirits; Dingyi is used to quell and pacify Jia Yen.

Planchette 扶鸞 fu-luan, spirit writing, by a medium possessed by a spirit

Po 魄 the yin aspects of the soul, seven in number, buried in the grave with the cadaver

Po-jun, 破軍, secret name of the seventh star of the big dipper. See also Gang-shen

Pole Star constellation 北斗 see Bei-dou, or Ursa Major

Primordial Breath, 元氣 (炁) See also Yüan-qi

Prior Heavens 先天 Xian-tien

Pu-lu 譜錄 list of spirit names, fifth segment of the 12 sections in each of the San Dong i.e., the "three Arcana" early Daoist Canon

Pu-shi 普施 Daoist ritual for "feeding" and freeing souls from the underworld; see Pu-du

Pu-du 普渡 Daoist ritual for "freeing all souls" during the Jiao liturgy of cosmic renewal

Qi 炁，氣，Primordial Breath, Dao as Birthing; "qi" or life breath

Qi men Dun-jia; 奇門遁甲, an esoteric Daoist manual; to be distinguished from a popular manual of the same name; used to summon the Six Jia Liu Jia 六甲神 spirits

Qien 乾 (trigram); used in burial ritual, Jiao ritual, and the sacred Hetu 河圖 dance

Qien Zhicai 錢枝彩, kindly Shenxiao Daoist of Hsinchu city, see Vols. 21-25 of ZLXDZ

Qien Tang 錢塘, city where Xu Huangmin, holder of the Shangqing manuscripts, died

Qing Jing 清靜 a Thunder-Vajra school of the Song dynasty

Qing zhou 清州 village near Daoist Long-hu Shan 龍虎山, home of Zhen-gyi Daoism.

Qing Xu 清虛 name for the Thunder-Vajra style of Taiyi 太乙 Daoism

Qing Ming 清明 Thunder-Vajra Qing-ming and Qingxu rites amalgamated with Zhengyi

Qing Shen 請神 Daoist ritual inviting orthodox spirits to the Jiao and Zhai sacred area

Qing Wei 清微 Thunder Vajra school, Tantric Daoism; founded by woman Daoist Zu Shu; similar to Shingon, Tendai texts from 805-845 Tang dynasty China.

Quan Zhen 全真 Taoist monastic school "Total Realization" school
Quan Tang-wen 全唐文 Classic collection of Tang dynasty Literature

Rang-chang 讓昌 taboo name for the fifth of the Liu Jia spirits
Ren 壬 the heavenly stem of the fifth Liu Jia spirit, Jia Chen
Redhead 紅頭 hongtou term for a popular Taoist, incl. Shenxiao, Lü Shan, Sannai

San-jiao 三焦 one of the 12 areas inside the body refined during inner alchemy meditation
San-qing 三清 "Three Pure Ones" Dao as Gestating, Mediating, Indwelling
San-huang 三皇 The "Three Emperors" of ancient China; Daoist primordial spirits
San-huang Chai 三皇齋 The sixth century Daoist rites for morning, noon, and night audiences
San-huang Wen 三皇文 Writ of the Three Emperors mentioned in apocryphal texts San Guan Jing 三官經 Three Officials Canons of merit
San Guan Bao-chan 三官寶懺 Three Officials litanies of repentance
San-nai Lü Shan 三奶閭山 popular Taoist sect. See also Lü Shan
San-Dong 三洞 Three Arcana; three sections of the earliest Daoist Canon
San-Dong Jing-shu Mu-lu 三洞經書目錄 Lu Xiu Jing's list of the early Daoist Canon
San-wu Du-Gong 三五都攻 Three-five Surveyor of Merit, Grade 6 Daoist
Sarvayana 一切經 "All in One" Canon also called "Ekayana"
Sha 煞 Minnan dialect, "soat"; evil force
Shaman 薩滿 travel in trance; not the same as medium possession 童乩; wu 巫 has both meanings; Orthodox Daoists are incorrectly called wu shaman in many western sources.
Shang-Qing 上清 Taoist meditation

school; differs from aberrant Mao Shan magic Yellow Court Canon, 黃庭 （內,外）經 are basic meditation texts in modern practice.
Shang-di 上帝 The Highest Heavenly Emperor in classical Chinese cosmology
Shao-hao 少暤 Spiritual Emperor of the West
Shen 參 27th of the 28 constellations
Shen 神 spirit, resides in the heart, governs the human will
Shen 申 9th of the 12 earthly stems, monkey
Shen-tu 神荼 one of the two Temple Door Spirit Guardians, see Yu Lü 鬱壘
Shen-qüan 神權 power to control a spirit, used with Jia-wu, fourth of the Liu Jia spirits
Shen-fu 神符 talisman used specifically to summon a spirit
Shen-Xiao 神霄 popular Taoist sect, called Redhead Daoists in north Taiwan
Shen-xian Juan 神仙傳 Biographies of Spiritual Immortals
Shen-nong 神農 Spiritual ruler of the south, Patron of farming, "Red" emperor
Sheng 生 life, to give birth see Sheng-men
Sheng-men 生門 Gate of Life; finding the, see ch. 4, and ch. 6, Thunder-vajra ritual
Shi 室 22nd of the 28 constellations
Shu 蜀 Szechuan province, one of the Three Kingdoms, 221-263 CE
Shu Ji-zhen 夊季真 famous Daoist and mandarin official, N-S period Song kingdom
Shu-jing 書經
Shu-wen 梳文 ritual document, "Rescript"
Shun 舜 second of the three ancient emperors, (Yao, Shun, Yü)
Shunt-di 順帝 Han Dynasty emperor, 126-145
Shuo-wen 說文 （說文解字）
Six Jia spirits 六甲 Liu Jia;

Six Ding spirits 六丁 Liu Ding, subjugate the Six Jia spirits, Ch. 4. *See also* Ding

Sixty-first Generation Heavenly Master, 六十一代天師

Su Qi 宿啟 ritual for implanting the Five Talismans, and refining the Five Elements

Sui-Yang-di 隋煬帝

Sun Yu-yüe 孫遊岳 ninth Mao Shan master, recipient of the Shang Qing texts

Song Shan 嵩山 Sacred Mountain of the Center

Song-shen 送神 Daoist ritual for "seeing off" the spirits

Song Wen-di 宋文帝

Sung Yin-tzu 宋隱子 Commentator of the *Huangting Jing* text, *Zhengyi Citan* collection

Si (Sz) 巳 sixth of the 12 earthly stems, 9 am to 11 am; snake

Si fu (Sz Fu) 四輔 four supplements to the three Arcana, San Dong of the daoist Canon

Si Ma Cheng-zhen 司馬丞真 Tang dynasty Daoist Master

Tai-ji 太極 same as the immanent Tao, Huntun 混沌

Tai-ji qüan 太極拳

Tai-ping Bu 太平部 fifth section of the Daoist Canon

Tai-qing Bu 太清部 sixth section of the Daoist Canon

Tai-xüan Pu 太玄部 fouth section of the Daoist Canon

Tai-yi 太乙 Daoist supreme deity-spirit who frees souls from hell/purgatory

Tai-ping qingling Shu 太平清领書 of the Han Dynasty Daoist Yu Ji (or Gan Ji)

Tai-ping Guangji 太平廣記

Tai-ping Yülan 太平御覽

Tai Shan 泰山 Sacred Peak of the East

Tai-shang Ganying Pian 太上感應篇

Tai-shang Laojun 太上老君

Tai-sui 太歲

Tai-zi Ye 太子爺

Taisho Shinshu daizokyo 大政新修大藏

Tan 壇

Tantric Buddhism 密宗 use of body-mouth-mind/shen-kou-yi 申口意 for enlightenment

Tao Hong Jing 陶弘景 ninth recipient of the Shangqing texts, Mao Shan scholar, d. 536

Taoist Canon 正統道臧 Zheng-tong Daozang, compiled between 1436-1445

Taoist monastery 觀 guan

Three Arcana 三洞 San-dong three-fold division of the earliest Daoist Canon

Three-five Surveyor of Merit 三五都攻 *See* San-wu Du-gong, grade 6 Daoist ordination

Three Officials Canon 三官經 *See* Sanguan Jing

Three Pure Ones 三清 *see* San-qing

Thunder ritual 雷法 (五雷法 Wu-lei Fa); used for purification and exorcism

Tian-shu 天樞 Celestial Pivot, esoteric name given to Qingwei Thunder-vajra registers, found in Mijue handwritten manuals used at Longhu Shan and Mao Shan

Tian-tai 天台 famous mountain in Jejiang province, Buddhist and Daoist practitioners

Transcendent Tao 無為之道 (*Wu-wei zhi Dao*); ritual of union with, *see Daochangzhengjiao*;

Tu-dui 鶉對 mantic name for Ding-wei, fourth of the Liu Ding spirits

Tui 兌 trigram of the west, "swamp"

Tong-shu 通書 Provincial and County level official records

Tong-zi 童子 "youth" or "yang" filled esoteric spirit, used to implant the Five Talismans

Tong-yüan 通元 esoteric name of Jia-chen, fifth of the Six Jia spirits

Twenty-eight Constellations. 二十八宿 *See* Er-shi-ba Su

Ursa Major. 北斗 *See* Pole Star constellation

Vajra 雷法 "thunder rites" used in Tantric Buddhist and Daoist ritual
Vajrayana - term for Tantric Buddhism, 密宗

Wai-juan 外卷
Wan-chao 晚朝 Daoist ritual for refining jing 精 intuition - Daode Heavenly Worthy
Wan-fa Zong 萬法宗 Daoist manual/register given to scholars, lay practitioners
Wang Zhong-yang 王重陽
Wang Ling-qi 王靈期
Wang Zi-hua, 王子華 Daoist Master of Thunder-Vajra ritual
Wang Wen-qing 王文卿
Wang Yeh 王爺 euphemistic term for spirits of pestilence "wenshen" 瘟神
Wang Yüan-zhi 王遠知
Wei 尾, 胃 18th, and 21st of the 28 constellations
Wei 未 eighth of the 12 earthly stems, sheep
Wei 緯 "weft" *or* proto-Daoist texts; See *Gu Wei-shu*
Wei Hua-cun 魏華存 woman founder of Inner Spiritual vision Daoism
Wei-yi 威儀 classic Daoist rituals, seventh section of the Three Arcana early daoist Canon
Wen 文 ritual and contemplative Daoism; see wu 武 martial, or exorcistic Daoist rites
Writ of the Three Emperors. 三皇文 *See San-huang Wen*
Wu 武 Emperor Wu of the NS period Qin dynasty, condemned the Wei Shu, in 267
Wu 吳 one of the Three Kingdoms
Wu 巫 possessed medium; Daoists are wrongly called wu mediums
Wu 午 seventh of the 12 earthly stems, horse
Wu-chao 午朝 classical Daoist ritual to refine shen spirit; Lingbao Heavenly Worthy

Wu-chen 午辰 fifth day of Liujia ritual, when two spirits are refined (six spirits subdued in five days)
Wu-dang Shan 武當山
Wu-di 五帝 *See* Five Emperors
Wu-dou Bao-chan 五斗寶懺 ritual chant, litanies of repentance
Wu-fa 無法 "no power" said of Daoist practice without a master's instruction
Wu-fang Zhen-wen 五方真文
Wu-ji 無（无極）Transcendent Tao, vs. Taiji 太極 Immanent (female) Dao
Wu-Jing-chun, 吳景春 brought Qingwei Thunder rites to Taiwan, 1823…
Wu-xian 午献 noon ritual offering of 9 items to the heavenly spirits; *see* wu-hong
Wu-hong 午弘 noon ritual offering
Wu-lao-yeh 五老爺 nickname of Lin Rumei
Wu-lei Fa. 五雷法 *See* Five Thunder ritual; Thunder Vajra Practice
Wu-shi Jia-pu 吳氏家譜 The Wu Family (Daoist) Records
Wu-wei 無為 (无為) transcendent act
Wu Yue Zhen Xing Tu 五岳真形圖

Xi dou jing 西斗經, Chant of Merit to the "Western Dou constellation"
Xiang Kai 襄楷 minister who gave Yu Ji's *Great Peace* text to Emperor Huandi , 147-168
Xiang Yü Ben Ji 項羽本記, *see* Sima Qian, Shi Ji, 司馬遷 史記
Xiao Lie 簫烈 name for summoning the fourth of the Six Jia spirits, Jia Wu
Xiao Bao Zhen 簫抱珍 Master of Tai Yi Daoism
Xiao Wen Di 孝文帝 Emperor of the northern Wei, mid fifth century.
Xiao Wu Di 孝武帝 Emperor of the N-S period Song dynasty, ca. 457
xie 邪 harmful magic, evil, unorthodox
Xie Guang Ji 叶光記 secret name for summoning the black emperor of the north

Xie Shen 謝神 Daoist ritual for thanking and seeing off spirits

Xian 仙 Daoist immortal, distinguish from *zhen* (真) and *sheng* (聖)

xin 心 17th of the 28 constellations, pictured with a fox

Xin 信 (name of a special ritual used to summon the fourth of the Six Jia spirits)

Xin Zhai 心齋 heart fasting, leading to union with the Tao; ch. 4 of *Zhuangzi*

Xing 星 16th star of the 28 constellations; also, the term used for a star in the heavens

Xiu 休 rest, technical term for "kan" 坎, the trigram of the north, "water" or winter rest

Xü 戌 14th of the 28 constellations, image of a "rat"; also jiaxu, 6:00 pm. The 11th of the 12 earthly stems, (11th year of 12 year cycle); symbolized by a dog

Xü 嘘 mantric seed word used to summon thunder spirits for healing

Xü Shun 許遜 legendary Daoist, popular throughout Taiwan and SE China

Xü Huang min 許黃民

Xü Hui 許翽, son of Xu Mi, nephew of Xu Mai, (Xu Mi's brother), Shangqing text recipients

Xü Lai-lei 徐來勒 semi-legendary Lingbao Daoist lineage master

Xü Mai 許邁 calligrapher and transmitter of Shangqing Daoist texts

Xü Mi 許謐 calligrapher and transmitter of Shangqing Daoist texts

Xüan 玄 "mysterious" associated with the color deep purple in Daoist Inner alchemy

Xüan-ho 宣和 reign years of the Song emperor Hui Zong, 1119-1126

Xüan Tian Shangdi 玄天上帝

Xüan Zong 玄宗 Tang Dynasty emperor, reigned from 713-756

Xüan Yi 玄嶷 Tang Dynasty Buddhist, critic of Daoism, see 甄正論 ch. 1, n34

Xün 巽 trigram for "Gate of Humans," in the southeast

Yang 陽 the male principle of the universe, spring and summer,

Yang Xi 楊羲 visionary author of Daoist texts

Yao 堯 one of three legendary rulers of ancient China (Yao, Shun, Yü)

Yellow Court 黃庭 Huang-ting: center of gravity in the Daoist body, xia dantian"

Yellow Court Canon 黃庭經 Huangting Jing; "Gold Pavilion"

Yellow Register 黃錄 Huang-lu, 2nd of 3 traditional Daoist registers, gold, yellow, jade

Yellow River 黃河 shaped like the Big Dipper, as it flows across north China

Yellow Turban 黃巾 early form of martial Daoism, destroyed as "rebels" in 185

Yi 翼 fourth of the 28 constellations

Yi-li 儀禮 "New Text" Confucian rituals, source of late Han Daoist rituals

Yi-mao 乙卯 6:00 am

Yi Qiu 乙丑 second in the 60 year calendar cycle, 2nd day of the Liu Jia cycle, summon jiaxu

Yi Pin 一品 grade one of Taoist perfection, knowledge of Shangqing rites and meditations

Yin 寅 third of the 12 earthly stems, tiger

Yin 陰 the female principle of the universe, birth, gestation, water, (autumn/winter)

Yin 殷 one of four Daoist marshal spirits, protector of the Wu-chao Daoist rite

Yin Fu Jing 陰符經 Popular Song dynasty Daoist manual

Yin-bing 陰兵 spirits of the water and fiery underworld, quelled by Daoist ritual

Yin-yang Five Element cosmology 陰陽五行說

Ying-huo 螢火 protector spirit of the planet Mars

Yu 酉 tenth of the 12 earthly stems, rooster; a direction from which Thunder is summoned

Yü the Great 禹 (Emperor Yü); China's Noah, stopped the floods by ritual dance

Yü 玉 joint in center of third finger of the left palm; controls spirits of the center

Yü-fu 玉府 code name for Zhengyi registers, licensed at Longhu Shan

Yü-huang Bao-chan 玉皇寶懺 Jade Emperor "Litany of Repentance"

Yü-huang Ben-xing Jing 玉皇本行徑

Yü Ji 于吉 founder of Taiping Daoism (also written Gan Ji 干吉)

Yü-jing 玉京 Code name for the highest Daoist Shangqing ordination

Yü-jüe 玉訣 secret teachings, third segment in each of the Three Arcana Daoist Canon

Yü-lan Pen 盂蘭盆 ritual for freeing all souls from hell-purgatory (Buddhist inspired)

Yü-luei 鬱壘 second of two protective spirits guarding temple gates

Yü-qing Xüan-tan 玉清玄壇 Daoist temple in Tang dynasty Luoyang city

Yü-shu Jing 玉樞經 Jade Pivot Canon

Yü Dao ho-I 於道合一

Yüan-de 元德 esoteric name for the 1st of the Liujia spirits

Yüan-qi 元氣 （元炁） *See also* Primordial Breath

Yüan-pao 元袍 Imperial robes, worn by the Liujia spirits

Yüan-shi Tian-zun 元始天尊 Primordial Heavenly Worthy, Dao as Gestating

Yüe 越 ancient kingdom, modern Fujian province

Yüe-jian 月建 esoteric Daoist method for controlling thunder spirits

Yüe-jüe Shu 越絕書

Yüeh-ling 月令

Zang Jing 藏矜 Lingbao Daoist, teacher of the tenth master of Mao Shan, Wang Yuanzhi

Zao-chao 早朝 "morning audience," Daoist ritual to refine yuan Qi, 元炁 primordial *Qi*

zhai 齋 a term used today for funeral ritual

zhang 張 constellation

Zhang Jiao 張角

Zhang Heng 張衡

Zhang Xiu 張修

Zhang Liang 張良

Zhang Lu 張魯

Zhang Daoling 張道陵

Zhang Ci yang 張紫陽

Zhang Wan fu 張萬福

Zhang Yüchu 張宇初

Zhao-xü 招婿

Zhao Tai 昭台 Tao Hongjing's residence on Mao Shan

zhen 軫 constellation

zhen-zheng Lun ch. 1, nn32-34 甄正論

zhen ren 真人

Zhen gao, 真誥

Zhen guan 貞觀

Zhen da 真大

Zhenwen 真文 *See also* Lingbao Zhenwen 靈寶真文

Zhen Yen 真言 mantic seed word, mantra

Zheng 正 "True" or "Orthodox" as opposed to"xie"邪 unclean, demonic, evil

Zheng Jiao. *See also* Daochang 正醮，道場

Zhengyi; 正一 orthodox one school, Meng-wei; (Heavenly Master Taoism, 天師道)

Zheng-i Meng-wei Lu 正一盟威籙

Zhengyi Bu, 正一部 seventh section of the Daoist Canon

Zhengyi Ci tan, 正一詞壇 association of Taiwan Celestial Master Daoists

Zhengtong Daozang 正統道藏 *See* Taoist Canon

Zhi 治 administrative district in late Han dynasty *Tianshi* 天師Daoism

Zhi 志 the will, located in the heart, in Daoist body cultivation

Zhu Xuan 朱軒 (egendary Huashan Taoist, mythical adept at Thunder rites)see *Zhen Gao*,

Zhuan Xu 顓頊 Daoist spirit-ruler of the North

Zhu-Ge Liang 諸葛亮
Zhu-sheng 祝聖 ritual summoning orthodox Daoist spirits
Zhuang, Daoist Master, 莊道師. *See* Zhuang-chen Deng Yün 莊陳登雲 (Teachings of)
Zhuang-chen Deng Yün; 莊陳登雲
Zhuang-lin Xü Daozang (ZLXDD) 25 vols, 1975; 2011; Zhuang-lin Supplement to the Daoist Canon
Zhuangzi (Zhuang-tzu) 莊子 third-and-fourth century BCE classical text, required reading for Daoist practice
Zhuangzi Neipian 莊子內篇, first seven chapters of the *Zhuangzi*
Zhong Zhi 重質 secret name of the second of the fierce Liu Jia generals, used in ch. 4
Zhong-hou 中候 "apocrypha" text, from the *Gu wei shu* 古緯書 ch. 1, n26, 27
Zhong shu 眾術 ninth of the classical Daoist Canon's 12 sections
*Zhong Dou Jing*中斗 經 "Canon of Merit" chanted second day of a Jiao ritual
Zi 子 first of the 12 earthly stems, rat, gall bladde pronounced "dz"
Zi-chang 子常 esoteric name of Tian-ren star spirit
Zi-cheng 子成 esoteric name of Tian-ying star spirit
Zi-jin 子金 esoteric name of Tian-qin star spirit
Zi-chin 子禽 esoteric name of Tian-feng star spirit
Zi-fei 子扉 style name of Jia Yan, sixth of the Liu Jia spirits
Zi-qiao 子翹 style name of *Tian-zhong* star spirit
Zi-qing 子卿 style name of Jia Wu, fourth of the Liu Jia spirits
Zi-wei Tan 紫微壇
Zi-xiang 子鄉 esoteric name of Tian-fu, star spirit
Zi-xü 子戌 esoteric name of *Tian-bing*, star spirit
Zi-zhong 子冲 esoteric name of *Tian-zu*, star spirit
Zi-xü Yüan-jun 紫虛元君 *Daoist name* of Wei Hua-cun
Zuo Dao 左道 *See* Tao of the Left; also called "sinister" Dao.
Zuo-wang Lun 坐忘論 "Sitting in Forgetfulness/oblivion"
Zu-qi 祖炁 "ancestral" primordial breath, nourished in the lower cinnabar field (belly)
Zu Shu 祖舒 woman Daoist, legendary founder of the Qingwei Thunder-vajra method
Zui 觜 23rd of the 28 constellations

Made in the USA
Las Vegas, NV
26 February 2022

44663997R00151